# THE BRIDGESTONE
# VEGETARIANS' GUIDE
# TO IRELAND

## JOHN McKENNA
## &
## SALLY McKENNA

*With illustrations by Ken Buggy*

**ESTRAGON PRESS**

First published in 1995 by
Estragon Press Ltd, Durrus, Bantry, Co Cork

© Estragon Press

Text copyright © John McKenna and Sally McKenna 1995
Illustrations copyright © Ken Buggy 1995
Cover photograph copyright © Lucy Johnston

The moral right of the authors has been asserted

ISBN 1 874076 12 X

Printed by Colour Books Ltd, Baldoyle, Co Dublin  Tel: (01) 832 5812
Designed by Karl Tsigdinos/Gold Star Media Ltd, Dublin Tel: (01) 260 0899
Typeset by Seton Music Graphics, Bantry, Co Cork  Tel: (027) 50742
Cover Photo by Lucy Johnston, Garville Lane Studios  Tel: (01) 496 0584

# *For Sarah*

*With thanks to:*

Des Collins, Karl, Lucy, Eddie, Elaine, Sarah Bates, Cynthia Harrison, Cathleen Buggy, Ray Buckley and John Harold, James O'Shea, Pat Ruane, Louis Lentin, Micky O'Neill, Ciaran Tanham, Pat Duffner, Maureen Daly, Caroline McGrath, Colette Tobin, Mary and Des Rainey.

*Some praise for* THE BRIDGESTONE VEGETARIANS' GUIDE TO IRELAND

"If you are visiting the Emeral Isle, of if you live there all year round, The Bridgestone Vegetarians' Guide to Ireland is invaluable. This is a well-researched book giving a personal flavour of both places and people, and killing the myth that vegetarians have few edible options in Ireland".
"BBC Vegetarian Good Food"

"Entries give much more than just the basic information you require; they are light-hearted descriptions of the food, the hosts, and the premises, and they make you want to pick up the phone and reserve a table on the spot".
"The Irish Vegetarian"

". . . the authors take you on a fascinating perambulation around the Emerald Isle and being the superb word painters that they are, introduce us to its culinary delights . . . the McKennas seem to cover the whole spectrum of places ranging from those for the connoisseur with disposable income, to the impecunious but well intentioned. Although this is a vegetarian guide, it doesn't fall into the trap of vege-elitism. Throughout the book the authors allow for the fact that our travelling companions may not be vegetarians . . . with this in mind we are informed whether eating places are 100% vegetarian or, as in some places, vegetarian meals need to be ordered in advance".
"Holiday Vegetarian".

**John McKenna** was born in Belfast and educated both there and in Dublin, where he practised as a barrister before turning to writing in 1989. His work appears in newspapers and magazines in Ireland and the U.K. He has won Glenfiddich Awards, as regional writer and for radio programmes, in 1993 and 1994.

**Sally McKenna** was born in Kenya, and brought up on the Pacific island of Fiji before coming to Ireland in 1982. She cooked professionally before turning to writing about food and restaurants.

**Ken Buggy** was born in Dublin in 1947 and has spent most of his working life abroad. He now lives in Kinsale with his wife Cathleen and their four children.

*JOHN McKENNA and SALLY McKENNA won the first André Simon Special Commendation Award in 1992 for the second edition of The Bridgestone Irish Food Guide. The third edition of The Bridgestone Irish Food Guide was short-listed for a Glenfiddich Award in 1994.*

The RTE television series "McKennas' Ireland" was written and presented by John and Sally McKenna, directed by Micky O'Neill, and produced for Crescendo Concepts Ltd by Louis Lentin.

# ＢRIDGESTONE

BRIDGESTONE IS JAPAN'S LARGEST tyre manufacturer and one of the top three in the world. Founded in 1931, the company has striven to maintain an emphasis on technological advancement and service while expanding the scale and scope of its operations. As a result the company is recognised as a leader in tyre manufacturing and technology.

Bridgestone tyres are presently sold in more than 150 countries. There are twelve manufacturing plants in Japan with others throughout the world including the U.S.A. and Australia. Bridgestone now also manufactures its tyres in Europe following the acquisition in 1988 of the Firestone Tyre and Rubber Company.

They manufacture tyres for many different vehicles, from trucks and buses to passenger cars and motor-cycles. Its commercial vehicle tyres enjoy a worldwide reputation for superior cost-per-kilometre performance, and its aircraft tyres are used by more than 100 international airlines. Many Japanese cars imported to Ireland arrive with Bridgestone tyres and a host of exotic sports cars including Ferrari, Lamborghini, Porsche, Jaguar and TVR are now fitted with Bridgestone tyres as original equipment.

Bridgestone is at the forefront of tyre research and development. Its proving ground in Kuroiso City, Japan covers 400,000 square metres and consists of a 3.5 kilometre banked test track and skid pan which together contain more than 40 different road surfaces. Bridgestone also operate an advanced R&D facility in Kodaira, Japan. Testing focuses on a wide range of features including directional stability, skid resistance, durability, abrasion resistance, riding comfort and noise reduction. All this data is then put to valuable use in the development of new and better tyres. Bridgestone is now the most technologically advanced tyre manufacturer in the world.

In June 1990 Bridgestone (Ireland) Ltd was established as a subsidiary of the multinational Bridgestone Corporation to take over the distribution of its tyres in Ireland. The company operates from its offices and warehouse in Tallaght in Dublin where it stocks a wide range of passenger car, commercial vehicle and earthmover tyres. Bridgestone staff also provide sales, technical and delivery services all over the country.

● *Bridgestone tyres are available from tyre dealers throughout Ireland. For further information contact Bridgestone (Ireland) Ltd., Unit A30, Greenhills Industrial Estate, Tallaght, Dublin 24. Tel: (01) 452 7766 Fax: (01) 452 7478*

MAP SHOWS COUNTY DIVISIONS AND PROVENCES.

# Contents

# How To Use This Book

ALL VISITS to the restaurants, hotels, country houses and B&Bs included in this book were made anonymously. All meals and accommodation were paid for and any offers of discounts or gifts were refused. Any food products bought from shops or growers were paid for.

Inclusion in "The Bridgestone Vegetarians' Guide to Ireland" is an implicit recommendation for each particular entry. Where producers, growers, shops, hotels or restaurants have been visited and found to be of an insufficiently high standard, or where they have recently changed hands, they have simply been excluded. We have not included restaurants and wholefood shops just because they cater for vegetarians: if the places have not matched up to our criteria, they have been excluded.

In a small number of cases, where we have encountered a producer, cheesemaker, grower, restaurateur or hotelier whose work represents a special and unique effort in terms of Irish vegetarian food and vegetarian food culture, we have marked these entries with a ★. These people are, simply, the very best at what they do.

In other cases where we felt the food was of special interest we have marked the entry with a ➠, meaning that the entry is worthy of making a special detour to enjoy the food.

Many Irish restaurants, particularly those in the south and west of the country, are seasonal. Many others change their opening hours during the winter. Even though opening hours are given for restaurants it is always advisable in Ireland to telephone in advance and check opening times when booking a meal.

# The Bridgestone Awards

## STARRED RESTAURANTS, SHOPS AND GROWERS ★

Café Paradiso, Cork, Co Cork
Drimcong House, Moycullen, Co Galway
Eden Plants, Rossinver, Co Leitrim
Gubbeen Farmhouse Cheese, Schull, Co Cork
The Ivory Tower, Cork, Co Cork
Penny and Udo Lange, Ballinroan, Co Wicklow
Lettercollum House, Timoleague, Co Cork
Mainistir House, Aran Islands, Co Galway
Manch Estate, Dunmanway, Co Cork
Organic Life, Kilpedder, Co Wicklow
Shiro Japanese Dinner House, Ahakista, Co Cork
Tir na nOg, Sligo, Co Sligo
West Cork Natural Cheese, Schull, Co Cork

## RESTAURANTS, SHOPS AND GROWERS WORTH A DETOUR ➡

Ardrahan Cheese, Kanturk, Co Cork
Ayumi-Ya Japanese Restaurant, Blackrock Co Dublin
Ayumi-Ya Japanese Steakhouse, Dublin, Co Dublin
Ballymaloe House, Shanagarry, Co Cork
Co-Op Shop, Manorhamilton, Co Leitrim
Corleggy Farmhouse Goat's Cheese, Belturbet, Co Cork
The Dublin Food Co-Op, Dublin, Co Dublin
Furziestown House, Tacumshane, Co Wexford
The Old Rectory, Wicklow, Co Wicklow
101 Talbot, Dublin, Co Dublin
Ow Valley Farm Shop, Co Dublin
Quay Co-Op, Cork, Co Cork
Rajdoot Tandoori, Dublin, Co Dublin
Truffles, Sligo, Co Sligo

# Introduction

THE EXTRAORDINARY renaissance which has swept through the world of Irish food and of Irish cooking in recent years, and which has gifted its energy to Irish vegetarian cookery every bit as much as mainstream cooking, has been founded on the simple, but utterly essential, idea of dialogue.

Firstly, there is the poetic interaction of climate and countryside, that bequest from nature which results in such startling, and startlingly delicious, diversity of flavour as you travel the country. The climate for producing food in Ireland is beatific, gentle, best summarised perhaps by that most optimistic of expressions, when rain will be described as "soft rain". Not wet rain, as you might expect, but soft rain.

In alliance with this, and of vital importance for the traveller in search of good food, is the fact that although a small country, Ireland has considerable diversities in climate — though the soft rain is consistent — temperament and characteristic. You might expect to find uniformity of food and of taste on such a small island, but you will be surprised.

This is one of the delights of the country, and it works hand in hand with farming practices which, to other Europeans, can seem almost prehistoric: small farms, dry stone walls, intelligent husbandry, a bristling outcrop of committed organic farmers. Ireland never followed the path of the U.K. after the last war, when the cheap food policy harmonised and, sadly, homogenised, farms and farming, creating a distance between those who produce food and those who eventually consume it.

For, when you find good food in Ireland, it evokes not just itself, but also something greater than itself. It evokes also its environment and background, the people who made it, the attitudes of care and concern which brought it to be. For anyone for whom it is essential also to have a clear conscience when it comes to enjoying food, and vegetarians with their clearly defined and orchestrated principles regarding animal welfare and environmental protection are chief amongst these groups, then the close relationship, the dialogue, in Ireland between those who produce food, those who cook food and those who finally eat food, is a blessing.

The best Irish food speaks glowingly and vitally of its place: the creamy milk of North Cork gives bloomy, rich cheeses which can age into mellow sweetness and fathom-deep complexities of flavour, whilst in Tipperary the crusty boggyness of the pastures makes for cheeses that are lactic and strappy in flavour, immediate and upfront.

The goat's cheese from County Waterford, on the east coast, is full and deep in flavour, whilst that from County Clare, directly opposite on the west coast of Ireland, is sharper, more flinty and direct, the produce of animals who graze on sea-swept, wind-swept pastures atop limestone rock.

Our favourite potatoes come from West Cork, but a good spud from Comber, in Northern Ireland, is something to savour and slaver. The first time you try oatmeal from North Cork it is one of the mightiest food surprises you can encounter. When you encounter porridge in Northern Ireland however, the surprise may be even greater: there is a tradition up there, which is fast becoming a habit, for a splash of whisky to be stirred into the breakfast brew before it is brought to table.

It is the breads found in B&B's and shops, hostels and guesthouses which may be the most famous aspect of Ireland's food, and the nuggetty richness of a well-made round of soda bread can seem elementally fine, and true in flavour. In truth, it is simple things like bread and butter, milk and cream, spuds and carrots which betray the graciousness of Irish food. They are rich in flavour, alive with complex and satisfying mineral riches and astute pleasures. We take them for granted, perhaps, but we do know how good they are, how important they are.

The skill and creativity of human touch then blesses these good ingredients. The environment in which food is produced in Ireland is uniquely caring and environmentally conscious, human in every way, small scale and personal, hands-on and, often, hand-held. In certain cases there will be no processes other than the use of human hands, and food which will have originated in its area will, eventually, be enjoyed in its area.

At the Saturday morning market in Galway city, for example, one finds vegetables, bursting with vigour, which will have been picked from the ground that morning, alongside salad leaves still flecked with dew. There will be fresh cheeses made only the previous day, the yellow slabs of creamy country butter produced in domestic kitchens, along with garishly decorated cakes and still-warm loaves of bread. It is a jamboree of colour and creativity, of fun and fine food, there every Saturday morning to be enjoyed and appreciated.

The dialogue continues, then, when we arrive at the doors of Irish restaurants. In the last decade, after a period when its restaurant culture lacked a distinctive national identity, Ireland's cooks have managed to evolve outwards from a cuisine which was fundamentally domestic and nostalgic, and have begun to create a cuisine which is contemporary and creative.

These men and women have hungrily seized on the rich culinary imprimaturs of regionality and proximity, and they have festooned the ingredients with their own individuality and creativity. They have hungrily plucked the classic foods of the past and reinterpreted them, brought to them a renaissance of new ideas and instincts and, of course, borrowed and adapted foreign influences to coincide with the trueness and sublime understatement of Irish ingredients.

This complicated interaction has always enjoyed an additional boon in Ireland, however. Vegetarianism, here, has never been saddled with the Bloomsbury, Ban-The-Bomb, G.B. Shaw baggage which has convinced so many vegetarians that it is necessary to be an ardent Shelleyan before you can foreswear eating animal products. The vegetarian food cooked in the best Irish restaurants comes unencumbered with anything other than a vocation to be as delicious as it can be. Vegetarianism, here, is seen as a culinary choice, and not an adjunct to a series of social and philosophical attitudes. If it doesn't taste good, no one wants to eat it.

If we think of some of the magnificent dishes eaten in Cork city alone within the past months — grilled chilli polenta with pepperonata; pumpkin squash and pesto soup; aubergine burrito with salsa and sour cream, or those aubergines used along with Puy lentils and goat's cheese in a charlotte with coriander custard — then one realises that we are discussing a cuisine which is as focused on food fashions in north and south America every bit as much as the necessity to have essential ingredients grown as close to the restaurant as possible.

The progresses in vegetarian cookery in the U.S have had a major influence here, as cooks move away from the idea that vegetarian food had to use pulses and grains to replicate animal products and have begun to use these ingredients in their own right. True, there are still restaurants where the vegetarian food is markedly old-fashioned, where imagination seems to be suppressed rather than liberated by the fact that there is no meat on the plate, but more and more it is vegetarian cookery which is at the cutting edge of creativity and originality in Irish kitchens.

It is on both sides of the swing doors of a restaurant kitchen, finally, that the dialogue of Irish vegetarian food rises to a crescendo of complementary voices. This works for a very simple reason: we have relatively few specialist vegetarian restaurants, but the younger generation of cooks enjoy the challenge of vegetarian cooking almost more than anything else.

The days when vegetarians were tolerated, at best, are gone, and even if a restaurant menu only offers a small selection of vegetarian dishes, these will be cooked with the same generosity and creativity which characterises the rest of their work. Indeed, it is likely that they will enjoy even greater attention than the conventional menu, a fact which has led to a situation where many folk who would not class themselves as vegetarian will only ever eat the vegetarian dishes on a menu when they eat in restaurants. For cooks, also, it is vitally important that you enjoy their food. Like our mothers, they anxiously watch the return of plates to check that everything has been eaten, and enjoyed.

This dialogue between cook, customer and food culture is entering a gloriously exciting phase, as a new wave of young cooks begin to flex their muscles and fight for attention. Indeed, these youngsters exhibit such restless creativity and urgent competence that one realises that the huge advances made in the last ten years are, in fact, little more than the initial rumblings, the early notes, of a true Irish vegetarian cooking. A cuisine of enormous pride, founded on the principles of dialogue and individuality, is rushing towards us at great speed.

But Irish food, and the enjoyment of Irish food, is always, and inextricably, founded on the principle of pleasure. The one thing which our cooks have never forgotten is the necessity of hospitality, the fact that food is a gift to be appreciated and enjoyed. Their cooking is creative, but not self-conscious. It is modern, but always instinctively generous. The delights of this renaissance are nothing less than thrilling, and they offer nothing less than a unique, uniquely delicious, experience.

John McKenna, Sally McKenna
Durrus, County Cork
January 1995

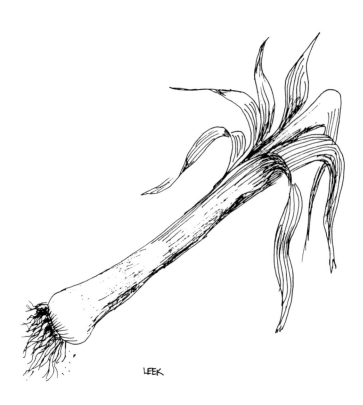

LEEK

# County Galway

# THE ARAN ISLANDS

## INIS MOR

Accommodation and Restaurant
### MAINISTIR HOUSE HOSTEL ★

*Kilronan, Aran Islands Tel: (099) 61169 Fax: 61351 Joël d'Anjou*

Why is Joël d'Anjou such a good cook?

Simple. Because he is an improviser. He makes it up as he goes along, cooking at all times without knowing precisely what he is going to finish up with. Like a great jazz musician, he takes a theme, then begins to shape it according to his own style. At the end, at the conclusion of the rollercoaster that is dinner in Mainistir, you know only that someone who implicitly, intuitively understands food has melded and moulded basic ingredients into these amazing dishes. But you might not be able to understand just how it has been done.

For no one else cooks like this man. No one else has enough savvy and confidence to simply let things unfold, to trust that it will all work out well. We watched, one summer day, as Jöel used the organic herbs which had just been delivered to the back door, to make an Aran Pesto.

Half a head of garlic and half a salad bowl of hazel-nuts were ground up with a predominance of parsley and basil, but chives, tarragon, coriander, dill, chervil and marjoram were all tossed into the pot with salt and vegetable oil. A far cry from the simplicity of Ligurian pesto, M d'Anjou produced a sauce that walloped you with its freshness, its greenness, its earthiness, its ruddy vitality. He simply made it up as he went along, but you never doubted for an instant that it would be anything other than outrageously good. Which it was.

Cooks, like any artists, are at their best when there is an element of exploration, of uncertainty, in their work, when they are still unsure of how something will finally turn out. That is what makes food interesting, and that is what makes Jöel d'Anjou's hostel, and his cooking, so special. Every dish eaten in a summer's week was perfection: spicy aubergines with a red onion relish; carrots in an orange sauce; a curry of lentils; mange tout with garlic and crystallised ginger. The nightly vegetarian buffets are events to remember.

Open for dinner 8pm sharp (7.30pm winter). Open for Xmas and New Year. Average Price: dinner under £7, B&B under £10–under £15. Visa, Access. No wine licence — wine available in shop in village. When you arrive on the pier ask for Mairtin.

## Jöel d'Anjou's Beetroot and Pumpkin Soup

**5 medium beetroot,**
    scrubbed and de-stalked
**half stalk of celery**
**1lb (450g) pumpkin flesh,**
    peeled and de-seeded
**1 large onion**
**2 cloves garlic**
**salt and pepper** to taste
**3 pieces of crystalized ginger**
**4 pints water**
**1 fl oz (28ml) oil**
**Sour cream** and **French parsley**
    to garnish

BEETROOT

In a large pot heat the oil and add to it the garlic, onions and celery. Fry gently until the onions are slightly caramelized. Add the water and bring to the boil. While waiting for the water to boil chop the beetroot and pumpkin. Add to the bubbling liquid and then simmer until tender. Finally, add the ginger. Put everything into the liquidiser to blend to a smooth thick purée. Put back on a low flame just to keep hot. Serve with a dollop of sour cream and some chopped French parsley.

Snack And Sandwich Bar
## PEIG'S
*Main Road, Kilronan Peggy Hernon*
Peggy Hernon's cracking little snack and sandwich bar has tables both inside and out, for days when the sun shines, and days when it doesn't shine. Good for bumper lunchtime sandwiches as well as muffins and carrot cake and other delicious sweet things. Friendly, and great fun.
Open 11am–6pm Tue–Sun. Lunch under £5. Just on the outskirts of Kilronan, heading towards Dun Aengus fort.

Pub
## JOE WATTY'S PUB
*Main Road, Kilronan Tel: (099) 61155 Rhoda Twombly*
Heart-and-soul-and-body-warming soups and stews come out of the kitchen in Rhoda Twombly's fine pub, just the fuel you need to get you back on your bike and, finally, up that hill out of Kilronan. Soups are spicy vegetable barley soup, gingered carrot soup, cream of mushroom or gardener's delight — a light summer soup of cucumber, tomato and potato. During the high summer there may also be chilli or vegetarian stews. Great sessions at night and sustenance — of the liquid kind — available all day.
Open pub hours, selling food from approximately 12.30pm–7pm (to 9pm in winter). Limited hours off season. Average Price: meals under £5. No Credit Cards. Just outside Kilronan, up the hill, heading towards Dun Aengus.

Organic Co-Op
## CILL EINNE

This splendid venture, kick-started by that guru of growers, Dolores Keegan, has begun to produce superlatively fine vegetables and herbs down at Cille Einne. Inquire from Jöel at Mainistir House, if you are perhaps renting a house on the island and want to enjoy food rich in the pure, untrammelled scents and tastes of Aran.

# INIS MEAIN

Crafts
## INIS MEAIN KNITTING COMPANY
*Inis Meain Tel: (099) 73009 Aine de Blácam*

The middle island is tricky to get to — the piers are absurdly short — and can be awkward to get off, but it would be worth swimming across in order to buy the lovely sweaters of the Inis Meain Knitting Company.

Shop open 8.30am–5pm Mon–Fri, open 7 days in summer. Visa, Access. Ask details at the pier.

# INIS OIRR

Accommodation With Meals
## BRID POIL
*Baile an Chaisleáin, Inis Oirr Tel: (099) 75019 Bríd Poíl*

There is no better base from which to seek out the measure of little Inis Oirr than Bríd Poíl's welcoming bungalow in the village of Baile an Chaisleáin.

Arrive in the morning and the swaddling smell of just-baked bread might meet you, served with that cup of tea you need to revive the limbs after you have hauled your bags up from the boat or the 'plane. At dinner time you can expect comforting mounds of spaghetti, or something inventive with pulses such as chick peas, for Mrs Poíl is a fine cook. Combined with excellent housekeeping and nonchalant comfort, it adds up to the ideal B&B.

Open for dinner for guests only, from 6.30pm, Closed Dec & Jan. Average Price: dinner under £10 B&B under £20. No Credit Cards. The house is near the airport, ask directions there or at the pier.

A PAIR OF APPLES

# CONNEMARA

# BALLYCONNEELY

Hotel and Restaurant
### ERRISEASKE HOUSE HOTEL & RESTAURANT

*Ballyconneely, Clifden Tel: (095) 23553 Fax: 23639 The Matz Brothers.*
Stefan Matz cooks with a dazzling mixture of discipline and daring, and his food is breathtakingly, startlingly delicious. Take, for instance, perfectly formed raviolis which come with pastas flavoured with tomato, or perhaps spinach, the large circles stuffed with ricotta cheese, fromage blanc with garlic and onions, or mushrooms with parsley; or the expert use of Filo pastry which flakes through a Greek spinach pie; or finely balanced sauces which can meld white wine, shallots, cream and lemon juice anchored with a base note of port or madeira.

Like his conventional cooking — and it has to be said, he is primarily a cook for the carnivorous — Stefan Matz's vegetarian cooking exhibits such iridescent flair and such implicit control that the food on the plate enjoys balance and brilliance in equal measure, and each concoction tastes truly organic: perfectly formed, perfectly allied, perfectly cooked.

But, just as delightful, is the fact that this food is not a shallow starburst of pyrotechnics and egotism: the proof lies in dishes as simple as homemade noodles in cream sauce with wild mushrooms, or the astute use of condiments and dressings in a salad, or a lemon tart whose pastry is of such inestimable thinness that it reminds one of a communion wafer, but one where the worthiness has been replaced by a melting, crumbling piece of perfection.

The cheeseboard in The Erriseaske sets Irish farmhouse cheeses in competition with their French counterparts, on a board arranged from sweet cheeses through to strongly flavoured ones. Both nationalities are served perfectly, with the Irish cheeses proving wilder and more vigorous than their more polite neighbours. The Hotel itself is a happy place, with kids and holidaymakers and locals, and with Mr Matz's brother Christian overseeing everything with his winning, shy style.

Open 6.30pm–9.30pm Mon–Sun. Closed Nov–Easter. Average Price: dinner under £30, B&B over £30. Visa, Access, Amex, Diners. The hotel is signposted from Ballyconneely village.

# CLIFDEN

Restaurant
## DESTRY'S

*The Square Tel: (095) 21722 Paddy & Julia Foyle*

It was Lord Beaverbrook, apparently, who said that the sight of Marlene Dietrich standing on a bar, in black net stockings, belting out "See What The Boys In The Back Room Will Have", in the great western "Destry Rides Again", was a greater work of art than the Venus de Milo.

They can't, of course, resurrect Dietrich to stand on the bar in Paddy Foyle's wonderful restaurant, but the occasional snatch of "See What The Boys . . ." does whoomp out from the music system every so often, allowing you and your friends to hold the ritual Dietrich Debate: could Marlene sing just one note? Or could she sing two?

Who cares. Dietrich was the most brilliant self-invented character of the century, and Paddy Foyle's admiration of the lady has extended not just to borrowing the title from the classic western in which she starred with James Stewart, he has also borrowed some of the lady's capacity for re-invention, and re-made his cooking and his style anew in Destry's.

A desire to simplify his food, to work in a funkier ambience, has led to this effortlessly enjoyable place. With a talented young chef, and the seamless lack of contrivance he and Julia Foyle gift to any venture, Destry rides along on good humour and an adrenalinated energy.

Clifden has needed a place like Destry's for a long time, somewhere that matches the exuberance of the holiday-maker, somewhere that lets tomorrow take care of itself. Sitting in Destry Rides Again, we all become The Boys In The Back Room, little Lord Beaverbrooks in the thrall of the Blue Angel.

Open noon–10pm Mon–Sun. Closed Nov–Easter. Average Price: lunch under £15, dinner under £20. Visa, Access/Master. Clifden town centre.

Restaurant
## HIGH MOORS RESTAURANT

*Dooneen Tel: (095) 21342 Hugh & Eileen Griffin*

Clifden at Eastertime. Happy locals, happy holiday-makers smile and say to themselves: High Moors is due to open.

Clifden at the end of September. Unhappy locals, unhappy out-of-season holiday-makers grimace and say to themselves: High Moors closed for the season. Roll on next year.

Unlikely as it may seem, for the Griffins' High Moors restaurant is nothing more than the sitting room of their bungalow revamped into a restaurant for the season, but High Moors is part of the social baggage and the culinary culture of Clifden. The reason why is simple: no one knows his customers better than Hugh Griffin and Eileen Griffin knows just what it is that they like to eat that will bring the hungry up the windy hill to the bungalow.

Eileen Griffin is a good cook, and she has the added security of using vegetables and herbs grown just down the road by Hugh. Vegetarian food is only available on request, but you will be guaranteed happy, simple cooking: baked potato gnocchi with a tomato ragout; cannelloni with spinach and ricotta; a fine filo pastry with goat's cheese and pine nuts.

Open 7pm–9.30pm Wed–Sun. Closed Oct–Apr. Average Price: under £20. Access, Visa. Look for the sign 1km from Clifden directing you to a side road off the main Ballyconneely road.

Restaurant
## O'GRADY'S SEAFOOD RESTAURANT
*Market Street Tel: (095) 21450 The O'Grady family*

For many visitors to the bric-a-brac town of Clifden, O'Grady's is as automatic a stop as St. Peter's in Rome or Mulligan's bar in Dublin. The food they serve, an unchallenging essay on getting good flavours from simple ingredients, explains why.

Everything is designed to make the diner feel comfortable, and to usher in a relaxed time. The lighting is low, the tables are intimately arranged if you want, socially arranged if you don't, service is charming. The business of the O'Grady family has always been to look after people, and, if you give them notice that you're a vegetarian, you'll find they look after you.

Open 12.30pm–2.30pm, 7pm–9.30pm Tue–Sat (open Sun Jun–Sep). Closed Dec–Feb (open for a few weeks around New Year). Average Price: lunch under £10, dinner under £20. Visa, Access, Amex. In the centre of Clifden.

Restaurant with Rooms
## THE QUAY HOUSE
*Clifden Tel: (095) 21369 Paddy & Julia Foyle*

The design of Quay House, from bedrooms through to dining room, is quite, quite wondrous. Upstairs houses an eclectic mixture of solid family furniture, "found" objects, gilt-framed dark Victorian paintings, shuttered windows with bright checked curtains and Lloyd loom chairs.

Downstairs, the main corridor boasts an avenue of deer heads and the massive skin of a tiger which, in its time, allegedly dispatched seven Indian women. The dining rooms are humorous, utterly individualistic. No one else could even begin to imagine a dining room so counterpointed in design. No one else could ever make it work. In The Quay House, it is just perfect.

And so are Paddy and Julia Foyle, and so is the young chef, Dermot Gannon, whose cooking is punchy and expressive, devoted to flavour. To get the best out of Quay House, do make it known to them that you are vegetarian when booking, as Mr Gannon tends to improvise dishes on the night rather than present a selection of vegetarian choices on the menu. That way, you enjoy the verve of this splendid organisation, and the verve of this talented young man's cooking.

Open all year except Xmas and Jan. Average Price: dinner under £20, B&B over £30. Visa, Access/Master. On the seafront at Clifden: drive around the town and take the road running down the hill.

Crafts
# CONNEMARA HANDCRAFTS
*Letterfrack Tel: (095) 41058*

Irish china, pottery, candles, table-cloths and a coffee shop in which to pause and peruse your purchases. Known as The Possibly Shop ("Possibly the best craft shop in the West"), as distinct from the craft shop near Clifden which came along sometime after and called itself "Probably the best craft shop in the West".

Open 9.30am–7pm Mon–Sat, 10.30am–6pm Sun. More limited hours off season. Closed Nov–Feb.

# ROUNDSTONE

Pub
## O'DOWD'S
*Roundstone Tel: (095) 35809*

A sepia of nicotine paints the chipped and aged wood of the walls and ceiling in this snugglesome bar, and sets the right tone for their good pints.

Open pub hours, food served all day 'till 9.30pm Mon–Sun. Closed mid–Oct–Feb (with limited opening times around Xmas and New Year).

Food Producer
## JOSIE MONKS
*Creeshla Farm, Cushatrower Tel: (095) 35814*

Josie Monks sells a fine soft goat's milk cheese, lovely fruity yogurts, cheesecake and milk as well as jams, chutneys and orange and lemon curd. Josie's daughter has joined the business and makes salad dips with home-made mayonnaise and goat's cheese. You can buy from the farm, and sometimes you might see them in the Clifden market on Friday or Saturday.

Open 8.30am–8pm Mon–Sun high season (limited hours and limited foods available during the winter). Look for signs about two and a half miles from Roundstone.

B&B
## THE ANGLER'S RETURN
*Toombeola, Roundstone, Co Galway Tel: (095) 31091*

The Angler's Return, once part of the Ballynahinch estate, enjoys a superb location for exploring this most indomitable, mysterious part of Connemara: close to Roundstone, close to Clifden, a scoot away from Maam, adjacent to the severe waters of Leenane. The house is quiet, peaceably run and simply furnished in muted pastels that show some happy signs of maturity. The beds are high and soft, the rooms are places in which to sleep deeply. Lynn Hill specialises in wholefood breakfasts: homemade muesli or granola, homemade yogurt, cheeses, brown bread and free-range eggs.

Open May–end Oct (out of season by arrangement) Average Price: B&B under £20. No Credit Cards. 4 miles down the Ballynahinch–Roundstone road (leading off the main Galway–Clifden road)

Crafts
## ROUNDSTONE PARK
*I.D.A., Connemara*

Along with crafts to decorate the table, you might find yourself buying a hand-crafted Bodhrán, made from goat's skin and decorated with a celtic design — the necessary accompaniment to good music and good crack.

# GALWAY

# AUGHRIM

## AUGHRIM SCHOOLHOUSE RESTAURANT
*Aughrim, Tel: (0905) 73936 Geraldine Dolan and Mícheál Harrison*

A friendly, youthful place set just off the main Dublin-Galway road as you drive past Aughrim, Mícheál and Geraldine work hard to satisfy the diverse appetites of locals and visitors. The cooking is imaginative, and a little notice will allow them to prepare something special for vegetarian eaters. Sunday lunch is good fun and good value.

Open Sun noon–3pm, Tue–Sat 6.30pm–11pm. Closed Xmas. Average Price: lunch under £15, dinner under £20. Visa, Access/Master. Look for the signs on the main Dublin/Galway road just past the village of Aughrim.

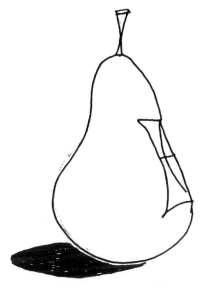

A PEAR

# GALWAY CITY

## The Galway Saturday Market

The surreal gaggle of the Galway Market manages to make everything, no matter how strange, seem integrated, straightforward.

Joachim Hess could be the lead guitarist in a rock 'n' roll grunge band, if he wasn't a vegetable grower and baker of good breads. The little canopy of the Brekish Dairy, laden with cheeses and yogurts and breads, has simply decamped from Northern Europe, but looks as if it has always been here. Gert and Vita Van den Brink's stall of organic vegetables, and Babs and Cait, the bubbly girls from the Connacht Growers, are camped beside the person selling beautiful driftwood, who is beside the kids with the Rice Krispie cakes and the mammies with the country butter.

It is all weird and wonderful, and you wish you were some sort of rural Stephen Sondheim so you could write a musical about them all.

Everything for sale is excellent: Dirk Flake's beautiful vegetables and herbs, the vociferous flowers, the flouncy-topped carrots, the home-baked cakes. This lovely jamboree, this strange confusion of people, is one of the delights of Irish food. Do not, if you are visiting Galway, miss the market on any account.

SOME OF THE PRODUCERS SELLING IN THE MARKET
*Brekish Dairy, Kylebrack West Tel: (0509) 45246 Hugo Zyderlaan*
Cheese, yogurts, butter, stout breads.

*Vita & Gert Van den Brink, Lough Ahorick Tel: (0509) 49215*
Organic vegetables.

*Connacht Organic Group, Cait Curran & Babs McMullan.*
Organic vegetables.

*Dirk Flake, Aughinish, Kinvarra.*
Organic vegetables.

*Joachim Hess, Brackloon, Ballyglunin, Tuam.*
Organic vegetables, bread.

*Avallo Apple Juice, Gort Tel: (091) 31860.*
Irish Organic Fruit Juices,

## Galway City Centre Restaurants

### THE COUNTRY BASKET
*Cross Street Tel: (091) 63236*
An all-day coffee shop serving stir fries, tofu-based dishes, vegetarian chilli, salads and some meat dishes.

Open 9am–6pm Mon–Sat. Average Price: meals and snacks under £5. No credit cards.

## FAT FREDDIE'S

*The Halls, Quay Street Tel: (091) 67279*

A pizza parlour, with some desserts made by Emer Murray of Goya's.

Open 11am–10.30pm Mon–Sun. Average Price: pizzas under £5. Visa, Access/Master.

## FOOD FOR THOUGHT

*3 Lr Abbeygate Street Tel: (091) 65854*

Vegetarian and wholefood restaurant. Lasagne, quiche, pizza, shepherd's pie, nut roast, none of them containing meat.

Open 8am–5.30pm Mon–Sat. Average Price: meal under £5. No credit cards.

## THE GRAIN STORE

*Lr Abbeygate Street Tel: (091) 66620*

Newly refurbished lunchtime restaurant.

Open 10am–6pm Mon–Sat, Average Price: meals under £5. No credit cards

## TIGH NEACHTAIN RESTAURANT

*2 Quay Street Tel: (091) 66172 Stephan and Maureen Zeltner-Healy*

Tigh Neachtain, in this delightedly frisky part of town known as Galway's "Latin Quarter", is famous not only for good pints but also for good music. It is now getting a name for good food.

This is thanks to Stephan and Maureen Zeltner-Healy. He is the chef, and she is always to be found front of house, amidst the burgundy walls, the open fires and the candle light. Curiously, for somewhere over a pub, Neachtain's has a sort of Country House Parlour atmosphere. It's not very formal: nobody bothers whispering in here, so it's a good place to pick up hot Galway gossip.

There are always vegetarian choices on the menu: good fresh salads to start, then a spinach crêpe stuffed with vegetables and served on a tomato sauce, perhaps, or one of the house specialities, Stephan's noodles.

Puddings are enjoyably classical: syrupy pears poached in red wine with a brandy parfait; some tangy stewed berries with mixed parfaits. The wine list is decent and decently priced, and Galway has needed this alliance of good food and great crack for some time.

Open 6.30pm–10.30pm Mon–Sat. Closed 1 week in Nov, Xmas. Average Price: dinner under £15. Visa, Access/Master. At the corner of Cross Street and Quay Street.

## PASTA MISTA

*2 Cross Street Tel: (091) 65550*

Pizza and Pasta.

Open 12.30pm–9.30pm Mon–Sat (coffee available from 11am), Average Price: pasta under £5. Visa, Access/Master.

## ROYAL VILLA

*13 Shop Street Tel: (091) 63450*
*Charlie Chan*

Upstairs, away from the crowds, the Royal Villa is a haven of waterfalls, step bridges, vivid Chinese shades and, most importantly, good food. There is a complete Vegetarian Menu with spring rolls and salads, soups of sweet corn and mushroom, or rainbow beancurd broth. Main courses mix vegetables with curry, sweet and sour, black bean sauce, or Szechuan sauce. With a detective's doggedness, Mr Chan hunts down the sweet, sharp, spicy flavours we love, and brings them to you on a plate.

Open 12.30pm–2.30pm, 6pm–midnight Mon–Sat (Fri & Sat 'till 12.30am), 1pm–midnight Sun. Closed Xmas. Average Price: lunch under £10, dinner under £20. Visa, Access, Amex, Diners. Galway city centre.

## SEVENTH HEAVEN

*Courthouse Lane, Quay Street Tel: (091) 63838*

Food from the Pacific Rim.

Open noon–midnight Mon–Sun. Average Price: meals under £10. No credit cards. Galway city centre.

## SUNFLOWER RESTAURANT
*Quay Street Tel: (091) 66320*
Politically Correct Grub.
Open 9am–midnight Mon–Sun. Average Price: meals under £5. No credit cards. Galway city centre.

## WESTERN TANDOORI
*Flood St Tel: (091) 65872*
The Western Tandoori offers a good selection of vegetarian food. Potatoes are a great staple, and come with cauliflower (aloo gobhi), chickpeas (aloo chole) or curry (curry). There is also stuffed okra, and dal with butter, onions, tomato and ginger.
Open 5pm-1am Mon-Thur and Sun, 'til 2am Thur, 'til 3am Fri. Average Price: meals under £15. Galway city centre.

# Galway Shops

Wholefood Shop
## EVERGREEN
*1 Mainguard St & High St Tel: (091) 64215 Aideen Hurley*
Not just your average corner healthfood shop, Evergreen sells vegetarian samosas, pakoras and spring rolls to take away, the wholesome Galway cheeses from Brekish Dairy, bread from Moyglass, the organic, locally-produced Avallo pure apple juice, fresh orange juice, and all the necessary dried goods: lexia raisins, Californian sultanas, oats, flours and porridges. Member of the IAHS.
Open 9am–5pm Mon–Sat. Galway city centre.

Wholefood Shop
## HEALTHWISE
*5 Lr Abbeygate St Tel: (091) 68761 Seamus Kelly*
Wholefood Shop which is a member of the IAHS.
Open 9am–5pm Mon–Sat. Galway city centre.

Bakery and café
# GOYA'S
*19 Quay Street Tel: (091) 67010 Emer Murray*

How does Emer Murray manage to do it? How can each detail of each biscuit, each cake and each bread represent such rarefied perfection? Individual Tira Misu redolent with chocolate; fig and walnut cake fine and distinct; individual cheesecakes balancing the high wire between sweetness and nourishment. Each cake, each loaf, from the vivid pink strawberry roulade to the miniature yeasted rolls, each are flawless in their execution.

But even though everything looks straight from the pages of a glossy publication, there is no artifice here, no tricks for the eye. For the ingredients used to construct these towers of taste are good flour, real butter, white wine, whole fruit, fresh cream.

Patisserie must be an indulgence, and be seen to be an indulgence, and from the Whoopii Pies — spiced biscuits flavoured with pumpkin purée and filled with a cream cheese icing — to the rhubarb crumble — icing sugared curves that look like the Burren mountains — Goya's cakes are an indulgence so fine, so much a lot of what you fancy, that they must be good for you.

Recently Emer has opened a coffee house, where all the above is available along with a limited lunch of vegetable soup (always a vegetarian stock), toasted sandwiches and bowls of salad. Coffee is freshly ground for each individual cup.

Open 9.30am–5.30pm Mon–Sat. Coffee House open 10am–5pm Mon–Sat (with possible extension of those hours during the high season). Average Price: under £5. No credit cards. Galway city centre.

Grocery and Delicatessen
# MCCAMBRIDGE'S
*38/39 Shop Street, Tel:(091) 62259 Pat McCambridge*

McCambridge's is a delightful shop, its shelves filled with interesting foods, the wine shop with interesting wines and spirits, but above all it is the cheese counter which is of greatest interest. You can find almost all of the Irish farmhouse cheeses, carefully cared for, carefully kept, carefully served, and they also maintain a good selection of cheeses from Europe.

Open 9am–6pm Mon–Fri, Sat 9am–5.30pm. Galway city centre.

Fruit Shop & Delicatessen
# SILKE & DAUGHTERS
*Munster Avenue Tel: (091) 61048 Brian Silke & Scott Ishmael*

Silke's has transmogrified over the years, with the wholesale side of their fruit and vegetable business slowly taking a back seat to Scott Ishmael's fine food venture, this part of the shop improving steadily and surely. Silke's is now an excellent place in which to find the best Irish artisan foods, cheeses in good condition, good bread and condiments, a good

selection of salads as well as the myriad varieties of fruits and vegetables that they have always sold.

Open 8.30am–6pm Mon–Sat. On the Strandhill side of the river on the edge of Galway
city centre.

# MOYCULLEN

Restaurant
## DRIMCONG HOUSE ★
*Moycullen Tel: (091) 85115 Gerry & Marie Galvin*
Whilst there is an element of the grandiose in Gerry Galvin's way of
thinking about his work in Drimcong House, his fondness for the
abstract and the romantic is, nevertheless, bedrocked in the reality of
running a professional kitchen, and in trying to figure out just what it
is that makes a restaurant work, trying to hit on the secret of just what
it is that makes people want to go out to enjoy a meal, just what it is
that makes a communion of food and wine and the environment of a
restaurant work together to produce the magic of enjoyment.

"We instil in our staff the idea that what we do is enjoyable and not
worth doing if it is not", he writes, and what is impressive about his
work is not just the pithy epithets he writes, it is the fact that they are
put into operation every night in Drimcong.

Perhaps most crucially, he writes that "We do strive to instil the
desire for excellence in our staff, being fully aware that very often the
excellence is in the effort rather than the achievement".

His restaurant, with its splendid staff and their obvious happiness
and pride in their work, was one of the first in the country to include a
daily five-course vegetarian menu, and his commitment to this school
of cooking — "My motivation and my guiding light is to experiment
and, being Irish, to try to build on what we have", he says — is as true
and as imaginative as the rest of his work.

Open 7pm–10.30pm Tues–Sat. Closed Xmas–Mar. Average Price: dinner under
£20–under £30. Visa, Access/Master, Amex, Diners. Drive out of Moycullen towards
Maam Cross, the restaurant is on your right.

# MOYGLASS

Bakery
## MOYGLASS WHOLEMEAL BAKERY
*Moyglass Tel: (0509) 49223 Norbet Illien*
The continental loaves you see around Galway town probably come
from the Illiens' bakery where they make rye bread, organic yeast
bread, sourdough loaves and sugar-free cakes.

Look for the breads and cakes in wholefood shops and delis in all the major towns
between Galway and Limerick.

# County Leitrim

The vine must suffer, in order to make good wine, is what they will tell you in Burgundy, what they will say in Bordeaux. Something of the same principle — spare the rod, spoil the child — must form the basis of the success of Rod Alston's twenty-year-old herb and vegetable growing operation in Rossinver. For his farm is set fast in shockingly inhospitable land, and yet his produce is unsurpassably marvellous, premiére cru quality, as fine as a First Growth.

Rod Alston, like others in Leitrim, works the land and the land works him. This countryside is demanding, but it rewards effort. Some years ago, the North Leitrim Vegetable Growers' Association produced a modest little cookery book and, in his introduction, the writer Michael Viney, after a learned discourse explaining why the Irish have historically been indifferent to vegetables, wrote of the curious fact that in "the quiet drumlin country of North Leitrim (not the first place you would think of as the garden of Ireland) a remarkable co-operative of small growers is selling vegetables in the local market town".

That town is Manorhamilton, and the Co-Op Shop is a treasure house of good food, food rich in the vibrant, zesty character which the Leitrim climate can bestow. Rod Alston's herbs and vegetables best exemplify this character: the vegetables are stubbornly flavoured, as if they have struggled to seize every element and nutrient from the earth, yet the tastes are not clumsy or brash, being instead fresh, typical. The salad leaves are frothy with life and arrogant with energy. The herbs — a huge range is listed in the Eden Plants herb catalogue, from Alpine Strawberry and Angelica to Sweet Woodruf and Yarrow — have fluent bouquets and distinct flavours.

If, thanks to the harsh terrain, everything must suffer as the vine must suffer, then the results are as pleasing and richly complex as a fine wine. A visit to the farm is nothing less than inspirational, a chance to see a vision made real. A visit to the shop, that "remarkable co-operative of small growers", is always a treat.

## THE CO-OP SHOP ➡

*Main Street, Manorhamilton Tel: (072) 55609*
Open 9.30am–6pm Mon–Sat (closed Wed from Oct–late Apr). Manorhamilton town centre.

## EDEN PLANTS ★

*Rossinver Tel: (072) 54122 Rod Alston*
The herb garden is open every afternoon from 2pm-6pm. Eden Plants is 7 miles north of Manorhamilton: in Rossinver turn right after the convent, where there is a sign to the herb farm. Eden Plants is the first turning on the left. Herbs can be bought by mail order: ring or write for a catalogue.

# County Mayo

## ACHILL

### ANNE FUCHS
*Dugort, Achill Island Tel: (098) 43233*
The milk from Anne's happy goats can be bought from her farm, a couple of miles outside Keel heading for the hills. Sometimes she has home-made cottage cheese for sale as well.

### O'MALLEY'S POST OFFICE
*Keel Tel: (098) 43125*
A reasonable selection of wines is sold here to perk up your picnics.
Open 9am–8pm Mon–Sat, 9am–2pm Sun.

## BALLINA

Shop
### BRENDAN DOHERTY
*O'Rahilly Street Brendan Doherty*
Shop here for home-made butter and good communion candles.

Jams & Preserves
### ETHEL'S HOMEMADE PRESERVES
*Ballyholan House, Downhill Road Tel: (096) 21853 Ethel Walker*
Ethel's Preserves, jams, marmalades and technicolour chutneys manage to retain an echo of the kitchen table and the kitchen sink, and are worth hunting down — from corner shops and supermarkets — whilst in the west.

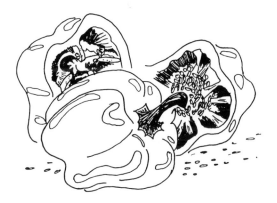

Shop
## T. MCGRATH
*O'Rahilly Street, (096) 22198 Mr McGrath*
A higgledy piggledy packed deli with a good cheese counter, select
comestibles and unexpected wines.
Open 9am–8pm Mon–Sat (winter times 'till 7.30pm), 10am–2pm, 5pm–8pm Sun.

# CASTLEBAR

Restaurant
## FLAVOUR OF INDIA
*Main Street, Castlebar, Co Mayo Tel: (094) 25738*
A new addition to the North West, Flavour of India re-interprets traditional Indian food by virtue of using and exploiting the flavours of
ingredients from this part of the country. Vegetarian dishes include
samosas, pakoras and onion bhajee, as well as creamed lentils with
aromatic spices, cooked with fresh tomatoes, ginger and garlic and the
usual clever combination of Indian cheese with spinach (saag paneer)
and peas (mutter paneer). There is also chana masala — chick peas;
aloo gobhi — cauliflower and potato, as well as home-made naan, plain
and flavoured with garlic and, of course, rice and chapattis.
Open 5.30pm–12.30am Mon–Thur, 5.30pm–1.30am Fri & Sat, 5pm–12.30am Sun.
Average Price: dinner under £10–under £15

# CONG

## ECHOES
*Main Street, Cong, Co Mayo Tel: (092) 46059 Siobhan, Tom & Helen Ryan*
Whilst Siobhan Ryan garners most of the attention in Echoes — quite
rightly, for she is the person who devises the dishes and is the instru-
mental force in getting them from stove to table — she could not do so
without her Dad, who takes care of all manner of supplies to the
restaurant, and young Tom, the brother, who is not above hopping
into the kitchen to rattle the pots and pans when Siobhan takes a
deserved break.

Siobhan's sister brings to the job of waiting on table a feline grace
and a skill which turns her work into an art form. Finally, Siobhan's
mother, who welcomes you, organises the bills and cooks breakfast in the
restaurant during the summer months, completes this extraordinary
picture. It's a family affair.

Together, the family all work to the benefit of the fine food you can
expect in Echoes, and vegetarians who give a little notice will find their
desires and demands expertly met.

This deeply comforting food, full of odoriferous scents and rich with
goodness, comes in grandly generous portions, and the happy family

affair of Echoes is as far removed from the self-conscious sense of denial that pervades Mayo as you could imagine.

Open 5pm–10pm Mon–Sun (shorter hours during winter season). Average Price: dinner under £20. Visa, Access/Master, Amex. Right in the centre of Cong.

# CROSSMOLINA

Country House & Restaurant
## ENNISCOE HOUSE

*Castlehill, nr Crossmolina Tel: (096) 31112 Susan Kellett*

Enniscoe is a relatively simple place, a modest country house which Susan Kellett is restoring slowly and lovingly, in a part of the country which is modest and under-celebrated. Things are done just right here, just so, and this desire to achieve correctness in simple things makes it a pleasurable house in which to while away some holiday time or an away-from-it-all weekend.

The bedrooms have enjoyed careful renovation. Those at the front of the house, overlooking the grounds, are truly the ones you want to stay in, with their quirky four posters and big lazy canopy beds.

At dinnertime, local ingredients are dotted through the menu: a vegetarian dinner could include grapefruit and grape cocktail, or peppers stuffed with sunflower seeds. Then there are quiches with locally grown courgettes, onion tarts, perhaps a brown rice and vegetable gratin, mixed salads made with fresh herbs. It is country house cooking, of course, but whilst in other places it might seem a little obvious, here it feels just right, friendly food within a friendly house.

Best of all, Enniscoe is a place it is easy to relax in, a place to enjoy time alone and apart from the real world, a house that is polite, vivid and perfectly expressive of the strengths of Irish country house hospitality.

Open for dinner if pre–booked. Closed mid Oct–Apr. Average Price: dinner under £25, B&B over £30. Visa, Access/Master, Amex. Two miles south of Crossmolina on the road to Castlebar.

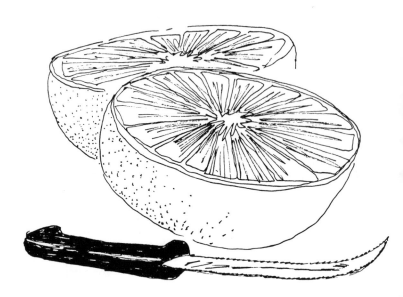

# WESTPORT

Restaurant
## BERNIE'S HIGH ST. CAFÉ

*High Street, Westport Tel: (098) 27797*

Irish breakfasts and high teas are served all day in Bernie's welcoming café in the middle of Westport. Expect to find omelettes, pastas, stirfries as well as pancakes with imaginative stuffing — sweet and sour, Chinese Vegetable or broccoli and cauliflower florettes. A truly modern caff, Bernie also serves Pacific rim specialities such as Mexican dip with tortilla chips. The all-day breakfast includes boxty as well as waffles with Maple syrup and croissants. Bernie was for a long time associated with the Quay Cottage, down at the waterfront. Her eponymous café is her very own venture.

Open 10am–10pm Mon–Sat 1pm–10pm Sun. Average Price: lunch under £10, dinner under £15. Visa, Access. Westport town centre.

Restaurant
# THE CORK
*nr The Octagon Tel: (098) 26929 Willie & Jutta Kirkham*

Willie and Jutta Kirkham have moved their restaurant from the Westport hills, where it was known as The Ceili House, to this location near the Octagon in the centre of town, a long, atmospheric run of a room. The menu includes dishes created especially for both vegetarians and vegans, including the ominously named Healthy Heaps. There is also a wine bar with an ever-expanding selection of wines. Non-smokers should note that the staff do not operate a no-smoking policy amongst themselves: smokers may, however, be delighted at this relaxed attitude.

Open 6pm–10pm Wed–Sun. Closed Xmas. Average Price: dinner under £15. Visa, Access/Master. Near the Octagon in the centre of Westport.

Restaurant
# O'MALLEY'S CHINESE RESTAURANT AND BAR
*Bridge Street, Westport Tel: (098) 27307*

Local vegetarians have a high regard for O'Malley's, the unlikely, but not impossible, name for the Chinese restaurant in the centre of Westport. The menu seems limited when it comes to vegetarian choices, but the upfront smack of flavours in their noodle dishes and stir fries, plus extras like spring rolls, makes up for the relative lack of choice.

Open 5pm–midnight Mon–Sun. Average Price: dinner under £15. Visa, Access/Master. Westport town centre.

Farmhouse Cheese
# CARROWHOLLY CHEESE
*Kilmeenacoff, Irma van Baalen*

Irma van Baalen's lovely Gouda-type cheeses are a valuable, enduring staple of the bubbly Thursday market in the Octagon in Westport, and during the summer she can also be found there on both Fridays and Saturdays. Both cow's milk and goat's milk cheeses, as well as some freshly made cheeses, are for sale.

Café
# CONTINENTAL CAFÉ AND HEALTHFOOD SHOP
*High Street Tel: (098) 26679 Wendy Stringer*

New proprietor Wendy Stringer has maintained the old favourites of the Continental Café — stuffed pitta bread sandwiches, warming soups and wholesome cakes — and the shop still maintains a wholefood slant whilst specialising in foods for those on special diets.

Open Tues–Sat 10.30am–6pm. Westport town centre.

Shop
# COUNTRY FRESH
*Shop Street Tel: (098) 25377*

A good general greengrocer, now celebrating twenty years of business. Look for organic herbs and vegetables grown by Chris Smith of Clogher.

Open 8am–6.30pm Mon–Sat ('till 7pm Fri & Sat). Westport town Centre.

Shop
# HEAVEN ON EARTH
*Bridge Street Tel: (098) 27127*
Recently moved and expanded from its location on High Street, Heaven On Earth still sells a large variety of wholefoods and healthfoods.
Open 10am–6pm Mon–Sat. Westport town centre.

Restaurant
# CIRCE'S
*1 Bridge Street Tel: (098) 27096 Antoinette Turpin and Corry O'Reilly*
Corry and Antoinette bake their own bread, serve organic salad leaves and local cheeses, and their careful sense of choice conspires to give Circe's a fleety holiday spirit and a rumbunctious western character.
Open 10am–10pm Mon–Sat, 7pm–10pm Sun. Closed Xmas and more limited hours during low season. Average Price: breakfast & lunch under £5 dinner under £15. Visa, Access. Westport town centre.

Restaurant
# QUAY COTTAGE RESTAURANT
*The Harbour Tel: (098) 26412 Peter & Kirstin McDonagh*
This intimate and pleasingly simple restaurant wisely focuses on local seafoods, but the professional spirit evident in the Cottage also means that they can offer decent vegetarian assemblies. Quality is high, given the prices, and the cosy atmosphere is particularly enjoyable at lunchtime.
Open noon–10pm Mon–Sat, 1pm–10pm Sun. Closed Xmas and Jan. Average Price: lunch & dinner under £15. Visa, Access, Amex. Down on the quays.

Organic Grower
# WESTERN HERBS AND VEGETABLES
*Westport Tel: (098) 26409 Chris & Brid Smith*
It is more than likely that the organic vegetables, leaves and herbs which you will find throughout Mayo in shops and supermarkets, and those you will hopefully enjoy in restaurants, will be those grown by Chris and Brid Smith on their few acres near Clogher. They produce almost fifty types of herbs and sell at the Thursday market at the Octagon in Westport as well as in Country Fresh greengrocers in the town.

Visitors to the farm are not merely welcome but encouraged: between May and September for the measly sum of £1.50 with the kids going free you can have a tour between 2pm and 6pm and see how the whole magical process works.
To find the farm take the Castlebar road out of Westport, turn left at the sign for Fahy, travel for one and a half miles when you will see the sign for Clogher and the farm is at the end of the road at the T-junction.

Shop
# WINE & CHEESE
*Bridge Street, Anne & Vincent Bourke*
Cottage renters and caravan-bound cooks will find much of interest in the Bourkes' unusual shop, with a great deal of the food home-made.
Open 10am–6.30pm Mon–Sat.

# County Sligo

## BALLYMOTE

Country House, Farm
### TEMPLE HOUSE

*Ballymote Tel: (071) 83329 Fax: 83808 Sandy and Deb Perceval*

The word you most often hear in connection with Temple House is "perfection".

What do people love? The food, says the acclaimed chef. The dinner party atmosphere, say your parents. The whacky and exotic rooms, say your friends. The friendship, say the people who have already been three times. Temple House is all things to all men and women, and all these things spell happiness.

The house itself is an artful confection, undeniably absurd and splendid, but it is the Percevals' gift to remove any strain of preciousness or pretension from Temple House which makes it work, and makes it appeal to those who love country houses and those who loathe them. Deb Perceval's cooking is an important element of the magic, for she manages always to produce dinners which are exactly appropriate, both for the evening and for the people with whom you share dinner: an onion and blue cheese tart, a chocolate meringue gâteau. "They are able to create a real kind of relaxed caring", says the lady from Germany sitting across from you at dinner. Yes, that's it.

Open for dinner for guests only. Closed Dec–Mar. Average Price: dinner under £20, B&B over £30. Visa, Access/Master, Amex, Diners. Temple House is 14 miles from Sligo and is signposted from the N17. If travelling from the east on the N4, then turn off the road to Ballymote, travel through the town and you will again see the distinctive blue signs.

## CLIFFONEY

Farmhouse Cheese, German Cheesecake, Sourdough Bread
### HANS AND GABY WEILAND

*Ballincastle, Cliffoney Tel: (071) 66399 Hans and Gaby Weiland*

Hans and Gaby grind flour, bake breads and cheesecakes, make cheese from cow's and goat's milk, grow vegetables organically and rent out their cottages, and they do everything with disarming charm and, best of all, with the joyous peal of Gaby's laughter adding a note of frothy irresistibility to their work. The bread, the cheesecake, the cheeses are all filled with joie de vivre, filled with the lovely flavour of zestful love of life. These are some of the finest foods of Sligo.

Cheese is only available in summer months. Telephone for more details of self-catering cottages (open all year, but they book up quickly). Hans' and Gaby's farm is up the narrow road on the right hand side of the road just before the village of Cliffoney, coming from the Sligo direction. Theirs is the fourth house on the left, with the cottage opposite. To order a cheesecake, ring in advance. Cheese and bread available in Tir na nOg in Sligo town.

MOUTHWATERING, FLAVOURSOME, TRADITIONAL MILKINESS, CREAMYNESS
WHOLESOME, NATURAL, PURE INDIVIDUAL, HANDMADE USING TRADITIONAL
METHODS, DEEP IN THE IRISH COUNTRYSIDE OF LUSH GREEN GRASS
FLAVOURED WITH WILD FLOWERS, FRUIT AND HERBS. EACH CHESSE
LOVINGLY 'REARED' AND PROTECTED, WATCHED EVERY HOUR OF
EVERY DAY DURING ITS AGEING PROCESS SO IT BECOMES ALMOST
CEREBRAL IN ITS OWN PLEASURE GIVING 'WHEY' THAT ONLY 'IT' CAN", IT
MELTS OBLINGINGLY AND ITS SWEETNESS FORMS A PERFECT ... (HEAVEN)
-BUT ITS A LIVE CREATION HERE ON EARTH. -NO FRENCH CHEESE-
MAKER COULD                              THESE, THEIR SUBTLE, SUPPLE
INTENSITY A                              THE VERY BEST ARISTO-
CRATIC CLARET                       NTAIN A DEPTH OF
COMPLEXITY                    SE          RANTLY
FULS                                    LK WITH
THESE FL                            ELSE.
THESE CHEESES REFLECT THE SMELLS AND SCENTS OF
A TRADITION GOING BACK IN TIME THAT HAS ALLOWED US A
MATURE AN IRONIC AND WELL VERSED FLUENCY — BUT CHEESES
OF SUCH DEEP DEEP CONCENTRATION OF TASTES AND FLAVOURS
THAT ARE SO TONGUE-READY AND UPFRONT THEY MAY LEAVE
YOU BEAUTIFULLY TONGUE-TIED.

# COLLOONEY

Country House and Restaurant

## GLEBE HOUSE

*Collooney Tel: (071) 67787 Brid and Marc Torrades*

Reading a newspaper article about Glebe House in Collooney, near Sligo — at the time a splendid ruin, and no more — led Brid and Marc Torrades to migrate to the west coast, and to two years solid slog to bring the unruly ruin back to some kind of shape.

By August 1990, they were open for business, quickly achieving popularity amongst the well-fed citizens of Sligo, a fame which has since spread steadily, by stealthy word of mouth. That quiet fame is well founded, for Ms Torrades allies a tenderly feminine skill as a cook with a rock-solid appreciation of fresh ingredients, most of them grown in the garden at Glebe by Marc.

Ask what her principal influence is and she replies, "Nature, I suppose. I'm very dependent on what is growing outside in the garden, what Marc is growing, and we try to be as self-sufficient as possible. I've always aspired to having fresh herbs and being able to cook using just them, getting the flavour of herbs. It's very simple cooking, I think, where it's simple and simply decorated, and you cook the food available at the time. Simplicity is the thing".

She cooks with great motivation, and has the too-rare gift of being as capable a baker as she is a cook: this means that the vol-au-vent case which cups some wild mushrooms will be melt-in-the-mouth soft, as soft as the bosomy lure of profiteroles with hot butterscotch sauce or a breakheart apple tart. The vegetarian options on the menu are typically thoughtful and appropriate: warm goat's cheese salad, a pancake of garden vegetables in a light mustard sauce will be dynamically flavoursome, escalopes of chickpeas with tomato and garlic, baked stuffed baby squash or a timbale of Puy lentils with a filo of vegetables.

Open 6.30pm–10pm (afternoon tea served from 2pm). Open for Xmas. Closed Jan. Average Price: dinner under £20, B&B under £25. Visa, Access/Master. Signposted from Collooney, just before the bridge.

# INNISCRONE

Bath House

## SEA WEED BATH HOUSE

*Pier Road Tel: (096) 36238 Edward Kilcullen*

We associate the Victorians with prudishness, but they knew something about sensuality. Why else would they have built these bath houses around the coast, and deigned to use sea weed to supply the natural oils in the water, had they not been captivated by the lubricious, evocative sexiness of the experience. Floating in sea-water with the unctuous oils lapping your limbs is a bawdy, wanton experience, altogether Rabelaisian.

Open noon–8.30pm Mon–Sun. Closed weekdays in Oct, and Nov–St Patrick's Day weekend.

# RANSBORO

Soft Fruit
## COLLEEN'S
*Ransboro Tel: (071) 68164 and (088) 562606 Colleen Bresnihan*
Look out for Colleen's strawberry season from mid-May to the end of July, and her raspberries which are available all through July and September. You'll find them in most of the fruit and vegetable shops in Sligo town as well as Kate's Kitchen and Gary Kilfeather's.

# RATHLEE

Dilisk and Carrageen Moss
## MELVIN'S SEA WEED
*Cabra, Rathlee Tel: (096) 49042 Frank and Betty Melvin*
Frank Melvin springs and leaps amidst the lumpen outcrop of the Long Rock in pursuit of edible sea weeds, in particular the fine sea-salty dilisk (known as dulse in Northern Ireland) and the tangly, khaki-brown restorative which is carrageen moss.

Packed in small plastic bags with the promise "Harvested in the North West of Ireland" on the label, the weeds are found mainly in health food shops throughout the country. By comparison to other weeds which are produced on a large scale, Mr Melvin's sea weeds are finer and more complete in both texture and taste.

The secret of the high quality of his sea weeds lies not just in the suitability of the Long Rock and its neighbouring outcrops, but also in his method of drying the weeds: "The weather will do the bleaching", says Mr Melvin. "All you need to do is pitch it out, for ten days. But, I believe, to do it right, it must be bleached all around, from the point of view that I can sell that and it won't go soft or go bad at room temperature. If I don't bleach it there will be a tendency that what won't get bleached will go soft'."

With the dilisk, says Mr Melvin, "Most of the people that I know just chew it, straight from the bag", though a handful of the chopped weed added to a soda bread mixture makes for a cake of bread that is particularly good with cheese.

The carrageen is used for cooking, the inevitable nursery school, blancmange-style pudding, of course, "though a lot of the people I sell it to use it for colds and flus, for the chest. There are many families even who I supply in the Ballina-Sligo area and they use a huge amount, give it to their kids and bring them up with it, they reckon they never have colds or sickness or anything, they swear by it".

As a restorative, indeed, carrageen is unbeatable, the weeds soaked and brewed up in water, then strained and mixed with honey and lemon juice. On Aran, notes the writer Tim Robinson, "Next to whiskey it is the people's most trusted cure for coughs and colds". A drop of the hard stuff tilted into some brewey carrageen, of course, is surely the perfect recipe for health and happiness.

Available in wholefood stores throughout the country.

# SLIGO

Wholefood Shop
## TIR NA NOG ★

*Grattan Street Tel: (071) 62752 Mary, John & Norah McDonnell*

Retailers tend, over the years, to mellow, to become timeworn by the pressures of business, the demands of customers.

They tend to lose the drive and the focus which motivated them in the beginning, the desire to sell the foods they love from the producers they respect.

Like any organic environment, a shop and its keepers need to develop and mature, and yet they need to hold fast to their principles, they need to refuse to allow their dedication to become subdued. In Tir na nOg, Mary McDonnell has clung on to her desire to do her best, has held fast to her right to get angry, has refused to mellow.

"Just look at this! They expect me to sell this!", she shouts, exasperated, and gets on the telephone to let some wholesaler or distributor know that nothing which comes in the door of the shop and which goes out the door of the shop is to be anything other than the best, and what on earth were they thinking about when they sent it?

Mary's fire is balanced by the gentleness of John and Norah but, like her, they are devoted to the idea of Tir na nOg as a place of good things, the best foods in their season, chockful of the vigour of the North West climate, the best of the farmhouse cheeses, the choicest dried foods. The shop is a personal reflection of the driven and devoted personalities of the McDonnells, and is an integral and essential part not just of the social culture of Sligo, but of the food culture of this island.

Open 9am–6pm Mon–Sat. Sligo town centre.

Restaurant
## TRUFFLES ➡

*11 The Mall Tel: (071) 44226 Bernadette O'Shea*

Bernadette O'Shea came to Sligo to open a restaurant which would specialise in pizzas, and everyone thought she was crazy.

Now, a few years down the line, in a new premises which has an artfully lovely wine bar above and the coolest staff serving the most exquisite food below, her success has led to the arrival of a host of imitators, folk who think Ms O'Shea simply spotted a trend and went for it, and who believe they can do the same.

They couldn't be more wrong. For Truffles is not simply the new thing, the latest fashion, a new twist on the sort of food people want to eat and a funky new way of serving it. It is, rather, a classic example of the application of the essential skills which every good cook must possess — toughness, determination, skill and dedication, good taste and judgement and a vision of one's work as an artistic enterprise — all of them applied, in the case of Truffles, to the creating and cooking of pizza.

And in Truffles, the creating is every bit as important as the cooking, for Ms O'Shea is an innovator, as restlessly creative as Alice Waters — and we should remember that the creator of Berkeley's Chez Panisse restaurant has a café upstairs over the restaurant which specialises in pizza and pasta — as obsessed with purity as Richard Olney, as devoted to detail as Joël Robuchon.

Each combination on top of the pizza is deliberately thought through to provide confluence and contrast, to offer the most pleasing and sympathetic tastes imaginable even when, in something like the Truffles' Best — roast garlic, roast peppers, ricotta, sautéed onions, parmesan, tomato sauce, olive oil and mozzarella — the list of ingredients becomes potentially overwhelming.

But whilst many of the Truffles' pizzas are culinary Baedekers, tablets of dough informed with all the funky happenings of both classic Italian tastes and New World improvisations — Chilli Pizza with hot chilli sauce with sun-dried tomatoes and three cheeses and a salsa of guacamole chutney on the side — Ms O'Shea is always looking to localise her work as much as possible. Thus the pizza with Seven Irish Cheeses or The Californian Classic with sun-dried tomatoes brought back home by the use of Irish goat's cheese. These extraordinary creations are nothing less than music for the mouth.

Open 5pm–10.30pm Tues–Sat, 5pm–10pm Sun. Closed Xmas. Average Price: pizza under £10. No credit cards. The Mall is an extension of Stephen's Street, on the main road to Enniskillen going in the direction of the hospital.

Pub
# HARGADON'S
*O'Connell Street Tel: (071) 42974 Pat Leigh Doyle*
Hargadon's has an atmosphere so womb-like wonderful that even the shelves are woozy. Lolling and sagging like Laurel and Hardy on a bender, they are surreally warped, and in Hargadon's they seem perfectly in place, just above the tea and spice boxes, just out front of the assignatory snugs, near to the ancient burner, across from the bar where

pints are respectfully pulled, tots of whiskey tilted out of bottles, conversations begun. Hargadon's is a crystalline vision of an Irish pub, frozen in time, preserved perfectly.

Delicatessen
## COSGROVE'S
*32 Market Street Tel: (071) 42809 The Cosgrove Family*
If you are no longer young, and prone to nostalgia, Cosgrove's shop may well have you whispering laments for the loss of the local shop, that denizen of carefully selected foods, that warren of excitements, that temple of gossip and information.

Cosgrove's is that shop, a splendid, handsome, loving place, with boxes of dried fruits and soft-smelling tumbles of bread and floorbound bags of salty fresh dilisk. Like Hargadon's pub and the Inniscrone Sea weed Baths, it is resplendently Victorian, an echo from a time now gone.
Open 9.30am–9pm Mon–Sat, 11.30am–1.30pm, 5.30pm–8pm Sun. Sligo town centre.

Farm Shop
## FARMHOUSE VARIETIES
*Wine Street Car Park Tel: (071) 70427 Tommy Breheny & Owen Downes*
A car park sounds like the last place you expect to find products from the farm, but here in Farmhouse Varieties you can buy good country butter and good country buttermilk and Irish farmhouse cheeses.
Open 8.30am–6pm Mon–Wed, 8.30am–7pm Thur, 8.30am–8pm Fri, 8.30am–6pm Sat. In the main Sligo town centre car park.

Traiteur
## THE GOURMET PARLOUR
*Bridge Street Tel: (071) 44617 Annette Burke and Catherine Farrell*
There isn't anything Catherine and Annette aren't game to have a go at, no taste venture they won't essay, no function too large for them to cope with, no party too small for them to furnish with food, no demand for Christmas cooking too awkward. This aching willingness to please, and the fineness of their work from bread to ice-cream, from patisserie to chutneys to quiches, has made them an essential addition to Sligo's quality-driven food culture.
Open 9.30am–6pm Mon–Sat. Sligo town centre.

Delicatessen
## KATE'S KITCHEN
*24 Market Street Tel: (071) 43022 Kate Pettit and Frank Hopper*
Kate's is the sort of shop that always reminds one of Christmastime. The shelves bulge with those jars of goodies which somehow seem indispensable at a time when you feel you should spoil yourself: aged vinegar, pickled walnuts, cranberry sauce, hand-made chocolates. There is also a catholic selection of wine, and various and plentiful cooked food to-go, for Kate and Frank are truly Irish traiteurs.
Open 9am–6.30pm Mon–Sat. Sligo town centre.

# County Carlow

Restaurant
## THE LORD BAGENAL INN

*Leighlinbridge, County Carlow Tel: (0503) 21668 James Kehoe*

The wine list in The Lord Bagenal, which may be the restaurant's greatest claim to fame, is a magnificent piece of work, a tender exposition of great wines described in splendidly commonsense language. "First and foremost, wine is made to be enjoyed" writes James Kehoe, the mastermind proprietor behind the list.

This is what is important about Mr Kehoe's splendid wine list, and his splendid restaurant. The list is not a bland recital of vintages and varietals, but is instead a careful canvas of fine wines, with the essentials of pleasure and accessibility underpining the reason why each bottle is on the list.

Truth be told, the greatest of Mr Kehoe's achievements is not just his wine list, but the fact that such a spiffing piece of work is put to play in the friendly, sociable and enjoyable bar and restaurant which is The Lord Bagenal Inn. They play classical music, hang splendid paintings by Irish artists on the walls, have linen tablecloths and good big glasses, but none of this is the slightest bit arch or reserved. The pleasure principle is what makes this place special, that and the fact that the enthusiasms which made Mr Kehoe go into the restaurant business when he was fifteen years old have never dimmed.

So, do make a feature of enjoying different wines with their vegetarian dishes: good tender omelettes; crisp savoury quiche and coleslaw and french fries, perhaps a fruit and vegetable curry, a stir fry, or a pineapple and almond pilaf. The wines and the food were made for each other, and in the happy embrace of the dining room one will be smitten by the delights of this caring, sharing, quaffing place.

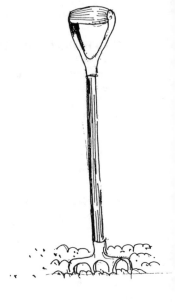

Open 12.30pm–2.15pm Mon–Sun, 6pm–10.30pm Mon–Sat, 6pm–9pm Sun.

Closed Xmas and Good Fri. Average Price: lunch under £10, bar lunch £5, dinner under £20. Visa, Access/Master. The Lord Bagenal Inn is signposted from the N9 a few miles south of Carlow town.

# County Dublin

## DUBLIN RESTAURANTS

## City Centre

### AYUMI-YA JAPANESE STEAKHOUSE ➡

*132 Lwr Baggot Street, D2 Tel: (01) 622 0233 Yoichi Hoashi*

The "steaks" of the restaurant's title are Teppan steaks, and refer to the manner in which they are cooked — over a hot iron griddle — rather than their cut, and vegetable "steaks" are a popular selection from the Teppan menu. Also available is a Kushi-age menu: where multi-varieties of veg are threaded onto skewers, breadcrumbed and deep fried.

But perhaps the best of many good reasons to eat in the Steakhouse is the noodles. These need all the concentration that they are habitually given by the regular clientele of Japanese businessmen who scoop and slurp in the correct fashion at the Soba, or buckwheat noodles, or the Udon, wheat noodles which bask in bowls of soup garnished with batter and deep fried tofu. Do enquire about the terrific Bento Box take-away service.

Open 12.30pm–2.30pm Mon–Fri, 6pm–11.30pm Mon–Thur ('till 12.30am Fri & Sat). Closed Xmas. Average Price: lunch and early evening menu under £10, dinner under £20. Visa, Access/Master, Amex. At the junction between Lr Pembroke Road and Baggot Street.

### BATZ

*10 Baggot Lane, D4 Tel: (01) 660 0363 Helen & Sarah Hackett*

A small, attentive lunchtime restaurant tucked just away from the office area of Baggot Street. The simple dishes are best achieved, the atmosphere splendidly unchauvinist. There are always vegetarian choices on the menu — omelette, various lasagnes — and don't miss the bread and butter pudding.

Open 12.15pm–2.30pm Mon–Fri. Closed Xmas/New Year. Average Price: lunch under £10. Visa, Access/Master, Amex. At the traffic lights where Lr Baggot Street meets Pembroke Road, turn left and Batz is on the right hand side.

### BEWLEY'S

*78–79 Grafton Street, D2 Tel: (01) 677 6761 Campbell Catering*

Part of the folklore and culture of the city, but the old Quaker idiom which once directed Bewley's is now long gone, replaced by a mercantile slickness. Enjoyable still, however, for tea and buns and afternoon idling.

Open 7.30am–1am Mon–Sun. Closed Xmas. Average Price: meals under £5. Visa, Access/Master, Amex, Diners. Bewley's is half-way up Grafton Street.

## BLAZING SALADS II

*Powerscourt Centre, Clarendon Street, D2 Tel: (01) 671 9552 Lorraine Fitzmaurice.*

Blazing Salads serve vegetarian food as well as gluten, dairy, yeast and sugar-free food with just that little bit of extra verve. The best way to enjoy the restaurant is to choose those dishes which offer a little more experimentation and individuality: vegetables packeted in arame sea weed, vegetarian couscous with fiery harissa. The staples of the restaurant are also reliable: the carrot cake, the hearty bakes, the potato salad. There is a small range of organic wine as an alternative to vegetable and fruit juices.

Open 9.30am–6pm Mon–Sat. Closed Xmas. Average price: meal under £5. No Credit Cards. At the very top of the Powerscourt Townhouse Centre.

## BU-ALI

*28 Lwr Clanbrassil Street, D8 Tel: (01) 454 6505 Ali Abbasali*

Even though it has smartened up in the course of the last year, as it has established itself as one of the most indispensable take-aways in the entire city, the Bu-Ali is changeless. Your eyes will likely go clammy with nostalgia, if you have ever travelled on the sub-continent and, back home, you walk in off the motorway which schisms and ruins this lovely part of Dublin and find yourself in Bu-Ali.

You can't eat memories, so it is just as well that the food in Bu-Ali is excellent: very real, very simple, very true, just what you might eat in the sub-continent, the rice in a vegetable biryani is baby-finger slender, each grain distinct; aloo cholay, a mix of potatoes and chick peas, is a sensation. With soft nan bread — and do try the nan which is doused with coriander leaves — it makes for a modest, splendid feast. And a feast of memories. Do note they deliver in the immediate radius.

Open 5pm–12.30am Mon–Sat, 5pm–midnight Sun. Closed Xmas. Average Price: under £10. No Credit Cards. 200 yards before the junction of Clanbrassil St and the South Circular Rd.

## RISTORANTE BUCCI

*7 Lwr Camden Street, D2 Tel: (01) 475 1020 Eoin Doyle*

Bucci is a laid-back, trés-cool, bare-boarded eating house, valuably sited on an increasingly neglected street.

It is modern in style and ethos, ambience and orientation and it deserves its success as somewhere that tries harder than many of the other mod-Italian dining rooms, a care one sees in the wine list, the sharp service, the astute music.

Open 12.30pm–2.30pm, 6pm–11.30pm Mon–Sun. Closed Xmas. Average Price: lunch under £5, dinner under £15. Visa, Access/Master, Amex, Diners. Halfway up Camden Street, across the road from the old cinema which you saw in "The Commitments".

STYRENE , EPOXY RESIN , BENZOYL PEROXIDE , E123 ,
MASTIC EPOXY RESIN , TRICHLORE THAN , CYANOACRYLATE ,
VAC PACKED AND WEIGHED , ZIP CODED AND 'BEST-
BEFORED', DATE STAMPED , BOXED , CHECKED , STAPLED
SEALED , STACKED , AND PUT ON PALLETS , NUMBERED
AND FORK-LIFTED INTO COLD STORAGE. — SOON THE CHEESE
WILL BE WITH US . THE PALLETS ARE DEFTLY RUN INTO THE
'CAVERN' OF A BIG SIXTEEN WHEELER BUILT TO CARRY
ANOTHER FORTY TONS OF THE HANDY SIZED PACKETS . THE
MIGHTY VOLVOS AND HINOS ARE QUICKLY LOADED , THE BIG
DOORS SWING CLOSED — THERE'S A CRASH OF COLD STEEL AS
THE BOLTS ARE R... ...S
SLAPPED A... ...S ARE
SECURED. ...D
BEFORE ...M FOAT
AND WOMB-LIKE WARM... ...S . THE BIG
DIESEL ENGINE TURNS RELUCTANTLY ONCE OR TWICE
BEFORE RUMBLING TO LIFE . THE DRIVER EAGERLY JABS
THE ACCELERATOR , AND IN PETULANT TEMPER THE ENGINE
ROARS BACK — THE TRUCK HISSES AND GROWLS ITS NODDING CAB
ROCKS ONCE OR TWICE — AND FORTY TWO TONS OF CHEESE
HIT THE N49 .

## CANALETTO'S

*69 Mespil Road, D4 Tel: (01) 678 5084 Terry Sheeran*

During the day Canaletto's is a neat café-cum-sandwich bar, with counter service and seating upstairs and down. Vegetable dishes of the day are always available: salads, filo pastry with spinach and feta cheese, or a butter bean and fennel bake are typical dishes.

At night, when piped music, vivid colours and candlelight turn Canaletto's into a sit-down restaurant, vegetarian options can seem to become more limited, but pastas can be customised and exotic and breads such as the oven-baked brushetta or the garlic bread with sundried tomatoes and basil are always on the menu.

Open 8am–6pm Mon–Fri, 6pm–11pm Mon–Sat. Closed Xmas. Average Price: lunch under £5, dinner under £15. No Credit Cards. Opposite the canal, near Baggot Street Bridge.

## CAPERS

*4 Nassau Street, D2 Tel: (01) 679 7140 Eddie Bates*

There will be many who will rejoice long and loud at the news that Eddie Bates has returned to his old stomping ground, upstairs over the vegetable shop in Nassau Street.

When Mr Bates cooked here some years back, he established a reputation for food which exhibited a modest flair and a knock-'em-dead understanding of flavour. Boldly amateurish and unconstrained by any formality, Capers always produced soulful, delicious food at the right price in the right place, with cool sounds and an enjoyably threadbare decor.

Well, for those who have missed it, here it is again: excellent roasted peppers stuffed with feta cheese, black olives and basil, then topped with a herb crust; grilled courgettes and tomatoes topped with Milleens cheese; tagliatelle with tomato, chilli and garlic sauce; cannelloni stuffed with spinach, walnuts and gorgonzola; spicy hazel-nut and red pepper rissoles with dahl and a yogurt and cucumber relish.

Mr Bates was a vegetarian himself for some years, and there is no one who so understands the need for invention, balance and variety in vegetarian food.

Open noon–3pm Mon–Fri, 6.30pm–late Thur–Sat. Closed Xmas and bank holidays. Average Price: lunch under £10, dinner under £15. No Credit Cards. Next to the Kilkenny Design Centre, above the Runner Bean shop.

## LA CAVE

*28 Sth Anne Street, D2 Tel: (01) 679 4409 Margaret Beskri*

A snatch of what might pass for a quayside bar in Marseille or a little café somewhere in Lyons, La Cave has a knockabout atmosphere — at any time of the day, it seems — and inexpensive food. The vegetarian cous cous with seven vegetables set beside fiery harissa sauce is simply the best thing on the menu.

Open 12.30pm–2.30pm Mon–Sat, 6pm–late Mon–Sun. Closed Xmas. Average price: meal under £10. Visa, Access/Master, Amex. La Cave is in a basement, just past the post office on Sth Anne Street: look for the sandwich board outside.

## CEDAR TREE

*11a Saint Andrew's Street, Dublin 2 Tel: (01) 677 2121 Ismail Sarhan*

The rich middle-eastern phrases of the Cedar Tree's proprietors, the Sarhan brothers, add a touch of poetry to the Lebanese staples which they serve in this Andrew Street basement.

The nature of this food, much of it constructed using beans and pulses, makes it a good place for vegetarians, and over the years the Cedar Tree has quietly established itself as a favourite haunt for anti-fashion followers, romantics, slackers, hackers and others of the demi-monde as the place in which to quaff richly tannic bottles of Lebanese wine, whilst munching from a seamless succession of mezzes which absorb the dark flavours of charcoal, legumes, spices and loads of garlic. Both the ambience and the food suit late-night assignations, conspiratorial amours, the private world of personal lives.

Open noon–5pm Mon–Sun, 5.30pm–midnight Mon–Sat, ('till 11pm Sun). Closed Xmas. Average Price: lunch under £10, dinner under £20. Visa, Access/Master, Diners, Amex. Beside the Old Stand pub.

## CHILI CLUB

*1 Anne's Lane, Sth Anne Street, D2 Tel: (01) 677 3721 Sharon Kenna*

Chillis and coconut milk, satays and skewered tofu, kaffir lime and sweet basil, the pungent and verveish tastes of Thailand are best enjoyed in The Chili Club, in a small dining room with a buzzy beat and a gameboy live-liness. This is fun food, gentle yet spicy, very enervating for the senses. But beware, strict vegetarians should counsel against shrimp paste and the oyster sauce, which are both prevalent in this cuisine.

Open 12.30pm–2.30pm Mon–Fri, 7pm–11pm Mon–Sat. Closed Xmas and 2 weeks in Jul. Average Price: lunch under £10, dinner under £20. Visa, Access/Master, Amex, Diners. Sth Anne Street leads off the middle of Grafton Street, and the Chili Club is on a laneway running south.

## CITY CENTRE

*23–25 Moss Street, Dublin 2 Tel: (01) 671 5907 Michael Creedon*

The City Centre is not, in fact, in the city centre, but it has a driven buzz and a fine energy about it that makes it seem smack up-to-the-minute, at the heart of things and chill-out cool.

A rag-painted-walls-and-columns room with minimal ornamentation and great big windows through which one peers at the world driving past, you will likely have to share this informal space with lots of uni-formed office grafters from the A.I.B. banking headquarters across the river, lured from their subsidised canteen by the tasty grub they can get up in here.

The City Centre may have elements which suggest post-hippy laid-back, but they know how to make a good spinach quiche with just enough nutmeg to give it a little kick-back and they appreciate how to dress a salad. There are dozens of places like the City Centre throughout Dublin, but this place has an edge that makes any return welcome.

Open 9am–6pm Mon–Fri,11am–4pm Sat. Closed Xmas week and bank holidays. Average Price: lunch under £5. No Credit Cards. Opposite the Matt Talbot bridge, across from the Custom House.

## THE COMMONS RESTAURANT

*85/86 St Stephen's Green, D2 Tel: (01) 475 2597 Michael Fitzgerald*

People come to the lavish and stylish Commons to celebrate those special moments of their lives — successfully achieved anniversaries or birthdays, colleges entered and exams successfully passed, deal clinching power lunches and lavish dinners to sway someone your way.

Whilst the food is very classical in the French style, they do, on request, offer vegetarian options: a pithivier of vegetables with sauerkraut on a tomato and leek sauce; a mille-feuille of vegetables and pasta with a saffron and sun dried tomato sauce, are just some of chef Micheal Bolster's creations. The paintings in the restaurant, by various contemporary artists, are splendid.

Open 12.30pm–2.15pm Mon–Fri, 7pm–10.15pm Mon–Sat. Closed Xmas and bank holidays. Average Price: lunch under £20 dinner under £30. Visa, Access/Master, Amex, Diners. Beside the Stephen's Green Church on St Stephen's Green South.

## COOKE'S CAFÉ

*14 South William Street, D2 Tel: (01) 679 0536/7/8 John Cooke*

The changes visited on John Cooke's eponymous café over the last year have been not just physical alterations — the restaurant has expanded both upstairs and down, with a new entrance and more spacious seating — but also intellectual changes, which have seen the promise of this fine space blossom into real, creative, food.

Where, previously, the menus disported themselves amidst the complexities of Cal-Ital cooking and brought forth a range of dishes that were usually well-achieved but which seemed to present endless problems of service, the newer menus are much more compact and intelligent, and the troublesome pasta dishes are confined to a scattering of choices: fettucine al vodka, or angel hair with grilled aubergines, tomato, basil and olive oil as starters; tortelloni au gratin as main courses. Salads, such as asparagus and avocado, are excellent, the crostini superb.

John Cooke's signature is a byword for stylish, groovy food. There are many other cooks in Dublin who are attempting something similar to Cooke's Café, but the original remains the best.

Open 12.30pm–6pm, 6pm–11.30pm Mon–Sun. Closed Xmas and bank holiday lunches. Average Price: lunch under £15, dinner under £30. Visa, Access/Master, Amex, Diners. At the back of the Powerscourt Townhouse Centre.

## LE COQ HARDI

*35 Pembroke Road, D4 Tel: (01) 668 4130/668 9070 John Howard*

One's estimation of John Howard's restaurant throughout its long history has always been of an archetypal bourgeois eating palace, somewhere that slings history right back to the days of César Ritz and Auguste Escoffier, an uninterrupted blow-out of classical cuisine and claret.

But, whilst this is largely true, they do, thoughtfully, offer a selection of vegetarian choices: asparagus spears and wild oyster mushrooms, in a light pastry pillow with lemon butter sauce, or strudel pastry filled with seasonal vegetables on a light curry sauce with mint. Great, and celebrated, wine list.

Open 12.30pm–3pm Mon–Fri, 7pm–11pm Mon–Sat. Closed Xmas and 2 weeks in early Aug. Average Price: lunch under £20, dinner over £30. Visa, Access/Master, Amex, Diners. On the right hand side when driving from Baggot Street towards Ballsbridge.

## CORA'S

*1 St Mary's Road, D4 Tel: (01) 660 0585 Mr & Mrs Basini*

A little Italian café, and a sweet, wholesome place. Bring the babies and let the female staff members scoop them from your arms and hand them around whilst you eat a little mushroom lasagne, some spaghetti with pesto, sip some wine.

Open 8.30am–6pm Mon–Fri, 9.30am–3pm Sun (closed Sat). Closed Xmas week and 3 weeks in Aug. Average price: lunch under £10. No Credit Cards. At the traffic lights where Lr Baggot Street meets Pembroke Road, turn left and Batz is on the right hand side.

## CORNUCOPIA

*19 Wicklow Street, D2 Tel: (01) 677 7583 Deirdre McCafferty*

Cornucopia has settled into the groove of Dublin life, its vegetarian pies, curries, bakes and salads appealing to both veggies and non-veggies, fulfilling a valuable role in the everyday goings on of the capital. Consistency has been the hallmark of the restaurant from the day it opened its doors.

Open 8am–11pm Mon–Sat. Closed Xmas. Average Price: under £5. No Credit Cards. Visa, Access/Master. Half way up the Grafton Street end of Wicklow Street.

## L'ECRIVAIN

*109 Lr Baggot Street, D2 Tel: (01) 661 1919 Derry & Sally-Anne Clarke*

Derry Clarke's food works because of the astute application of oodles of common sense, a strain of common sense which ushers food out to the customer in a pristine, lively state, full of taste, full of tense, alert flavours. And no exception is made with his vegetarian menu: grilled goat's cheese with crisp toast salad in filo pastry; fresh asparagus spears in butter; avocado and pear salad with deep fried vegetables; a tartlette of leek and carrot; wild mushrooms with vegetables and nuts en croute; pasta with good olive oil and sweet peppers.

Mr Clarke's staff could give Masterclasses in the art of waiting on table. Mr Clarke himself could give Masterclasses in the art of culinary common sense. The family also now run Parker's Restaurant in the Lansdowne Hotel on Pembroke Road, where the menu retains some classical influences but also offers pasta and vegetarian dishes and draws on the funky flavours of the Mediterranean.

Open 12.30pm–2pm Mon–Fri, 6.30pm–11pm Mon–Sat. Closed Xmas. Average Price: lunch under £20, dinner under £30. Visa, Access/Master, Amex, Diners. In a courtyard across from the bank of Ireland.

## ELEPHANT & CASTLE

*18 Temple Bar, D2 Tel: (01) 679 3121 Liz Mee & John Hayes*

At any time of day or night, the Elephant & Castle serves the food you want and becomes the place you want it to be. From 8 in-the-morning omelette breakfasts, perhaps after you've just got off the boat, are going into work or have just wrapped up the night shift, to a mid-morning gouter, to a pasta lunch with a girlfriend, maybe a late afternoon pick-me-up, and onwards to a late night romantic rendezvous with a loved-one, perhaps a family table for Sunday brunch.

All of the foods for all of these occasions can be found here. You can even, indeed, eat in the E&C more than once a day, and find it is different, find the style of food will have changed to suit the time of day.

The food is democratically priced, but never cheap: with these ingredients it could never be.

On the face of it, the Elephant and Castle seems an ideal restaurant for vegetarians. The daily special is often a wonderful vegetarian concoction from the far east — often chosen by non vegetarians for its deliciousness as well as its appropriateness. The general menu offers omelettes, salads and pastas, great chips and sparklingly good desserts.

Open 8am–11.30pm Mon–Thur, 8am–midnight Fri, 10.30am–midnight Sat, noon–11.30pm Sun. Closed Xmas. Average Price: under £10. Visa, Access/Master, Amex, Diners. In Dublin's Temple Bar, just on the south side of the River Liffey.

## FITZERS CAFÉS

*24 Upper Baggot Street, D4 Tel: (01) 660 0644; Dawson Street, D2 Tel: (01) 677 1155; The RDS, Ballsbridge, D4 Tel: (01) 667 1301 Frank Fitzpatrick*

The dynamic, spirited organisation which is Fitzers expands year-by-year. The latest venture, following on from their funky new outlet in Dawson Street, is a café in the RDS, in Ballsbridge. Add on the film catering arm of the organisation, and you have an outfit responsible for an extraordinarily large volume of meals.

Happily, these meals are good, and the democratic and easy-access attitude of Fitzers makes it easy to pick and choose just the sort of food you want.

The culling of influences in their food is extraordinarily universal. Beginning on the west coast of the 'States, their grab-bag of influences then proceeds out in search of coriander, limes, and the red spices of

Indonesia, before travelling even further afield to add the culture of Indian dishes and, finally, with the occasional detour to Africa for a purloining of chilli cooking, it all comes home to roost with the techniques and flavours of the Mediterranean: crisp French-style baguettes and plenty of pastas, which makes the Café very vegetarian-friendly.

Open Baggot St: 8am–11.30pm Mon–Sat; Dawson St: 9am–11.30pm; RDS: noon–3pm, 6–11pm Mon–Sun ('till 10.30pm Sun). Average Price: Baggot St: lunch under £10, dinner under £15; Dawson St: lunch under £15, dinner under £15; RDS: lunch £15, dinner under £30. Visa, Access/Master, Amex. Between Searson's pub and the Baggot Street hospital; half-way up Dawson Street; and in the RDS building in Ballsbridge

## FURAMA CHINESE RESTAURANT

*88 Donnybrook Road, D4 Tel: (01) 283 0522 Rodney Mak*

At weekends, the Furama is full of Dublin 4 types — weekend-access fathers spoiling their kids, rugby souls already tanked up on a few bevies of beer, skinny women discussing their career curves — all of them enjoying the lush accents and sensual flavours which Freddie Lee's food delivers to the diner. Vegetarians should seek their advice, and they will happily amend the menu.

Open 12.30pm–2pm Mon–Fri, 6pm–11.30pm Mon–Sat, 1.30pm–11pm Sun. Closed Xmas. Average Price: lunch under £10–under £15, dinner under £20. Visa, Access/Master, Amex, Diners. Opposite Bective rugby ground, near the Shell Garage.

## GOTHAM CAFÉ

*8 South Anne Street, D2 Tel: (01) 679 5266 David Barry*

Although the Gotham Café is a sister-ship of the famed Independent Pizza Co, of Drumcondra, they have begun recently to separate the identities of the two outlets, tied as they were previously by a bold smattering of pizza styles.

Where, before, there was a large range of gourmet pizzas and calzoni, the menu now is moving in the direction of a modern Cal-Ital style: calzoni stuffed with roasted peppers, olives, tomato, mozzarella and basil; foccaccia; goat's cheese crostini, and especially with their pasta dishes: linguini with pesto; penne with tomato and fresh basil.

Open 11am–midnight Sun–Thur, 11am–12.30am Fri–Sat. Closed Xmas, Good Fri. Average Price: lunch under £10, dinner under £15. Visa, Access/Master. South Anne St. runs between Grafton St and Dawson St.

## RESTAURANT PATRICK GUILBAUD

*46 James Place, Baggot Street Lwr, D2 Tel: (01) 676 4192 Patrick Guilbaud*

Whilst you might be surprised to learn that a restaurant as classically French as M. Guilbaud's is a safe haven for vegetarians, it is. Simply give them notice, and the vegetarian choices can prove to be splendid.

Open 12.30pm–2pm, 7.30pm–10.15pm Tues–Sat. Closed Xmas. Average Price: lunch under £20, dinner under £30. Visa, Access/Master, Amex, Diners. Behind the Bank of Ireland on Baggot Street.

## LITTLE CAESAR'S PIZZA

*5 Chatham House, Balfe Street, D2 Tel: (01) 671 8714 Adel Samy*

A one-up, one-down pair of rooms just across from the Westbury hotel and just off the strip of Grafton Street, the hungry energy of the proprietors and the generous, hunger-zapping food of Little Caesar's make for somewhere that makes it easy to enjoy yourself.

Pizzas are the speciality, obviously, and you can improvise, invent, mutate or minimalise any manner of pizza topping you wish, then watch some skilful, slap-happy exhibitionism in action as the pizza man hurls circles of dough into the air before bedding them down with ingredients and shooting them into the pizza oven.

Open 12.30pm–12.30am Mon–Sun. Closed Xmas, Easter. Average Price: Pizzas under £10. Visa, Access/Master, Amex, Diners. Opposite the Westbury Hotel.

## LOCKS

*1 Windsor Terrace, Portobello, D8 Tel: (01) 454 3391 Clare Douglas*

Clare Douglas works closely with the organic grower Marc Michel, who maintains one enormous tunnel on his farm in Wicklow with fruits and vegetables grown just for the restaurant.

This professional and careful approach to her supplies runs right through Ms Douglas' approach to the restaurant itself, one of the most meticulous and professional operations in the city. There's nothing startlingly original for vegetarians here but, like everything else, the veggie food offered is professionally put together, meticulous and generous: Mediterranean salad of Marc's lettuce, goat's cheese, olives and grapes; melon with strawberries and mint; or pastas with blue cheese, tomato or creamy vegetable dressing.

Open 12.30pm–2pm Mon–Fri, 7.15pm–11pm Mon–Sat. Closed Xmas. Average Price: lunch under £15, dinner under £25. Visa, Access/Master, Amex, Diners. Between Portobello Bridge and Harold's Cross Bridge, facing the Grand Canal.

## MARKS BROS

*7 South Great George's Street, D2 Tel: (01) 677 1085 Simon McWilliams*

Marks Bros is a place of eternal youth. It doesn't change, age does not alter it a jot. It does the same thing and it does it well. As the students and adolescents who are its punters grow older and move on, new kids take their place on the block, in the long lunch queue. Their fave bands may be different, they may crave new drugs and lower-rate mortgages, but their need for Marks Bros' sandwiches and soups remains a constant.

The soups, trusty enemies of hangover hunger, are reliable vegetarian concoctions, the sandwiches are reliable doorsteps. Simon runs the show and, it seems, lets the place run itself, the next generation of kids come and go, talking of Michelangelo, wondering what The Love Song of J. Alfred Prufrock is all about.

Open 10am–5pm Mon–Sat. Closed 25–26 Dec, Good Fri. Average Price: lunch under £5. No Credit Cards. At the Dame St end of Sth. Gt George's St.

## THE NATIONAL MUSEUM CAFÉ
*Kildare Street, D2 Tel: (01) 662 1269 Joe Kerrigan*

The enchantingly lovely room which the Museum Café occupies is a happy, handsome space in which to enjoy cooking which one Dublin journalist, appositely and accurately, described as "simple, unpretentious food . . . cooked with care and attention".

Those factors of care and simplicity have always been the hallmark of Joe Kerrigan's cooking, and throughout his work you see the mark of someone who respects the mantra that one must respect the intrinsic flavour of a dish and work only to bring it to its best. This is, indeed, simple and unpretentious food, for Kerrigan has no arrogant ego, and wants only to make food that will satisfy and give pleasure. There are many treasures in the National Museum, and the Café is the latest one.

Open 10am–5pm Mon–Sat, 2pm–5pm Sun. Closed Xmas. Average Price: lunch under £5. Visa, Access/Master. Signposted in the Museum buildings.

## NICO'S
*53 Dame Street, D2 Tel: (01) 677 3062 Graziano Romero*

Ageless tratt food, which suits buckets of wine, flaming sambucas and suits the lovers of all sexes who love Nico's for its grand guignol and its piano player. The waiters are a theatre of chauvinism and panicked cool.

Open noon–2.30pm Mon–Fri, 6pm–12.30am Mon–Sat. Closed Xmas. Average Price: lunch under £10, dinner under £20. Visa, Access/Master, Amex, Diners. Just down from the Central Bank on Dame Street (travelling away from Trinity).

## OMAR KHAYYAM
*51 Wellington Quay, Dublin 2 Tel: (01) 677 5758 George Sabongi*

It is most often vegetarians who sing the praises of Omar Khayyam, an Egyptian restaurant on Dublin's quays which is one of a trio of places owned by George Sabongi, a restaurateur who also tries his hand at Italian food, in La Scala, and at conventional bistro fare in his eponymous Bistro and Piano Bar, on South Frederick Street.

The vegetarians prize its mix of pulses and spices, wrapping up the warm colours and flavours of the Middle East in pitta breads, or layers of filo pastry. For the main part the food is simple and whilst the restaurant doesn't have the ambience of an Alexandrian balcony — you won't find record company wheeler dealers with portable 'phones on Alexandrian balconies, or at least not often — many enjoy its youthful style and energy.

Open noon–midnight Mon–Sat. Closed bank holidays. Average Price: lunch under £10, dinner under £15. Visa, Access/Master, Amex, Diners. A few yards down from the Ha'penny bridge, on the south side.

## 101 TALBOT ➡
*100–102 Talbot Street, D1 Tel: (01) 874 5011 Margaret Duffy & Pascal Bradley*

101 Talbot has grown into one of the essential restaurant spaces in the city, and for a very simple reason: the cooking speaks of personal care

and personal preferences, the big room oozes quiet charm, and the calm personalities of Margaret Duffy and Pascal Bradley make it feel like a restaurant where the owners are more than overly concerned that you should have a good time, enjoy the food, and want to come back.

Margaret Duffy is one of those cooks who bring a meticulous feel for goodness and taste to their cooking, so the culinary grab-bag of foods which 101 offers — Italian pastas, Provençal bakes, up-to-the-minute sandwiches, Yankee desserts, stir-fried vegetables — never lose track of true flavours. At any time of the day, this food is a delight, and the space is perfect for solo diners of both sexes, babies, paramours, theatre-goers, cineastes. Even your mother. Maybe.

Open 10.30am–10.30pm (Mon 'till 4pm) pasta served all day, Lunch menu noon–3pm, dinner menu 6.30pm–11pm. Closed Xmas. Average Price: lunch under £5–under £10, dinner under £20. Visa, Access/Master. Between the Abbey Theatre and the Pro Cathedral.

## PIZZERIA ITALIA

*23 Temple Bar, D2 Tel: (01) 677 8528*

No-nonsense Italian tratt grub, pastas and pizzas, all the old standbys to be drunk with rough red wine that is happily priced as rough red wine. Its Italian colours flag the beginning of the Temple Bar cobblestones and the counter seating is suited for looking out and looking in. If the toasty smell of rising pizzas doesn't drag you into the restaurant, you can buy yourself a wedge-to-go from its side street kitchen window.

Open noon–11pm Tue–Sat. Closed Xmas/New Year, last 2 weeks in Jun. Average Price: lunch under £10, dinner under £10. No Credit Cards. In Temple Bar, on the corner where it becomes Fleet Street.

## THE RAJDOOT TANDOORI ➡

*26–28 Clarendon Street, Westbury Centre, D2 Tel: (01) 679 4274*

Not just the best Indian cooking in the city, but one of the most consistent restaurants in the country. The Rajdoot is part of a small chain of Indian restaurants based in the U.K., but there is no feeling of factory-line production here.

The food is reverberantly lush in the northern Indian Moghul style, with their daals delicate and creamy, their curries a serene meld of butter and tomatoes, yogurt and cashew nuts and not the jumble of junk so many Indian restaurants are content to serve, the biryanis fluffy and precise, each element distinct. Breads are marvellous, vegetarians are almost spoilt for choice, service is perfect, and prices are keen.

Open noon–2.30pm, 6.30pm–11.30pm Mon–Sat. Closed Xmas/New Year. Average Price: lunch under£10 dinner under £20. Visa, Access/Master, Amex, Diners. At the back of the Westbury Hotel.

## ROLY'S BISTRO

*7 Ballsbridge Terrace, D4 Tel: (01) 668 2611 Roly Saul*

Roly Saul's eponymous venture has proven to be the biggest hit in Dublin's restaurant culture in recent times, and the clever calculation behind it all reveals the shift in eating styles which is driving through the restaurant trade.

For a start, though called a bistro this is really a brasserie — the upstairs dining room is handsome and endearing — but the prices belong almost to a café with lunch, in particular, a whacking great bargain. Secondly, the food betrays no tension between care and necessary speed of service. The cooking, however, is well crafted: no matter whether you are eight or eighty, the secret of Roly's success is that you can extract from it what you want: a quick lunch or a lingering dinner, a family party, maybe impressing the kids at the weekend when you have access and they don't want to go to the zoo again.

Open noon–4pm, 6pm–11pm Mon–Sun. Closed Xmas. Average Price: lunch under £15, dinner under £20. Visa, Access/Master, Amex. On the corner between Ballsbridge and Herbert Park, just down from the American Embassy.

## SHALIMAR

*17 South Great George's Street, Dublin 2 Tel: (01) 671 0738 Mr Anwar*

The Shalimar has acquired a very hip reputation for its food, and it is deserved in many ways. The food has a fine understanding of North Indian and Pakistani cooking — the owners hail from central Pakistan, so tandoori dishes are spicy, and their "exquisite dishes" are sinfully gorgeful with cream and nut sauces, tomato and butter emulsions.

As with most Indian restaurants there are excellent choices for vegetarians, and these are always good places to take kids.

Open noon–2.30pm Mon–Sat, 6pm–midnight Mon–Thurs & Sun, 6pm–1am Fri–Sat. Closed Xmas. Average Price: lunch under £10, dinner under £20. Visa, Access/Master, Amex, Diners. Opposite the Central Hotel, on the corner of Exchequer Street.

## LA STAMPA

*35 Dawson Street, D2 Tel: (01) 677 8611/677 3336 Paul Flynn*

Paul Flynn is such a fine cook that one wishes he had a benefactor who would grant him a small restaurant, a large kitchen brigade, and a beautiful room in which to serve his creations.

Well, he has the last of this trilogy of dreams — La Stampa, a converted guildhall, is the most glorious restaurant room in the city, in fact in the country.

But, in the real world of commerce in which restaurants must work, Mr Flynn cooks in a restaurant which turns over very large numbers of covers. And he manages it with a small brigade.

And Mr Flynn is such a good cook that, despite the pressures of this system, he still creates good food: baked aubergines with pesto; croustade of goat's cheese; rigatoni with four cheeses, or with a pesto cream; feuillete of seared spring vegetables; roast vegetables with lemon and cous cous. As you might expect in a beautiful room, the beautiful people are one of the staples of La Stampa, which makes the restaurant slightly self-conscious. The staff are also slightly self-conscious, except for the restaurant manager, Declan Maxwell. Mr Maxwell is a genius at people-handling, and it is purest joy just to watch him at work.

Open 12.30pm–2.30pm Mon–Fri, 6.30pm–11.15pm Mon–Sun ('till 11.45pm Fri & Sat). Closed Xmas. Average Price: lunch under £15, dinner under £30. Visa, Access/Master, Amex, Diners. Opposite the Mansion House at the St. Stephen's Green end of Dawson Street.

## TOSCA

*20 Suffolk Street, D2 Tel: (01) 679 6744 Norman Hewson*

Tosca features endlessly in gossip columns, on account of its attraction to visiting starlets and rock stars, which means the food garners too little attention. A pity, because whilst the modern Italian influences are obvious, there can be interesting tastes in Aongus Hanly's cooking: smoked garlic and broccoli to accompany some pasta, or perhaps a trio of pestos, and the staff are excellent.

Open 10.30am–midnight Mon–Sun ('till 1am Thur–Sat). Closed Xmas. Average Price: lunch under £5 dinner under £10. Visa, Access/Master, Amex, Diners. Half-way up Suffolk Street.

## TROCADERO

*3 St Andrew's Street, D2 Tel: 677 5545/679 2385 Rhona Teehan*

An integral and unmissable part of Dublin culture. The food is just what you will expect it to be, but the crack will be a whole lot better. There's no set vegetarian option, but they'll put something together, they promise. So go very late and join the thespians, rock'n'rollers, paparazzi and assorted night owls. Don't worry about the food, don't worry about your hangover.

Open 6pm–12.30am Mon–Sat, 6pm–11.30pm Sun. Closed Xmas. Average Price: dinner under £20. Visa, Access/Master, Amex, Diners. St Andrew's Street runs between Wicklow Street and Suffolk Street.

## THE WELL FED CAFÉ

*Dublin Resource Centre, Crow Street, D2 Tel: (01) 677 2234 Michael Long*
Now one of the great staples of vegetarian eating in the capital, the Well
Fed is a friendly, valuable place where the cooking can be both old-
fashioned — veggie burgers — and decidedly modern — Mexican tacos,
perhaps, or some other improvisation from the Pacific Rim. Very child-
friendly, solid as a rock

Open 10.30am–8.30pm Mon–Sat. Closed Xmas/New Year and bank holidays. Average
Price: under £5. No Credit Cards. In the Temple Bar area, parallel to Fownes Street, beside
the Central Bank.

## THE WINDING STAIR BOOKSHOP AND CAFÉ

*40 Lwr Ormond Quay, D1 Tel: (01) 873 3292 Kevin Connolly*
Kevin Connolly's Winding Stair has always sold coffee and cakes to
enable you to while away hour after hour in this beautiful second-hand
bookstore, listening to music, perusing the shelves, peering out the
window at the River Liffey.

Recently, since Kevin's sister Eileen began to cook soups and to
make bumper sandwiches at lunchtime, the shop has begun to attract
hordes of the hungry and these, too, have succumbed to the innocent
seductiveness and chippy hilarity of the Winding Stair. The atmosphere
is so unpretentious and crystalline calm, the girls and guys cooking and
serving the food so full of sappy sang froid, that the Winding Stair is
irresistible.

Open10.30am–6pm Mon–Sat, Soup served from noon; coffee, cake and rolls and
sandwiches available all day. Closed 25th Dec–1st Jan and bank holidays. Average Price:
under £5. No Credit Cards. The Winding Stair looks down from the North side of the River
Liffey onto the Ha'penny Bridge.

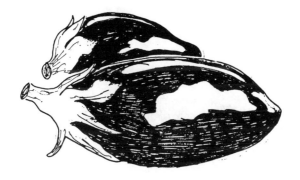

# South County Dublin

# BLACKROCK

### AYUMI-YA JAPANESE RESTAURANT ➡

*Newtownpark Avenue, Blackrock Tel: (01) 283 1767 Akiko Hoashi*

The parent of the Ayumi-Ya Steakhouse in Dublin city, and one of the longest established restaurants in the county, the Ayumi-Ya continues to move through the years with grace and the promise of good food. Mrs Hoashi's food is as ornamented and as fine as one expects of Japanese cooking, whether you choose the Teppan-Yaki tables and have the food cooked immediately in front of you, or decide to go native and sit on the floor and enjoy the calming service by the waitresses.

The set menus are excellent value, but sometimes it is fun to allow the restaurant to compose a menu for you — they even suggest that first-timers choose the Omakase-Menu, where the chefs select the food — and to indulge in a succession of sublime and sinuous and sympathetic dishes: tempura with its clamouring batter, tofu with its mellow indifference sharpened by deep-frying or mixed with sesame oil. Vegetarian dishes are excellent.

Open 7pm–11pm Mon–Sat, 6pm–10pm Sun. Closed Xmas. Average Price: dinner under £20. Visa, Access/Master, Amex, Diners. At the Blackrock end of Newtownpark Avenue, amongst the small group of shops.

### LA TAVOLA

*114 Rock Road, Booterstown Tel: (01) 283 5101 Bahaa Jaafai*

Excellent service, great atmosphere, nice spicy arrabbiata for penne, crisp and well-balanced pizzas, fresh, lively salads, super ice-cream. Good value.

Open noon–11.30pm Mon–Sat. Closed Xmas. Average Price: meals under £10–under £15. Visa, Access/Master. The Rock Road is part of the main thoroughfare between Dublin and Dun Laoghaire, opposite Booterstown DART station.

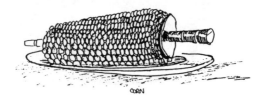

CORN

# DUN LAOGHAIRE

## KRISHNA INDIAN RESTAURANT

*47 George's Street Lwr, Dun Laoghaire Tel: (01) 280 1855 Paul Sahota*
The lighting is almost dusky dark, but the food is bright with careful flavours and personal care. The use of organic vegetables is diligent and typically thoughtful, and vegetarian dishes expert.

Open noon–2.30pm Mon–Sat, 6pm–midnight Mon–Sun ('till 1am Fri and Sat). Closed Xmas. Average Price: dinner under £20. Visa, Access/Master, Amex, Diners. Upstairs, a few doors up from Dunphy's pub.

## MORELS

*18 Glasthule Road, Dun Laoghaire Tel: 230 0210/230 0068 Alan O'Reilly*
The intention of Morels is to reflect the splashes of colour that festoon this high-ceilinged room with atmosphere and light, back onto the plate with a mixture of Californian and Mediterranean cooking.

The room, designed by Frank Ennis and featuring paintings from artists Emer Diamond and Killian O'Connell, certainly lifts your spirits. The food could be a little more free and easy in its execution, but its simplicity gives it a goodness and trueness that ultimately wins your attention. Vegetarian meals are not built into the menu, but the kitchen, which is in full view of the dining room, will adapt and amend the wealth of good ingredients on offer: cous cous, field mushrooms, rocket, white truffle oil, aged parmesan and goat's cheese ravioli.

Open 6.30pm–10pm Mon–Thurs, 6.30pm–10.30pm Fri & Sat, 12.30pm–2.30pm, 6.30pm–9pm Sun. Closed Xmas. Average Price: lunch under £10, dinner under £15. Visa, Access/Master. Above the Eagle House pub.

## ODELL'S

49 Sandycove Road, Dun Laoghaire Tel: (01) 284 2188 John Waddell

The cooking here is smooth-edged and friendly, and this suits the modest ambitions of Odell's. They are able to achieve good flavours, and create a peaceful ambience to help one to enjoy an evening. Vegetarian food includes Baked St Killian with ground tropical nuts, pineapple and muscatel chutney, grilled aubergine salad with sweet peppers and red onions in a ginger rosemary vinaigrette, or a vegetarian pasta with seasonal vegetables in a garlic soy orange sauce.

Open 6pm–10.30pm Tue–Sun. Closed Xmas. Average Price: dinner under £20. Visa, Access/Master, Amex, Diners. Upstairs, opposite Fitzgerald's pub in Sandycove.

# STILLORGAN

## CHINA-SICHUAN RESTAURANT

*4 Lower Kilmacud Road, Stillorgan Tel: (01) 288 4817 David Hui*

The China-Sichuan is not some sizzling-dishes-with-curry-chips sort of an establishment, it's the real thing. Both chefs and ingredients are imported from the People's Republic and the imaginative vegetarian menu includes first courses of hot and sour soup, as well as genuine vegetarian spring rolls, to be followed by spiced beancurd, fried Chinese Cabbage and something curiously called Fried Twin Delight — try it and see.

With these, some voluptuously slinky Dan-Dan Mein noodles, or maybe some clean boiled rice. Expect to cough, occasionally, as the toxic charge of chillies hits the back of the throat: apply Australian Chardonnay immediately. For dessert, some gloriously cool almond bean curd, the taste like an incredibly exotic marzipan, comes as a delicious surprise, the perfect ending to a series of surprisingly accessible and delightful tastes.

Open 12.30pm–2.30pm, 6pm–11pm Mon–Fri, 6pm–11pm Sat, 1pm–2.30pm, 6pm–11pm Sun. Closed Xmas. Average Price: lunch under £10, dinner under £20. Visa, Access/Master, Amex. On the Kilmacud Road, just up from the Stillorgan Shopping Centre.

# North County Dublin

# DRUMCONDRA

## INDEPENDENT PIZZA CO

*46 Lower Drumcondra Road, D9 Tel: (01) 830 2957 Jackie Keating*

The Independent Pizza Co has been working well for years now, simply because they know that the secret of pizza is to take painstaking care both with preparation and production.

If you want to laze at home with a six-pack, a brace of videos and the remote-control, then their "Pizza Pick-Up" allows you to telephone, make your order, and they will have it ready for you when you arrive, along with comprehensive instructions on how to re-heat it at home. On request, Pizzas to go and to be re-heated are undercooked and uncut.

Real pizzaficionados, of course, will abjure the charms of the cinema of James Cameron and John Woo and eat in, savouring the unbeatable zing of pizza as it arrives piping hot from the oven, enjoying the funky atmosphere, savouring the excellent value.

Open: noon–1am Sun–Thur, noon–2am Fri–Sat. Closed Xmas. Average Price: Pizza under £10. No Credit Cards. The Drumcondra Road is the beginning of the main N1 to Belfast: Independent Pizza is right at the traffic light junction.

# HOWTH

## ADRIAN'S

*3 Abbey Street, Howth Tel & Fax: (01) 839 1696 Catriona Holden*
The restaurant should, perhaps, be more accurately called "Catriona's", for it is Adrian Holden's daughter who is the firebrand with the frying pan in her hand

Ms Holden is a young woman who looks like a teenager, cooks with the vitality of an adolescent, and the control of an expert. Her skills enjoy a broad template, untrammelled by any conservatism: three pepper gâteau; koulibiaca with a sorrel sauce; parsnip and cauliflower gratin with a little salad; youthful snappy cooking, and Ms Holden manages to prime each dish so that the flavours are clambering out. Never mind the shoestring decoration of the place, the informality: this is real cooking.

Open 12.30pm–3pm Mon–Sat, 6pm–9.30pm Mon–Sun ('till 8pm Sun). Closed 25–26 Dec, Good Fri. Average Price: lunch under £10, dinner under £20. Visa, Access/Master, Amex, Diners. At the end of Howth village, past the pier, where the road broadens out, Adrian's is just a short stroll up the hill.

PARSNIP

# MALAHIDE

## BON APPETIT

*9 St. James Terrace, Malahide Tel: (01) 845 0314 Patsy McGuirk*

There are clever and ingenious specialities in Patsy McGuirk's cooking, and the restaurant pulses with the attentive concern of the chef-proprietor. This same concern is directed to the vegetarian who will be made to feel welcome, and pampered with creamy concoctions of pasta.

Open 12.30pm–2.30pm Mon–Fri, 7pm–11pm Mon–Sat. Closed Xmas and bank holidays. Average Price: lunch under £15, dinner under £30. Visa, Access/Master, Amex, Diners. At the crossroads take the coastal road back to Dublin. Bon Appetit is one of the houses on the long Georgian terrace on the left.

## OLD STREET WINE BAR

*Old Street, Malahide Tel: (01) 845 1882 Gail Sinclair*

Gail Sinclair's menu suits the style of her little place, whether you find yourself there on a quiet Monday lunchtime or late on a bumptious Friday night when the buzz is good. There are placid vegetable soups—good mushroom, a more energetic curried parsnip — quiches that enjoy good pastry, a vegetable and ginger stir fry.

There is, naturally, a chocolate biscuit cake, apple pie from Mum, and even apple and strawberries together in a tart. It is a thoughtful menu — there are always at least four or five vegetarian options — and it doesn't require more than a second's thought to decide that you want to go back to Old Street and enjoy it again.

Open noon–3pm, 6pm–11pm Mon–Sun. Closed Xmas. Average Price: lunch under £5, dinner under £15. Visa, Access/Master. Turn left before the traffic lights, just after the Church. The wine bar is on the left.

# SWORDS

## OLD SCHOOLHOUSE

*Coolbanagher, Swords Tel: (01) 840 2846 Brian Sinclair*

The ambitions of The Old Schoolhouse explain the reasons for its enduring success. In here, the intention is to provide food which is enjoyable without presenting any unfamiliar challenges. People like The Old Schoolhouse: its unpretentiousness, its feminine efficiency and feminine charm, its simple food, which can be effective and tasty: avocado and hazelnut tossed salad; baked filo parcels filled with ratatouille; nut loaf with fresh tomato and basil sauce; potato pancake stuffed with spinach and blue cheese in a nutmeg sauce.

Open 12.30pm–2.30pm Mon–Fri, 7pm–10.30pm Mon–Sat. Closed Xmas and bank holidays. Average price: lunch under £20 dinner under £20. Visa, Access/Master, Amex, Diners. The Old Schoolhouse is just off the main street in Swords, down the hill, five minutes from the Airport.

# DUBLIN SHOPPING GUIDE

## Dublin City Centre

Asian Food Store
### THE ASIA MARKET
*18 Drury Street, D2 Tel: (01) 677 9764*
The Asia Market is the place to go to find a paradise of ingredients. One of Dublin's greatest shopping adventures is to seek out and find some queer foodstuff that, until you read Yan Kit So's recipe for Almond Bean Curd or Julie Sahni's Gobhi Masallam, you'd never heard of and certainly never cooked with before. Despite its size, you could be cooking every day of the year and still find some new exotica on the groaning shelves of the Asia Market with which to experiment: white fungus; lotus root; ginseng extract, chillies by the kilo bag, it's all here.
Open 10am–7pm Mon–Fri, 11am–6pm Sat and Sun.

Chocolates
### BUTLER'S IRISH
*51a Grafton Street, D2*
One of the very first Irish made chocolate companies, Butler's Irish are distributed throughout the country from their small factory at Unit 5 Enterprise Centre, Pearse Street, D2 Tel: (01) 671 0599. Recently they acquired their own shop at the top of Grafton Street, from where you can buy their entire range.
Open 9am–7pm Mon–Sat (Thur 'till 8pm).

Chinese Food Store
### CHINACO LTD
*67 Bride Street, D8 Tel: (01) 478 4699*
Chinaco is reminiscent of the Chinese supermarkets in London's Soho, a bit of a barn of a shop spilling over with giant woks and spatulas set beside colourful tins and taffeta-green flourishes of bok choy. Part warehouse, part retail outlet, from the outside you might not imagine that the shop is even open to the public. The service within is cool — it's sensible to have an exact idea of what you want before you get here, because advice is seldom given.
Open 10am–6.30pm Mon–Fri, 11am–6.30pm Sat & Sun.

Bakery
### COOKE'S BAKERY
*31 Francis Street, D8 Tel: (01) 549201*
*32 Dawson Street, D2 Tel: (01) 6772270 Fax: (01) 6790546*
Walking into Cooke's bakeries is, in bread terms, the equivalent of stepping out of monochrome into the charged fission of Technicolor.

Forget the sober, simple stuff on which you were reared, the no-nonsense sliced pans and dour soda breads, for the breads in here are day-glo dizzy, acid-crazed hallucinations that seem to have sprung more from a Salvador Dali dreamscape than from the fusion of flour and water.

There are torridly coloured breads with tomato and fennel seeds. Shiny, egg-washed sourdoughs. Sternly brown rye breads. Flour-flecked sodas. Great big whirls of foccaccia dotted with tomato. Threaded lengthy plaits of white bread, the whole kit and caboodle of them as bright with vivid colour as some pop art poster.

Open Francis Street: 10am–5pm Mon–Sat, 10am–2pm Sun, Dawson Street: 10am–5.30pm Mon–Sat.

Growers' Market
## THE DUBLIN FOOD CO-OP ➧

*St. Andrew's Centre, Pearse Street, D2 For membership Tel: (01) 872 1191 Fax: 873 5737*

We polarise neatly into two distinct and diametric camps, those of us who line up each second Saturday morning for the Dublin Food Co-Op.

There are, firstly, the hard-working volunteers whose zealotrous energy keeps this ingenious show on the road. These selfless souls shovel oat flakes into bags, weigh out shoals of aduki beans on the little scales, diligently arrange the rice crackers in their boxes beside the Ecover bleaches and the wholewheat spaghetti. They line up the alternative magazines, pin up notices for shiatsu and house-sharing, before scooting around the Saint Andrew's Hall with their power purchasing leaflets, hoovering up the necessary Tanzanian coffee, sesame oil, miso and brown rice.

They are a diverse crew: beards, Doc Marten's and Traidcraft dresses. All around the hall their day-glo kids are alternatively meek and mischievous as they cavort together. They are the backbone of the Co-Op: dedicated to an idea of alternative purchasing which has created an aspect of community around the whole venture.

And, then, there are the hedonists.

We are here to buy some of Silke Cropp's wanly wonderful goat's milk cheeses, driven down from Cavan by the cheesemaker herself. We are here for Nicky Kyle's mum's eggs, those hearty, muck-speckled orbs of delight which glare at you from the Sunday morning frying pan with their defiant freshness. And, today, Nicky's mum also has pâté and hummus, pickles and chutneys, and box-bursting duck eggs.

We line up to see just what organic herbs and plants Laura Turner has for sale, then splurge politely on fragrant mint and lissom tarragon, spruce thyme and — we have been waiting for this — some aristocratic basil. Next door Deirdre O'Sullivan has freshly dug spuds with some Kildare soil still on them, or deep-green cabbages or lovely Swiss chard which will go into that favourite Raymond Blanc tart recipe with some Gruyère cheese.

Penny Lange's table of biodynamic produce groans with unimpeach-ably wonderful vegetables which, a few hours ago, were snugly embedded in Wicklow soil. Here one finds the curious rarities such as salsify and scorzonera, purple baby cauliflowers, yellow finger-size courgettes. Our greedy eyes feast, our swiftly evacuating wallets and purses disgorge once more, our bags are filled up and up.

All around us the hard work of the Co-Op carries on, but we hedonists are locked into oblivion, thinking of nothing further than lunch, then dinner, then Sunday lunch and Sunday dinner. Some of the basil will go towards a fresh pesto sauce for pasta, the goat's cheese will be barbecued gently, the spuds and baby turnips and celeriac milled into a white purée. If, at the stall where the Inisglass community sell their flours and breads, we can find some of their yogurt mixed with fresh fruits, then dessert is a cinch.

The workers fortify themselves for more work with aduki bean pasties from the little stall manned by Sage foods. We hedonists, famished by our expedition, do the same, and promise ourselves that, one day, we will come along and volunteer and do some work and help out and keep the whole thing going. But that, well, that will have to be next time. For now, it is lunch, and dinner, and lunch, and dinner, and that is as much as matters.

The Dublin Food Co-Op is open from 10.30am–5pm every Sat. St Andrew's Hall is half way down Pearse Street.

Patisserie
# THE GALLIC KITCHEN
*49 Francis St Tel: (01) 454 4912*
Sarah Webb is a superb baker. Not a trace of ego or arrogance gets in the way of her search for flavour, for savour. Where other patissiers like to show off with façile complication, Sarah Webb sticks to the basic tenet of pleasurable deliciousness as the goal of her work.

So, pain au chocolat is crumbly and fulsome; the baby quiches with their flecks of spinach are the perfect picnic lunch. The white breads with their mantle of browned egg wash are serene and sweet, the potato bread so confoundedly delicious that you curse yourself for the fact that you cannot emulate them, but console yourself with the fact that Ms Webb turns them out, perfectly, every time.

A dogged, professional consistency explains why Ms Webb's business gets bigger every year. Year in, year out, winter, spring, summer or fall, all you have to do is call here and, after the initial delightful assault on the nostrils, you can bet your bottom dollar that the pear tart this time will be as good as last time, the crunchy pizzas just as terrific as every-thing else.

Open 9am–5pm Tues–Sat.

Wholefoods
## THE GENERAL HEALTHFOOD STORE
*93 Marlborough Street, D1 Tel: (01) 874 3290*
A small, friendly wholefood shop with an interesting range of breads and good snacktime cooked foods — spring rolls, vegetarian pasties, lentil burgers.
Open 9.30am–6pm Mon–Sat.

Greengrocer
## HERE TODAY
*25 South Anne Street, D2 Tel: (01) 671 1454 and the Corporation*
*Markets, D7*
The laid-back, slap-dash service aside, Here Today is an essential place for every manner of fruit and vegetable, especially for a good selection of organically grown produce.
Open 6.30am–6.30pm Mon–Sat (Market shop open 5am–2.30pm Mon–Sat).

Kitchen Shop
## KITCHEN COMPLEMENTS
*Chatham House, Chatham Street, D2 Tel: (01) 677 0734*
Ann McNamee's shop spills over with the sensual, superb stylings and designs of the finest makers of kitchenware, the producers of the most alluring and must-have pots, pans and paraphernalia. On two floors intersected by a steeply winding staircase, you will find, and will be charmingly helped to find, any and every necessity to transform you from a kitchen Cinderella into the new Alice Waters. Calphalon pans, Sabatier knives, crushingly complicated texts for cake decorating, every little fidgety item and finickety necessity you need to unleash the huge culinary potential that lurks within you is to be found here.
Open 10am–6pm Mon–Sat ('till 7pm Thurs).

Chocolates
## LIR CHOCOLATES
*IDA Enterprise Centre, East Wall Road, D3 Tel: (01) 878 7800*
Lir truffles are veritable orgies of confected intensity, narcotic in their sweet splendour, profound in their ability to reduce the eater to the state of gluttonous chocaholic in seconds. Finely balanced between sweetness and fruit intensity, they are aristocrats of the sweetie world: ordinary chocs compare to Lir truffles as Mantovani compares to Mozart.

Recently Lir have also begun to produce a gift-wrapped box of chocolates for Quinnsworth and Crazy Prices. Each box in the Cliona range contains sixteen chocolates, with evocative names such as Cupid's Delight, Cameo and Ivory Shell and the fact that they are now stealing the space traditionally allocated to foreign chocolates is just one of their pleasures.

Delicatessen
# MAGILL'S
*14 Clarendon Street, D2 Tel: (01) 671 3830*
An excellent cheese counter with French and other European cheeses alongside the best Irish farmhouse cheeses; Stone Oven bread brought in every Thursday morning and every manner of oil, preserve, salad and condiment make up the splendid selection of Magill's long-established deli. Prices are generally on the steep side, but with such a satisfying array of foods on offer who minds the extra few shillings.
Open 9.30am–5.45pm Mon–Sat. Opposite Powerscourt Townhouse Centre.

Greengrocer
# OW VALLEY FARM SHOP ➡
*Powerscourt Townhouse Centre, D2 Tel: (01) 679 4079*
An absolutely invaluable little place for finding the most unusual doo-dahs: girolles, good olives, fruits and nuts, tomatoes on the vine in season, smoked garlic. Sean McArdle gets the foodstuffs that others only dream about and, best of all, is always amenable to new suggestions, new ideas, new foods.
Open 8.30am–6pm Mon–Sat ('till 7pm Thur).

Greengrocer
# THE RUNNER BEAN
*4 Nassau Street, D2 Tel: (01) 679 4833*
The trestle tables of this busy shop spill out into Nassau Street under a couple of great big canopies, and it is always busy with both the mundane and the magnificent of the fruit and vegetable world.
Open 8am–6pm Mon–Sat ('till 7pm Thurs).

Cheese Stall
# RYEFIELD FOODS
*Mother Redcap's Market, Back Lane D8*
Ann Brodie's happy stall of cheeses benefits not only from the younger-than-springtime nature of the lady herself but also from the expert eye of a cheesemaker, for Mrs Brodie is responsible for the fine Ryefield cheeses, made back home on the farm in County Cavan and, you guessed it, available here.

But, then, so is almost every other Irish farmhouse cheese you can think of, all in expert condition and sold in conjunction with breads and cakes, pickles and jams, hand-made sweets and a host of other delicacies. Mrs Brodie manages to cull the best foods from her neighbours, meaning that everything here is charmed with natural, instinctive, organic flavours.

At Christmastime, especially, the Ryefield Foods' stall is invaluable for real Christmas cakes and puddings, crumbly sweetmeat pies, all the fare of the festive season.
Open Mother Redcap's 10am–5.30pm Fri–Sun.

Kitchen Shop
## SWEENEY O'ROURKE
*34 Pearse Street, D2 Tel: (01) 677 7212*

Whilst it is mainly professional cooks, on the hunt for a brace of ladles or a giant-sized sieve, who habituate Mr Sweeney and Mr O'Rourke's lovely kitchen shop, the domestic cook has much to gain from a visit here, not least the keen prices and the fact that the shop aims to cater for every culinary need. So, if the design of the shop is higgledy-piggledy, this only adds to the fun of hunting through mountains of stainless steel in search of the right sized mixing bowl, or pulling through boxes to find the right pestle and mortar.

Open 8.15am–5.15pm Mon–Fri (closed for lunch).

# North City

Italian Food Shop
## LITTLE ITALY

*68 North King Street, D7 Tel: (01) 872 5208*

An essential place for anyone with a copy of Ada Boni, Giuliano Bugialli or Marcella Hazan. Good dried pastas from De Cecco, good dried porcini, good Lavazza coffee, a belting range of Italian wines and liqueurs, and essential cheeses. Many restaurateurs use the shop to stock up on the necessities of take-away and trattoria food, but in amongst the tomato purée and the cooking oil there are lots of good foods to be found.

Open 9am–5pm Mon–Fri, 10am–1pm Sat.

# South City

Japanese Foods
## AYUMI-YA

*Newpark Centre, Newtownpark Avenue, Blackrock, Co Dublin*
*Tel: (01) 283 1767*

If you have eaten the — cooked — ingredients in Mrs Hoashi's restaurant underneath the Ayumi-Ya shop, you may be tempted to try your hand at this ethereal and intricate cuisine. This is where to begin assembling the soya, beancurd, seaweed, marinated plums and other staples which will, assuredly, see you on the road to success.

Open 5pm–7pm Mon–Sun (Sat 1pm–5pm).

Bakery
## BRETZEL KOSHER BAKERY

*1A Lennox Street, D8 Tel: (01) 475 2724*

The more moderne bakeries which have opened in Dublin in the last few years have not knocked the venerable Bretzel out of its stride. Just take a peek in the window and you see that all the old favourites survive, today as ever: great big hanks of gloopy pizza, milky coffee-coloured onion rolls, bug-eye gingerbread men, foldaround croissants, sugar-smack cakes, rustic rye breads. The confectionery here has a happy, kiddyish concept of sweet foods, with more piled on top of more in the pursuit of surfeit and a happy disregard for patissier's finesse.

Open 9am–5.30pm Mon–Sat.

Traiteur
## DOUGLAS FOOD CO.

*53 Donnybrook Road, D4 Tel: (01) 269 4066*

An eye of intricate discrimination rules over Richard Douglas's lean, minimal shop in Donnybrook.

The Spanish olive oil they sell from the barrel is soft and fat tasting, neither too spicy nor florid. The cheeses, artisan French abetted with farmhouse Irish, will be in pristine condition: a pungent Brie, an unguent Gaperon, an urgent Roquefort, a Gubbeen in immaculate prime. The bread, from Cooke's Bakery, cannot be bettered. The chocolate, the coffee, the vinegars, the olives and the essential what-nots are all chosen for their finesse.

The sense of discrimination is unerring, so you shop with confidence, allowing the Co. to take the slog out of a dinner party or allowing yourself the benefit of a night off, with nothing to do but warm the food through when you get it home. There are good wines — at caution-causing cost, admittedly — to complete the menu.

Open 10am–7.30pm Mon–Fri, 9am–6pm Sat.

Greengrocer, delicatessen and wholefoods
## FITZPATRICK'S
*40A Lower Camden Street, D2 Tel: (01) 475 3996*
Fitzpatrick's was one of the first good food shops in the city, and it retains its essential status by virtue of diligent and dedicated hard work, patiently expanding its range whilst maintaining precise standards with everything it stocks. Along with an ever-present range of vegetables and fruits from Organic Foods, there is a choice array of wholefoods, a good cheese counter and fine breads for sale. So much good stuff, in fact, that Fitzer's is almost a one-stop shop.

Open 8am–6.30pm Mon–Sat.

Delicatessen
## FOTHERGILL'S
*141 Upr Rathmines Road, D6 Tel: (01) 962511*
Terry and Breda Lilburn's shop has such a sweetie-pie air of innocence about it that it seems like a cake kindergarten, inviting you to Please Look After This Chocolate Sponge Cake.

The innocence, however, ends with the Lilburns and their splendid staff: many indeed have been the customers who have come in here with the intention of giving a decent home to a chocolate torte or a chocolate bombe or a selection of drooling eclairs or what-have-you, only to then pass it off to their coffee morning cronies or dinner party dilettantes as their own work. Would that they were half such talented bakers as this quiet and hard-working couple, who augment their sweet thing skills with excellent savoury foods — you can make up a very fine picnic or sandwich here at lunchtime — and choice deli foods and wines.

Open 9.30am–6pm Mon, 9am–6.30pm Tue–Fri, 9am–6pm Sat.

Greengrocer and Delicatessen
## ROY FOX
*49a Main Street, Donnybrook D4 Tel: (01) 269 2892 Roy Fox*
Tumbling out onto the pavement there is an imaginative display of fruits and vegetables — priced in groups, like a market: "6 limes for a pound"

— inside there's a fruitful display of deli goods: Silke Cropp's fresh cheeses from Cavan, breads from Cooke's Bakery, plus nuts, spices, rices and other such niceties.

Open 9am–7pm Mon–Sun.

Delicatessen
## THE GOURMET SHOP
*Rathgar Road, D6 Tel: (01) 970365*

A strange shop that happily appears to be almost time-warped, and which quietly offers some fine, locally baked foods, salads and some excellent, unusual wines.

Open 9am–7pm Mon–Sat.

Delicatessen
## KIM CONDON
*99B Rathgar Road, D6 Tel: (01) 492 9148*

Though Kim Condon's deli is spanking new, the shop has the confident feel of someone who knows the business inside out, for Ms Condon is a scion of the family who run Magill's, in the centre of town, and she knows all there is to know about fine foods. So, expect great breads, olive oils, pristine cheeses, everything your heart could desire.

Open 9am–6pm Mon–Sat.

Supermarket
## C MORTON & SON
*15 Dunville Avenue, D6 Tel: (01) 497 1254*

There is something distinctly bright and breezy about Morton's lovely supermarket, and the bright and breezy nature of the place comes from what is on the shelves, and the careful selectivity which puts it there: Cooke's Bakery bread in all its splendiferous glare, Drumiller yogurt, Marc Michel's organic produce from County Wicklow; a host of berries, cherries and currants in season; crème fraîche and buffalo mozzarella and the other essentials of a cool cabinet; a selection of wines which runs from cheap Argentinians and Bulgarians to decent Medocs and other interesting clarets; and then, naturally, those necessary little bits and bobs for the house and the garden.

You get the impression in Morton's that they want to sell these foods because they are proud of them.

Open 9am–6.30pm Mon–Sat.

Italian Shop
## NATURALLY NICE
*Dunville Avenue, D6 Tel: (01) 497 411*

From the outside, with its trays of fruit and veg nestling under a canopy, Naturally Nice looks like a conventional shop: nothing more, nothing less. But, in fact, its speciality is Italian foods, and most anything from mozzarella to Montepulciano d'Abruzzo is for sale. Beside serried rows of familiar foods, they prepare a selection of their own speciality dressings.

Open 9am–7.30pm Mon–Sat, 9am–2.30pm Sun.

Asian and African Store
## UNIVERSAL FOODS
*11 Upr Camden Street, D2 Tel: (01) 478 4617*
Shiny shards of ginger, chillies that throb with lurid red and green vibrancy, shaggy coconuts, Brazilian coffee, rice of all manner of origin and specie sold from big buckets: there is always a torrent of quizzically arousing foods in the Universal, the best place in town to find the more unusual African and Asian foods. The shop itself has all of the splendidly disorganised air of someplace in Karachi or Bangalore.

Open 10am–7pm Mon–Sat, 2pm–6pm Sun.

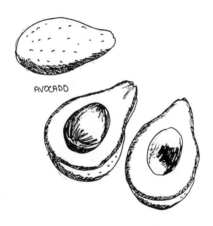

AVOCADO

# South County Dublin

Delicatessen
## CAVISTON'S DELICATESSEN
*59 Glasthule Road, Sandycove, Co Dublin Tel: (01) 280 9120*
Venture into an argument about which is the best shop in Dublin and the County and the chances are that, after many names and places have been canvassed, most considerate souls will agree that Caviston's is hard to beat.

Not just because it has everything you desperately need and desperately want, though it has all of those things, but it also has the breezy, busy-bee atmosphere of the best shops, that helpful, running-here-and-there air of young folk working hard, preparing, assisting, serving.

This is the factor that makes it special, the very deliberate hands-on policy of the Cavistons themselves, their intimate knowledge of each and everything they sell, their desire that you should be happy with each thing you buy and that you should always get what you want. This is a very old idea of service, done with a smile, and it makes it great fun to shop here.

Open 9am–7pm Mon–Sat.

Traiteur
## THE GOOD FOOD SHOP
*Glenageary Shopping Centre, Glenageary, Co Dublin Tel: (01) 285 6683*
Sue Farrell's shop is as bright and fresh-faced as the proprietor herself, a carefully considered traiteur filled with cooked food, and with the added bonus of a boulangerie, for Ms Farrell bakes excellent breads on the premises.

Open 9.30am–6pm Mon–Sat.

Wholefoods and Spices
## MONKSTOWN FINE FOOD CO
*16a Monkstown Crescent, Monkstown,*
*Co Dublin Tel: (01) 284 4855*
Anne Kendrick's shop is a friendly little place with an eclectic mixture of wholefoods and spices, but it is of especial interest because of the broad range of dried spices she sells. You want three different types of paprika? This is where you will find them, available to buy in modest amounts so they won't go stale on you. There are dozens and more to choose from, so even the most recalcitrant recipe specification is likely to be satisfied here.

Open 10.30am–6.30pm Mon–Sat.

Delicatessen
## THOMAS'S DELICATESSEN
*1 Cornelscourt Village, Foxrock, D18 Tel: (01) 289 6579*
This long narrow warren of a shop is a pleasing place in which to find judiciously chosen foods, both in their raw state and cooked. There are good breads and excellent cakes and assorted bakes, a fine cheese counter selling many of the Irish Farmhouse cheeses alongside their Continental colleagues, and there are plenty of quaffable wines at decent prices. Thomas's always feels like a keen, eager place, somewhere to find the good things.

Open 8.30am–7pm Mon–Sat, 10am–2.30pm Sun. Right at the end of a strip of shops in Foxrock village.

# DUBLIN WINE SHOPS

## FINDLATER'S
*The Harcourt Street Vaults, 10 Upper Hatch Street, D2 Tel: (01) 475 1699*
These vaults below the old Harcourt Street railway station are unquestionably handsome and venerable, the air is agreeably cool, of course, a great boon should you wish to splash out on something special or be a subscriber to Findlater's clever Cellar Plan, where you pay a certain amount of money each month and choose wines from the lists which they recommend twice a year.
Open 9am–6pm Mon–Fri, 10.30am–6pm Sat.

## THE LORD MAYOR'S
*Main St, Swords, Co Dublin Tel: (01) 840 9662*
This is a surprisingly fine wine shop, with an excellent range of plonk and fine beers and spirits to chase each other.
Open 10.30am–10.30pm Mon–Sun ('till 10pm Sun).

## THE MARKET WINERY
*George's Street Arcade, D2 Tel: (01) 677 9522*
Tony Ecock's wine shop is sister to the Vintage shops described later.
Open 10.30am–6pm Mon–Fri

## MCCABE'S
*51–55 Mount Merrion Avenue, Blackrock, Co Dublin Tel: (01) 288 2037*
*(Also at Vernon Avenue, Clontarf, D3 Tel: (01) 833 5277)*
Jim McCabe's shops are splendid homes to the great wines of the world, pleasing places that entice and lure you into a love affair with the bottle. There are often good-value fine bargains to be had amidst the battalions of good bottles from all over the world and, if you are on the hunt for a serious vintage, this is one of the most promising places to come. The staff, as you would expect, are excellent.
Open 10.30am–10pm Mon–Sat, 12.30pm–2pm, 4pm–10pm Sun

## MITCHELL'S
*21 Kildare Street, D2 Tel: (01) 676 0766*
The great lure of Mitchell's is not just that it is a splendidly clubbish place in which to buy wines, but also the fact that their recent additions to the range seem to have been chosen with care and an eye for distinctiveness. The shop gives the feeling that it is not excessively concerned with fashion, with chasing down the latest bright star to get splashed across the pages of the wine press. They work to their own pace and rhythm, and are to be congratulated for it.
Open 10.30am–5.30pm Mon–Fri ('till 8pm Thur), 10.30am–1pm Sat

EAPPLE
&S

CONTENTS
PINEAPPLE
ENRICHED WITH
NOURISHING
MARROW BONE JELLY
FIBRES E.8143

## MOLLOY'S LIQUOR STORES

*Greyhound Inn, Blanchardstown, Co Dublin Tel: (01) 821 012 Also at Crumlin Shopping Centre (453 1611), Nutgrove Shopping Centre (493 6077), Block 3, The Village Green, Tallaght (459 7599), Penthouse, Ballymun (842 8189) and Clondalkin Village (457 0166)*

Though their supermarket 'n' suburb locations may lead you to expect little from the Molloy's shops than clearing houses for beer and plonk, they do have a fine range of wines.

Open 10.30am–11.30pm Mon–Sat (11pm winter), 12.30pm–2pm, 4pm–11pm Sun.

## O'BRIEN'S

*30–32 Donnybrook Road, D4. Tel: 269 3033 Also at Blackrock (288 1649), Dun Laoghaire (280 6952), Bray (286 3732), Dalkey (285 8944), Sandymount (668 2096), Greystones (287 4123), Vevay Road (286 8776)*

The style of the O'Brien's shops follows a pattern of large windows and glass doors which open out onto simple floor spaces littered with boxes and wooden crates, spanning everything from the very best clarets to a huge range of negociant wines. The shops are usually reliable sources of unusual spirits, and their prices are very keen.

Open 10.30am–9pm Mon–Sat, 12.30pm–2pm, 4pm–9pm Sun.

## SEARSON'S

*The Crescent, Monkstown, Co Dublin Tel: (01) 280 0405 Fax: 280 4771*
This simple little room has nothing so formal as a counter, just stone walls, a high ceiling and bottles of good stuff arrayed around the walls and stacked on a fine big sideboard. Frank and Charles Searson have a reputation as serious claret men, chaps who only ship stuff that comes in wooden crates, but this image belies the reality. They have a good, inexpensive house wine in Domaine de Bousquet and have begun in recent years to expand their range to include wines from California and Australia, Spain and Portugal, and to begin to include excellent French country wines alongside their Burgundies and Bordeaux.

It is possible, therefore, to drop in on the way home from work and to pick up something for dinner that evening, and it is possible to stop by and discuss the staying power of a vintage, should you have come into some Money From America and want to fill your shelves with something fine.
Open 10.30am–7pm Mon–Sat.

## SUPERQUINN

*Blackrock Shopping Centre, Blackrock, Co Dublin Tel: (01) 283 1511*
Irish supermarkets have tended to lag behind the revolution which has energised the wine departments of so many English supermarkets, but Superquinn is a proud exception and the range at Blackrock, their flagship shop, is impressive and keenly priced.

The reason for this is simple. The chaps who are given the run of the wine sections of Superquinn are all enthusiasts, many of them with personal preferences which mean that one shop will have, say, more Portuguese or Spanish or Chilean bottles than another, simply because that is how the local man likes it. Jim Hammond has a keen eye for Portuguese wines and offers a splendid range in the Blackrock shop, but there are also good clarets and Burgundies and fine wines at steep and not-so-steep prices.
Open 9am–6pm Mon–Sat ('till 9pm Thurs & Fri) Walkinstown and Swords open 'till 7pm.

## TERROIRS

*103 Morehampton Rd, D4 Tel: (01) 667 1311, Fax: 667 1312*
Françoise and Sean Gilley's new temple of quaffing, Terroirs, on Donnybrook's Morehampton Road, is pure heaven for imbibers. Mrs Gilley is the daughter of a winemaker and has spent the last few years working for Clos De Val Winery in California. Mr Gilley will be well-known to anyone who has frequented Verling's wine shop, in Clontarf, in recent years. They stock not merely fine wines, but also all the essential wine accessories and a fine range of speciality foods.

## VERLING'S

*360 Clontarf Road, D3 Tel: (01) 833 1653*

There is always a great buzz about Verling's, the sort of shop where bottles are always being opened and glasses handed round for the customers to taste some chirpy new arrival, some exciting newcomer that has everyone bright with delight. Jim Verling runs a splendid wine shop, the kind of place where it is all too easy to loiter and all too easy to spend all too much money.

Never mind. Drinking the results of your splurge will always prove to be delicious, for their wide selection is chosen with care and sound knowledge and the great and the good of the wine world are here, as well as many good bargains: Verling's often proves to be a shop where you can pick up some good quaffing stuff at a keen price. If that happens, of course, you will simply buy more of the booze at a keen price, instead of less of the booze at a costly price. Either way, you win. At least until the monthly bills drop through the letterbox.

Open 10.30am–10pm Mon–Sat, 12.30pm–2pm, 4pm–10pm Sun.

## THE VINTAGE

*Newtownpark Avenue, Blackrock, Co Dublin Tel: (01) 283 1664, 149 Upper Rathmines Road, D6 Tel: (01) 496 7811*

The Ecock brothers' shops have acquired a swisher, more assured completeness in the last few years, and none more so than the shop in Rathmines which always has a busy, commodious atmosphere, doubtless partly helped by the wine appreciation classes which they run from time to time. They import the complete Fetzer range of wines from California, and many other pleasantly surprising wines from Europe.

Open 10.30am–10pm Mon–Sat, 12.30pm–2pm, 4pm–10pm Sun.

# County Kildare

# ATHY

Shop

## WHOLESOME HARVEST

*Leinster St, Athy*

Wholesome Harvest is the wholefood shop of Athy, and it effortlessly lives up to its name selling, amongst other goodies, the organic vegetables and produce of the Innisglass Trust community in County Wexford.

# CARBURY

Food Producer
## DEIRDRE O'SULLIVAN AND NORMAN KENNY
*Nurney House, Carbury Tel: (0405) 53337*

Both Deirdre and Norman come from conventional farming back-grounds, "traditional beef and cattle and tillage", but have started what Norman insists will be a Commercial Farm selling organic vegetables in bulk to supermarkets through the Dublin organisation Organic Foods.

They have learned not to panic as their various experiments have led them to live and learn about these difficult and labour-intensive methods of humane food production, and all the while they are refurbishing a house that has not been lived in for twenty-five years. It's a difficult life, but the happy personalities and sheer bravery of these two people is inspiring. Naturally, the vegetables are delicious.

Deirdre sells her produce in the Dublin Food Co-Op, where she is one of the essential regulars, as well as in Healthy Image in Naas. Otherwise if you buy organic food from Superquinn and Quinnsworth it might well be Deirdre and Norman's carrots or parsnips that you have been lucky enough to come across.

# KILCOCK

Farmhouse Cheese
## MARY MORRIN
*Kilcock Tel: (01) 628 7244 Mary Morrin*

Mary Morrin adheres to the disciplines of both organic and bio-dynamic farm-ing, and, using the milk of her Hereford cow, makes a cream cheese, sometimes flavoured with fresh herbs, sometimes flavoured with dried herbs and cumin seeds. She also makes country butter.

You can buy the produce of Mary's farm at the Naas Country Market, Fri mornings, 10.45am–12.15pm.

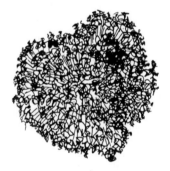

RED 'LOLLO'

# LEIXLIP

Shop
## THE HEALTHY WAY
*2 Ralph Square Linda Southgate & Mary Manning*
Wholefood Shop which is a member of the IAHS.

# NAAS

Shop
## HEALTHY IMAGE
*4A Basin St, Naas Tel: (045) 97210*
Cindy and Larry Quinn run a small health food shop in Naas, where you
might find Deirdre O'Sullivan's organic vegetables along with all the
other wholefood staples.

# MOYVALLEY

Roadside Diner
## MOTHER HUBBARD'S
*Moyvalley Tel: (0405) 51020 John Healy*
Mother Hubbard's is the trucker's equivalent of restaurant Paul Bocuse.
Just as, if you eat in M. Bocuse's famous restaurant near Lyons, you are
confronted with images of the great man on every wall, on the wine
bottles, on the plates, in bronze sculptures, photorealist paintings, everywhere — someone once described it as like eating with Stalin — so John
Healy's Mother Hubbard's shouts loud and clear the message and the
moniker.

The t-shirts which the staff wear advertise their place of employment,
and you can buy them for yourself, to further broadcast its fame. The
name is on the napkins. It is on the biros which they leave for you to fill
in the little questionnaire enquiring if you are happy with their efforts.
There are pictures of the diner on the table-mats and the name is further
emblazed on cigarette lighters, key rings and car stickers. Outside there
are a couple of signs beaconing the name in neon. M. Bocuse simply
cannot compete with Mother Hubbard's. Who needs culinary rosettes
when you have this much confidence?

They are unlikely to collect any culinary rosettes in Mother Hubbard's,
but if your image of a roadside diner is someplace where someone
shoves something like food in your direction whilst straining to keep
their cigarette ash out of the pot, think again. This is one of the most
thoughtful, pristine, efficient places you will find in Ireland. True, it's
someplace which truckers swear by and largely dominate, but the food is
properly done, the tea contains tea leaves (unless you specifically ask for
tea bags), the service is solicitous, there are splendid facilities for
changing baby, they broadmindedly provide condom machines in both
the loos, and there are showers and telephones and newspapers, and
some refuge from the road.
Open from 6.30am–11pm Mon–Sat, Sun 8am–11pm. On the N4 to Sligo and Galway, a
few miles before the road divides at Kinnegad.

# County Kilkenny

## BENNETTSBRIDGE

Flour Mill
### KELL'S WHOLEMEAL FLOUR
*Bennettsbridge Tel: (056) 28310 Billy Mosse*
The River Barrow powers the wheel which grinds Billy Mosse's flour, giving it sagacious, deep tastes which many professional chefs appreciate. You need to buy it in 10 kilo bags, or otherwise content yourself with the widely available brown bread mix which can be found in shops and supermarkets.

Café and Craft Gallery
### THE MILLSTONE
*Bennettsbridge Tel: (056) 27644 Eavan*
*Kenny & Gail Johnson*
This clever venture is organised by the Mosse family, famous for their pottery, but is run by Eavan and Gail, who both have backgrounds working and cooking at Ballymaloe. The menu is reassuringly short and achievable — kibbled wheat scones, watercress soup, pasta with tomato and basil, lemon roulade, chocolate fudge pudding — and the surroundings are charming.
Open noon–6pm Wed–Sun, 6pm–9.30pm Thur–Sat.

Pottery
### NICHOLAS MOSSE POTTERY
*Bennettsbridge Tel: (056) 27126 (shop) 27105 (factory) Nicky Mosse*
Nicky Mosse's work fuses a gentle Edwardianism in his palette of colours — baking bowl brown, soft blues and greens — with a delicate, plainness of design that is ruddily functional. His work is quietly distinctive, made from Irish clay, fired by water power, a very homey and consoling series of earthenware.
Open Jul & Aug 10am–6pm Mon–Sat, 2pm–6pm Sun.

Pottery
### STONEWARE JACKSON POTTERY
*Bennettsbridge Tel: (056) 27175 Michael Jackson*
Handsome tableware, also porcelain and stoneware.
Open 9am–5.30pm Mon–Fri, 9am–6pm Sat. Closed lunch 1pm–2pm.

# INISTIOGE

Restaurant
## THE MOTTE

*Inistioge Tel: (056) 58655 Alan Walton & Tom Reade-Duncan*

The Motte is a charmingly regressive space, just what you want a restaurant dining room to be when you are out for that special night, just how you want a restaurant dining room to appear when you walk in out of the evening. Drapes tumble and flow to the ground and shudder up to the ceiling, the art on the wall is full of presence, the music is whacky, linen is crisp and tactile. Vegetarians must give twenty-four hours notice — because there's nothing on the set menu that would suit. But, with advance warning, the care and individualism which is Alan and Tom's trademark will be in full flow, and a typical example of one of Alan vegetarian dishes is a rich nut roast, layered with wild mushrooms.

Open 7pm–10pm Mon–Sun ('till 9pm Sun). Closed Xmas. Average Price: dinner under £20. Visa, Access/Master.

# KILKENNY

Greengrocer
## THE AUBERGINE

*74 High Street Tel: (056) 63274 Mr Farrell*

Locally grown organic vegetables can often be found in Mr Farrell's shop, with a full complement of conventionally produced produce. The L&N supermarket across the road also sells organic produce.

Open 9am–6pm Mon–Sat ('till 7pm Fri).

Craft Shop and Café
## KILKENNY DESIGN CENTRE

*Castle Yard Tel: (056) 22118 Kathleen Moran*

The shop sells the most gorgeous Irish crafts from all over the country, the restaurant sells clever, simple food for those who are almost dropping from the shopping. Good for reviving coffee and cakes.

Open 9am–5pm Mon–Sat (10am–5pm Sun). Closed Xmas and on Sun between Jan and Mar. Average Price: under £5. Visa, Access/Master, Amex.

Restaurant & Accommodation
## LACKEN HOUSE

*Dublin Road Tel: (056) 61085 Eugene & Breda McSweeney*

You could select any dish from the menus which Eugene McSweeney prepares and cooks in Lacken House, the homely restaurant with rooms just on the outskirts of Kilkenny, and no matter what the choice — a vegetarian cous cous with chick peas, ginger and tomatoes; a "lasagne" made from layers of filo pastry with puy lentils on a fresh tomato sauce; a puff pastry parcel with vegetables and nuts — you will find yourself always confronted by the fact that with everything he cooks, Mr McSweeney exploits the long-learnt skill of the professional cook to extract flavour, to reveal the character and essence of a food.

You will also find that the cooking shows someone who has never lost touch with the scents, attractions and satisfactions of the garden and the ground: he likes to spirit the green, wild tastes of herbs and leaves such as nettles and parsley into dishes to offer a counterpoint to the luxury of rich sauces and complex tastes. Mrs McSweeney complements the fine food with expert knowledge and service with wines. Rooms are super-comfy, staff only brilliant.

Open 7pm–10.30pm Tue–Sat. Closed Xmas. Average Price: dinner under £30, B&B under £30. Visa, Access/Master, Amex. On the Dublin Road, just as you go into Kilkenny from the Dublin direction.

Delicatessen
## SHORTIS WONG
*74 John Street Tel: (056) 61305 Mary Shortis & Chris Wong*
The name sounds like a fusion of Irish and eastern, and thus Chris and Mary's shop has the perfect title for somewhere that bakes great soda bread — Mary Shortis has an assured, light touch in her baking — or perhaps super spicy samosas — Chris Wong has a demon touch when it comes to street food — and which otherwise offers all the good things of the area with every manner of spice, seasoning and soul food from around the globe also for sale. A restless, endlessly reinvented shop, one of the treasures of the area.

Open 9am–7pm Mon–Sat, 10.30am–2.30pm Sun.

Wine Shop
## THE WINE CENTRE
*15 John Street Tel: (056) 22034 Maureen & Eamonn O'Keeffe*
An excellent range of wines and a shop with the sort of cloistered atmosphere that makes it a pleasure to browse amongst the bottles.
Open 9am–6pm Mon–Sat (closed 1pm–2pm lunch).

# LAVISTOWN

Farmhouse Cheese/Mushroom Hunts
## LAVISTOWN FOODS
*Lavistown Tel: (056) 65145 Olivia & Roger Goodwillie*
Olivia Goodwillie's Lavistown cheese is a subtle thing, refined where other cheeses are blowsy, cerebral where other cheeses are ruddy. It is made in a style which approximates to an English Caerphilly, so the texture is pale white and slightly crumbly, and the cheese seems to be made up, when it is young, like a series of curd pieces joined together like the chains of an atom.

A little ageing alters this curdiness, and the cheese then dries slightly and takes on softer, more lengthy flavours. It is perfect, then, to match with red wine, but is also very good for cooking, for it melts obligingly and its sweetness forms a perfect cloak for gratins and bakes.

Lavistown also doubles up as a study centre, when Roger Goodwillie runs courses on organic gardening and related green and environmental matters. They also organise mushroom hunts when the season is on, and these are mighty fun indeed.

Lavistown cheese is distributed throughout Ireland.

# PILTOWN

Honey
## MILEEVEN
*Owning Hill Tel: (051) 43368 Joe and Eilis Gough*
Joe and Eilis add various spirits to their honey — everything from Evening Primrose Oil to Passion Fruit Juice — but, truth be told, the Mileeven honeys have little need of any spicing up, for the subtle scents of clover which they exhibit are narcotic enough in their own right. Do look out, also, for the wonderful honey and cider vinegar which they make, a sweet, rich, altogether joyful splash of vigour to contribute to any salad.

# STONEYFORD

Hand-blown Glass
## JERPOINT GLASS STUDIO
*Stoneyford Tel: (056) 24350 Keith & Kathleen Leadbetter*
The Leadbetters' glassware is intended for the table, so those seeking distinctive hand-made glasses for quaffing and swallyin' should take themselves down to Stoneyford, near to Mount Juliet.

Open 9am–6pm Mon–Fri, 11am–6pm Sat.

# County Laois

# ABBEYLEIX

Pub
## MORRISSEY'S
*Abbeyleix Tel: (0502) 31233 P.J. Mulhall*
A pub like Morrissey's, of Abbeyleix, if one were to transport it to Dublin or Galway, would quick become a pickled tourist trap, somewhere famous for being famous. In Abbeyleix, this extraordinary pub simply gets on with the business of serving drink, as it has done for decades, refusing to allow time to change it, still with a counter of foods, still with

the old biscuit tins, still with the respect for a fine pint of stout which they have always pulled.

# BALLACOLLA

Farmhouse Cheese
## ABBEY BLUE BRIE
*Ballacolla Tel: (0502) 38599 Pat & Joan Highland*
Abbey Blue Brie — a soft blue cheese, rather like Cambozola — is an effective, tasty, surprising cheese which, allowed a little ageing, develops salty and complex flavours, but is always an unassuming, modest thing.

# MOUNTRATH

Country House
## ROUNDWOOD HOUSE
*Mountrath Tel: (0502) 32120 Frank & Rosemary Kennan*
In Frank and Rosemary Kennan's Roundwood House, an air of pleasure-filled idyll pervades, and you could almost believe it was the product of the air that sweeps down Slieve Bloom, such is the ease with which this house operates.

Roundwood is so story-book super, with its commingling ducks and its horses, its wide rooms with tall windows, you might imagine yourself transported to some never-never land.

Open for dinner and Sun lunch for guests, and for non-residents if pre-booked. Closed Xmas. Average Price: dinner under £20, Sun lunch under £10, B&B over £30. Visa, Access/Master, Amex, Diners. Roundwood House is signposted from Mountrath. If in doubt follow signs for Slieve Bloom.

# PORTLAOISE

Shop
## THE FRUIT & NUT PLACE
*Tara Court Tel: (0502) 22239 Statia Wellwood*
Wholefood shop, a member of the IAHS.

Restaurant
## JIM'S COUNTRY KITCHEN
*Portlaoise, Tel: (0502) 32616 Jim Tynan*
A friendly, very popular lunchtime place which is packed out with locals. The dishes are arranged on a central plate and you simply help yourself from the salads and bakes. Cosy in wintertime, thanks to the warming fires, and always good fun.

Open 9am–5pm Mon–Sat.

# County Louth

## CARLINGFORD

Pub & Bistro
### JORDAN'S PUB & BISTRO
*Newry Street, Carlingford Tel: (042) 73223 Harry and Marian Jordan*
A genuine bistro where, with County Louth typicity, everything is served with a generous spirit, cleverly but never too seriously, and the happy style of the food colludes charmingly with this disarmingly seductive village. Vegetarian food comes in the form of stir fries or veg baked in a cheese and wine sauce.
Open 6.30pm–7.30pm early bird menu summer months, 7pm–10pm Tue–Sun. Closed two weeks in Nov. Average Price: dinner under £10. Visa, Access/Master, Amex.

## DROGHEDA

Grocer
### KIERANS' BROTHERS
*15 West Street Tel: (041) 38728 Mark Kierans*
This fine shop can appear, initially, to be indistinguishable from the slough of supermarkets and other retailers which cluster around West Street, but there are good breads and other carefully selected foods to be found amidst the standard plastic-clad produce from dairy and farm.
Open 9am–6pm Mon–Wed, 9am–8pm Thur, 9am–9pm Fri, 9am–6pm Sat.

## DUNDALK

Shop
### ONLY NATURAL
*Stockwell Street Tel: (046) 24302*
A fine wholefood shop.

SPROUTS

Organic Farm
### PHILIPSTOWN TRUST
*48 Cloonevan, Clermont, Dublin Road Tel: (042) 21763 Ollan Herr*
This splendid scheme is managed by a trust who farm 13 acres of land near Ravensdale, in north County Louth, and who then operate a direct-purchase system, whereby families pay a lump sum and are supplied directly with vegetables for 8–9 months of the year. Those who wish to order for only two people pay less. Vegetables are delivered the day they are picked. A splendid idea and surely, the way the future lies.

# DUNLEER

Flour Mill
## WHITE RIVER MILL
*Dunleer Tel: (041) 51141 Gerard O'Connor*

A slow, ponderously powerful stone wheel grinds Gerard O'Connor's flour and bran in the White River Mill, and anyone who seeks the solace of an elemental pace should call here to buy some flour and to watch this beautiful process at work.

Nationally, the wholemeal flour is sold under the Lifeforce label, but locally you can find both it and the bran sold under the White River Mill label.

# KNOCKBRIDGE

Farmhouse Cheese/Country Butter
## TARA CHEESE
*Dunbin, Knockbridge Tel: (042) 35654 Caroline Meegan*

Ever since she began to sell her wanly yellow country butter in Superquinn, Caroline Meegan has been barely able to keep up with demand. Even though the milk she uses is pasteurised, the flavour of the butter is soft and lactic, perfect as a sauce just melted in its own right over some asparagus. Caroline's cheese, Tara, is likewise mellow in taste, a gentle Louth gouda, and as it is very low in fat is perfect for those who are weight conscious.

The butter is for sale in the Ryefield Stall in Mother Redcap's market in Dublin and in Superquinn stores. Tara cheese is widely available.

# RIVERTOWN

Whiskey Distillers
## COOLEY DISTILLERY
*Rivertown, Dundalk Tel: (042) 76102 David Hynes*

Cooley Distillery's single malt takes its name from the famous single malt made originally in Derry by the company of A.A. Watt, a firm which, late in the last century, ran the largest distillery in Ireland. Revived since 1986 by the Cooley Distillery, the Tyrconnell Single Malt is a beautiful whiskey. The first sip impresses with the distinguished, almost amazing softness of the spirit, before muted floral aspects enter into the taste frame.

Two new blends, Locke's and Kilbeggan, have just been newly launched onto the market. They are pleasant, but it is The Tyrconnell which should not be missed.

# TERMONFECKIN

Restaurant
## TRIPLE HOUSE RESTAURANT
*Termonfeckin Tel (041) 22616 Pat Fox*

Pat Fox's keen interest in wine spills over happily into his cooking, and, indeed, his vegetarian food: wild mushrooms with shallots and Madeira, or wild mushrooms baked with garlic butter; spinach filled pancakes baked with a tomato parmesan sauce or home made noodles. Mr Fox is a quiet, characterful man, and his food is thoughtful and unshowy.

Open 1pm–2pm, 7pm–9.30pm Tues–Sat (early bird menu 'till 7.30pm). Closed Xmas. Average Price: lunch under £10, dinner under £20. Visa, Access/Master, Amex. 5 miles north east of Drogheda on the Boyne River road.

# County Meath

Restaurant
## HUDSON'S
*Railway Street, Navan Tel: (046) 29231 Richard & Trish Hudson*

Richard and Trish Hudson opened this funky, informal bistro in September 1992 and their imaginative menu is adaptable not only to various diets, but also to various food allergies: Richard is allergic to cheese and Trish is a vegetarian with an allergy to wheat.

So, the same spirit that dreamed up spicy Thai chicken, or Hong Kong chicken stir fry has the wit and the skill to create similar dishes without fowl — spicy Thai chickpeas, or Hong Kong cashew nut with Chinese mushrooms. Prawn fettucini can become pine kernel fettucini.

Other vegetarian dishes which are always on the menu include deep fried potato jackets with either aioli or a Mexican spicy dip, hummus, spaghetti tossed in homemade pesto, aduki burgers and ratatouille.

But the real speciality of the restaurant is actually the desserts. chocolate terrine, a meringue galette and, in season, a classic summer pudding. A fun spot, affordable, good for families.

Open 6.30pm–10.45pm Tue–Sun. Closed Xmas. Average Price: dinner under £20. Visa, Access/Master.

Restaurant
## COASTGUARD RESTAURANT
*Bettystown Tel: (041) 28251 Maureen Hassett*

There are always four or five vegetarian options on Maureen Hassett's menu: Fettuccini with a Provençal Sauce, a Crêpe filled with vegetables served on a cheese sauce, various concoctions with nuts and pulses.

If, however, you ring in advance then extra special care will be taken to deal with personal requests, and this will give them time to prepare the like of nut roasts. But, because everything is cooked to order, requests can always be dealt with sympathetically.

Open 7pm–late Mon–Sat. Closed Xmas. Average Price: dinner under £20. Visa, Access/Master, Amex, Diners.

Flour Mill
## MARTRY MILLS
*Martry, Kells Tel: (046) 28800 James Tallon*
A great County Meath speciality to look out for is James Tallon's super-coarse Martry Mills flour.

Ecology Centre
## SONAIRTE ECOLOGY CENTRE
*The Ninch Farm, Laytown Tel: (041) 27572 Mary Perry*
Sonairte has an interesting garden and an obscure selection of apples come the season, with other vegetables for sale during the rest of the year.
At Julianstown on the main N1 road take the sign for Laytown. The centre is about a mile down the road on the right hand side.

Self-catering Cottages
## THE COTTAGES
*Seabank, Bettystown, Co Meath Tel: (041) 28104 Liz Lyons*
Liz has six cottages available for rent, and there are organic vegetables available not only from the garden but also from the nearby Sonairte Centre. Write for a brochure.

# County Westmeath

# ATHLONE

Wholefood Shop
## THE HONEYPOT
*Athlone Tel: (0902) 72965 Matt & Tina Kennedy*
Good range of wholefoods and miscellaneous items.

Restaurant
## THE WAREROOM RESTAURANT
*Bastion Street, Athlone Tel: (0902) 94446 Anthony & Emer McKay*
The Wareroom, in the centre of Athlone, opens daily for lunch, and offers a weekend evening menu from Thursday to Saturday. "We have lots of Vegetarian dishes" they promise on the menu, and options include tostados — a homemade chilli sauce served with crispy tortillas, shredded lettuce, olives, tomatoes and finished with grated cheese and sour cream. There are also vegetable filled crêpes which come with sour cream and olives and garlic potatoes.
Open noon–3pm Mon–Fri, noon–5pm Sat, from 6.30pm Thurs–Sat. Average Price: dinner under £20, Sun lunch under £5. No Credit Cards. Bastion Street runs down to the river in the centre of Athlone.

# GLASSON

## THE GLASSON VILLAGE RESTAURANT

*Glasson, Athlone Tel: (0902) 85001 Michael Brooks*

Michael Brooks' restaurant is famed in the locale for his imaginative and personal style of food. Vegetarians should try to give some notice. It is a generous, fun place.

Open 7pm–10.15pm Tue–Sat, 12.30pm–2.30pm Sun. Closed Xmas. Average Price: dinner under £20, lunch under £10. Visa, Access/Master, Diners.

## WINEPORT RESTAURANT

*Glasson, Athlone Tel: (0902) 85466 Ray Byrne & Jane English*

No one can try harder than the owners and staff of The Wineport. No request, no event, is too small not to summon their best efforts and their instinctive thoughtfulness, and their choices for vegetarians show the generous charm which has made the place such a success.

The vegetarian dishes which Therese prepares include Cashel Blue, celery and potato soup; mushroom caps stuffed with fresh herb cheese with a fruity gooseberry sauce; fresh winter fruits with an aromatic mint vinaigrette; vegetable risotto of crisp winter vegetables and nuts steamed and finished with a creamy sauce and wholegrain rice; buckwheat and vegetable pies.

Open noon–10pm Mon–Sun. Closed Xmas and winter hours 6pm–10pm Mon–Sat, noon–10pm Sun. Average Price: lunch under £10, dinner under £20. Visa, Access/Master, Amex.

# County Wexford

# BALLYEDMOND

Restaurant, Pub Food and Take-Away

## EUGENE'S RESTAURANT

*Ballyedmond Tel: (054) 89288 Eugene & Elizabeth Callaghan*

Eugene's Restaurant sits beside a pub, with a take-away sandwiched in the middle. Hardly auspicious. The dining room of the restaurant is a simple, four-square space, the colours are pastel-quiet, the loos are immediately at the end of the room which has enough tables to seat thirty or so.

If this all seems a bit glum, then fear not. Strange to relate and even stranger to believe, in Ballyedmond, not too far from Wexford town, Eugene's Restaurant, beside the chipper beside the pub, is run by Eugene Callaghan, winner a couple of years back of the Roux Brothers' Young Chef of the Year title, until recently right-hand man to Paul Rankin in Belfast's Roscoff, and one of the hottest culinary talents to be found anywhere in Ireland. In this fine trio of establishments that he cooks not just for the restaurant, but for the bar and for the chipper.

Whilst there are no vegetarian dishes on the menu, Mr Callaghan will cook vegetarian food given some advance notice: all soups are vegetarian, and a broad range of pasta dishes and warm vegetable dishes show his stunning expertise. He simply, intelligently uses what is available to create a dish, say, baked vegetables with balsamic vinegar and shaved parmesan, or vegetables in puff pastry. Both the restaurant and the bar are adaptable to vegetarian demands, whilst the chipper uses vegetable oil to fry the chips.

Open 12.30pm–2.30pm Mon–Sun, 7pm–9.30pm Mon–Sun (closed Tues evenings). Bar lunch and evening meals, takeaway open 'till 12.30am. Closed Xmas. Average Price: Bar lunch under £10, lunch under £10 dinner under £20. Visa, Access/Master, Diners. Ballyedmond is on the R741 between Gorey and Wexford.

---

### Eugene Callaghan's Roast Beetroot
Wash and trim the stalks and leaves of the beetroot. Wrap each bulb individually in aluminium foil and bake in a low to medium oven for approximately two hours, until the beetroot are slightly soft to the touch. Unwrap, and Eugene suggests you use them as follows: Drizzled with crème fraîche; in a salad dressed with hazelnut oil; or in a vinaigrette — liquidised with 1 cup of vinaigrette and half a teaspoon of walnut oil.

---

# BLACKWATER

Farmhouse Cheese
## CROGHAN CHEESE
*Ballynadrishogue, Blackwater Tel: (053) 29331 Luc & Ann van Kampen*

"Goats are natural foragers, not grazers" says Luc van Kampen. Just walk behind his happy herd as they return to their fields after milking and you soon see what he means, for the greedy curiosity of the goats quickly transforms them from behaving like an unruly dragoon of squaddies, lazily sauntering out after a lazy lunch, into a busy raggle of foragers, bounding up ditches and hedgerows like so many basketball players pitching for a basket.

Mr van Kampen, meanwhile, will be likely back at work, beginning to create the curd from which Croghan will eventually emerge. "It's a process, it's alive, it's a creative thing really", he says and the sense of excitement and pride which this gentle, almost Doonesburyish man takes in his work is palpably evident in his cheese. Croghan is a masterly food: handsome to look at in its ice-curl shape with a mottled, bluey-pink rind caused by being rubbed with Bacterium Linens for a few days, inside it is pure white and tender, with a tense lactic thoroughness that delivers a powerful aftertaste. As Luc points out, "there are no indigenous Irish recipes for cheese and though most are based on a Continental model, they take on their own character after a while".

None more so than Croghan (pronounced, alternatively, as "Crockan" or "Crowan": the name refers to a mountain in north Wexford). The cheese resembles a Reblochon, but no French cheesemaker could arrive at tastes like these, their subtle, supple intensity a perfect parallel for a fine, aristocratic claret. Croghan reaches its best at about six weeks old and it is the autumn cheeses, made in September and October, which are perhaps the most characteristic, though the out-of-slumber freshness of the cheeses made in April and May is delicious.

# CROSSABEG

Organic Flour, Vegetables, Bread & Yogurt
## INISGLASS TRUST
*The Deeps, Crossabeg Tel: (053) 28226 Anthony Kaye*
Much of the produce of the Inisglass Trust makes its way up to Dublin for the fortnightly Dublin Food Co-Op, whilst the Inisglass flour is widely available in good wholefood shops throughout the country. One good reason to make the trip to Wexford, however, is the fact that they have an excellent nursery of fruit trees for sale, so those with the patience to begin planting for the next generation should head for Crossabeg.
The Dublin Food Co-Op holds its market every Saturday. See Dublin chapter for more details.

# ENNISCORTHY

Farmhouse Cheese
## CARRIGBYRNE FARMHOUSE CHEESE
*Adamstown, Enniscorthy Tel: (054) 40560 Paddy Berridge*
Paddy Berridge's cheese is the biggest selling, and probably the most widely available, of the farmhouse cheeses, recognisable instantly by the multi-sided little wallets in which the Saint Killian brie is sold. If you have the patience to allow the cheese to age a little, for, typically, wholesalers and retailers always sell the cheese when it is still sprightly young, it can mature into something rich and creamy in flavour. So, make a deliberate policy to buy a Saint Killian when it is right at its Sell By Date, then leave it alone in a cool room for a while, then open a bottle of red wine.

# GOREY

Restaurant
## GOREY CHINESE RESTAURANT
*50 Main Street Tel: (055) 22104*
The cooking here is greatly more authentic than most Chinese restaurants.
Open 12.30pm–midnight Mon–Sun. Closed Xmas. Average Price: lunch under £20 dinner under £20. On the main street in Gorey.

Shop
# THE HONEY POT
*4 Main Street, Gorey Tel: (055) 20111*
Bread from Arklow, good coffee and crafts.
Open 9am–6pm Mon–Sun.

# TACUMSHANE

B&B with Full Board
## FURZIESTOWN HOUSE ➡
*Tacumshane Tel: (053) 31376 Yvonne Pim*
It is the inherent thoughtfulness she brings to everything that makes
Yvonne Pim's house so special, and Mrs Pim's care and concern for her
guests has elevated the house into one of the most highly regarded places
to stay in the country. You feel welcome. Mrs Pim spoils you. You love it.

And you will love the food: Mrs Pim organises scrumptious menus for
vegetarians — mushroom croustades on a bed of mixed greens, chick peas
in spiced lentil and coconut sauce with mixed rice, then a carrageen moss
mousse — and for vegans — carrot and apple salad, then sesame tofu with
stir-fried vegetables and mixed rice with courgettes and cashews. One
friend described Furziestown to us as "perfect", and that may just be right.
Open for dinner for residents only. Closed end Nov–Feb. Average Price: dinner under £20, B&B
under £20. No Credit Cards. Signposted from Tacumshane (telephone for detailed directions).

# WEXFORD

Wholefood Shop
## GREENACRES
*56 North Main Street Tel: (053) 22975 James G. O'Connor*
A copious array of vegetables.
Open 9am–6pm Mon–Sat.

Wholefood Shop
## HUMBLE NATURAL FOODS
*Walker's Mall, North Main Street Tel: (053) 24624 Heike Weiehagen*
Heike's shop has all the potions and lotions and pulses of wholefoodery,
but you can also find organic vegetables, real breads and, occasionally,
very good honeys.
Open 9.15am–6pm Mon–Sat.

Hotel
## FERRYCARRIG HOTEL
*Ferrycarrig, Wexford Tel: (053) 22999*
During the Opera Festival, the Ferrycarrig is the place to go when you're
in your fab evening gear. At other times of the year the bar enjoys good
views and a sunny location.

But, it is also good for food: "The meals I had while staying here were probably some of the best I have ever been served in twenty years of being a vegetarian", writes a correspondent, who singles out a delicious vegetable strudel, and especially impressive breakfasts: hot cakes with maple syrup and melted butter; kiwi and grapefruit cocktail topped with natural yogurt and sprinkled with toasted muesli; French cinnamon toast with caramelised fresh fruit.

Bar open 10am–11pm Mon–Sat, noon–11pm Sun.

# County Wicklow

# ARKLOW

Bakery
## THE STONE OVEN BAKERY
*65 Lower Main Street Tel: (0402) 39418 Egon Friedrich*
"The secret of good bread is heat, and steam", says Egon Friedrich.

If only it were that simple. The secret of the fine breads which Mr Friedrich produces lies not just in the correct, quick application of thunderous heat to make the bread rise, followed by the play of steam in order to achieve a correct crust. It lies also in the happy co-mingling of those traditional skills — flour-milling, hand-kneading, natural proving, wild yeast sourdough starters — which announce a style of bread diametrically opposed to the spongy, supermarket gunge made by the Chorleywood process.

The Stone Oven Bakery is a veritable balm. The grey bread loaves — which are not grey, of course — sit in little Moses baskets, quietly proving. There are the joyful party rings, large spirals of white bread dotted with seeds that contribute a warm oiliness to the palate as you crunch through. In the window of the shop, cheerfully hanging by coloured ribbons, are crunchy pretzels, and buying some bread here means that one can enjoy the pain of feeling famished, as the odour of apple strudel has your nose puckering the air.

A modest, amusing man, his business philosophy is simple: "You make sure nothing goes on the counter which isn't fit for sale. We all make mistakes, but so long as you're not trying to sell them, and trying to take someone else's money for it, you're okay", and as straightforward as his modesty: "I think the oven is the secret", he says. "It forgave me all my mistakes, it always baked the stuff good and it's encouraging to bake with something like that. You put something in and it works".

Open 9.30am–6pm Mon–Sat, closed half day Wed.

# AVOCA

Craft Shop & Tea Room
## AVOCA HANDWEAVERS
*Avoca Tel: (0402) 35105 (Also at Kilmacanogue Tel: (01) 286 7466)*
A useful and enjoyable stop, not just to peruse the desirable crafts, but
also for revitalising cups of tea and cake and some very clever, enjoyable
and creative lunchtime cooking. The food in the Avoca Handweavers
shops is far superior to most food found in craft shops, and attracts
people from miles around at lunchtime, so make sure you arrive early.
Open Avoca: 9.30am–5.30pm Mon–Sun; Kilmacanogue: 9am–5pm Mon–Fri, 9.30am–
5pm Sat & Sun.

# BRAY

Restaurant
## ESCAPE
*1 Albert Walk, Tel: (01) 286 6755 Patrick O'Conner*
Escape is a simple, unadorned little space — bare tables with little flower
vases and candles in wine bottles, prints and paintings on the wall, a
guitarist to fret away the evening time peacefully — and their vegetarian
cooking is imaginative and impressive.

There are no menus, as they change them daily, so the waitress will
list the details for the evening — creamy hummus to begin, maybe deep
fried garlic mushrooms on a bed of spicy tomato sauce, or an onion
bhaji. Main courses might be an aubergine richta — layers of sliced
aubergine and potato on a bed of spinach, generous in both volume and
flavour — or a woodland pie — a meld of courgettes, carrots, turnips and
chestnuts, served with a chestnut sauce.

They also make a good cashew risotto, and the variety of dishes show
a restaurant which is enjoying its experiments, experiments which work
especially well with desserts: a lemon and banana crunch of elfin lightness,
a spiced apple pie tricked out with sultanas. Portions are quite enormous,
and it might be an idea to have a lighter selection of vegetable dishes to
accompany pies which are trencherman stuff. Some thing might also be
done about a no-smoking policy, at the very least for the staff.
Open noon–10.30pm Mon–Sat, noon–8.30pm Sun. Closed Xmas. Average Price: lunch
under £5–under £10, dinner under £15. Visa, Access/Master. On the seafront, 50 yrds
from the National Aquarium.

Greek Cypriot Restaurant
## THE TREE OF IDLENESS
*Sea Front Tel: (01) 286 3498 Susan Courtellas*
Susan Courtellas has continued to run the 'Tree, following the death of
her husband Akis, and, assisted by devoted staff, she has made the
transition smoothly. The menu is still composed of dishes which Akis

Courtellas either created or upon which he stamped his interpretation — vegetarian dishes include wild mushrooms with a carrot sauce, grilled ewe's milk cheese with a tahini sauce, whilst the great standards of the Eastern Mediterranean — Imam Bayildi, hummus and puffy home-made pitta bread — are given an ever-new interpretation. The great dessert trolley, an Archimboldesque explosion of exotic fruits with accompanying ices and desserts, is unique, the wine list deeply serious and rewarding.

Open 7.30pm–11pm Tues–Sun ('till 10pm Sun). Closed Xmas and 2 weeks in Aug/Sept. Average Price: dinner over £30. Visa, Access/Master. The Tree Of Idleness overlooks the seafront in Bray

Shop
## THE NUT KEG
*The Boulevard, Quinnsboro Road Tel: (01) 286 1793 Roger White*
Wholefood shop which also has lots of good organic vegetables during the summer season. Sister to the shops in Swords and Tallaght in Dublin.
Open 9am–6pm Mon–Sat ('till 7pm Fri).

# DONARD

Study Centre
## CHRYSALIS RETREAT AND WORKSHOP CENTRE
*Donoughmore Tel: (045) 54713 Claire Harrison*
The array of courses they run in the Chrysalis centre is dauntingly impressive, and forms the backbone of their work, but they also do mid-week bed and breakfast in the summertime, and the cooking is based on the use of organically grown foods, some of them coming from no further than their own garden, to create a wholefood cuisine. An Introduction to Vegetarian Cookery is just one of the courses they offer, (there is another interesting course on food and healing) but there is much else, everything from Iyengar yoga through meditation and alchemy to the Enneagram.

13 miles after Blessington, go over a bridge into Donard. Bear right in the village, and half a mile further take the right fork. Chrysalis is two miles from here, and signed.

# ENNISKERRY

Wholefood Shop
## NATURE'S GOLD
*Killincarrig Road Tel: (01) 2876301 Brod Kearon*
Locally grown organic vegetables, a thoughtfully serene atmosphere and intelligent choices amongst the various foods sold, mean it is always a pleasure to visit Brod Kearon's shop.

> ## Wicklow and South Dublin Country Markets
>
> None of the other Country Markets held throughout Ireland seem to buzz with the same sense of possessive pride as those of Wicklow and south County Dublin. On Saturday mornings, in modest church halls and simple community centres, gangs of ladies, and the occasional gentleman, assemble, tense with expectation, wicker baskets readied, granny elbows sharpened, to fight their way through yet another bruising encounter with their neighbours and friends.
>
> Their quarry is the spanking fresh salad leaves and soil-laden spuds, still-warm breads and cakes, jars of jam, conserves and chutneys, armfuls of flowers and occasional niceties like farm-made buttermilk, which these splendid organisations assemble for the committed and the curious. In Roundwood, the atmosphere is that of a polite jamboree, in Kilcoole it is cooler, a little more sedate, in Kilternan it is little other than warfare, a thunderous, adrenalinated struggle to grab as much as you can in the shortest possible time.
>
> They are exhilarating adventures into the soul of a community, surprising glimpses of the just-under-the-surface social tensions which make life worth living. Forget the gentility with which this part of the eastern seaboard is traditionally associated: the Country Markets are for those who relish the shout and the shove and the fight of real life, the physical and spiritual charge of real shopping. Camaraderie between neighbours is set aside, family is enlisted in the dedicated, concentrated pursuit of fresh, hand-made foods, and may the devil take the hindmost.
>
> Kilcoole, North Wicklow Country Market, St Patrick's Hall (10.30am–11.30am Sat).
>
> Roundwood Sunday Market, Parish Hall (Mar to Dec, 3pm–5pm Sun).
>
> Kilternan Country Market, Golden Ball, Kilternan, Co Dublin (10.30am–noon Sat)

# KILMACANOGUE

Goat's and Cow's Milk Yogurt
## COPSEWOOD YOGURT
*Kilmacanogue Tel: (01) 286 2081 Edward Drew*
Copsewood is perhaps the longest-established yogurt in the country, and one of the best. Both cow's and goat's milk varieties are made, and they are widely available in both Wicklow and Dublin.

# KILPEDDER

Organic Farmer
## ORGANIC LIFE ★
*Tinna Park House Tel: (01) 281 9726 Marc Michel*
Marc Michel compares to the standard organic farmer as Yves Montand compares to Bing Crosby. His pony mane of blond hair could get him a

gig with any garage band in San Francisco. His cowboy boots could get him a bit part in "Hud" and, whilst his torn jeans signify age and hard work, they have the sorts of holes and patches which suggest the slashes of the fashion pages. He is a modern vision of the Organic Grower as Rock'n'Roller, the Rolling Stone of the compost crowd.

Mr Michel markets his superb produce with a marketing-man's wizardry, zaps it out under the banner "Organic Life" in bright big boxes, in smart packs with his signature clearly visible. Not only is the produce superb, packed tight with the elegant and understated flavours which the Wicklow air and the Wicklow climate gift to his graft, but they look cool, hip. You want these chunky little tomatoes with their soft red skins, those flouncy lollo rossos, the rainbow-bright peppers in red and yellow, the noble Home Guards with their dusting of soil, and you want them not just because they are full of goodness and will do you good, but also because they are hip, fashionable. The spud as fashion accessory. Organic vegetables as part of your World of Interiors.

Organic Life produce is widely available in Supermarkets and Healthfood Shops in Dublin and Wicklow.

# KILTEGAN

Bio-dynamic Growers
## PENNY & UDO LANGE ★
*Ballinroan House, Kiltegan Tel: (0506) 73278*
Penny and Udo Lange farm thirty-six acres in County Wicklow according to the principles of Bio-Dynamic farming, a code of practise first suggested in a short series of lectures in 1924 by the educationalist Rudolf Steiner.

Some of the steps they take in their farming practices can seem arcane, even obscure-for-the-sake-of-it, but there is a delightful, delicious conclusion to the hard work they so assiduously undertake. Their produce, quite simply, is stunning: full of flavour, full of heart, full of real scents and mineral elements, full of simple goodness, a term so easily forgotten — so deliberately sidelined — in today's boisterous food world.

We have seen people look at Penny Lange's produce with nothing less than amazed stupefaction as she sets up her stall in the fortnightly Dublin Food Co-Op. Strong-veined fennel with long, wavy fronds that reek of caramelly scents. Glistening, rubied broccoli and tightly nuggeted cauliflower. Celery that actually has an odour, a clean, vibrant smell. Everything — from salad leaves to cut herbs to root vegetables — has such vigour, such ruddy health. And this is before you talk about the carrots, chunky, crunchy dangles of pure health, which have achieved an almost legendary reputation.

Udo Lange describes the principles of bio-dyn as designed to promote the idea of each farm as an "individuality": "We look at farming as an organism and what we strive for is towards a healthy, complete organism", he says. "We call each farm an individuality". And, he adds, "I think a plant which is raised in a particular place is more able to give what it is supposed to give when it is raised, planted and then harvested all in the same place".

The Langes lived abroad for some years and on returning to Ireland they were struck by the fact that the country "still felt untouched" and thus a perfect environment in which to farm bio-dynamically. Their foods, grown in harmony and rhythm with the land, seem imbued with these simple processes, seem suffused with the very life force.

The Langes' vegetables are sold in the fortnightly Dublin Food Co-Op on Pearse St, and in certain branches of Superquinn and Quinnsworth.

# WICKLOW

Restaurant & Country House
## THE OLD RECTORY ➡

*Wicklow Tel: (0404) 67048 Fax: 69181 Paul & Linda Saunders*
If Linda Saunders did not exist, then the citizens of the County of Wicklow would have had to invent her.

A vital and essential asset to the town and the county, her character seems to sum up this delightful place — quietly complex, slightly reserved, but pretty bloody determined behind it all — and her effusive and intricate cooking is a perfect reflection of the strengths and delights of Wicklow.

She uses fine organic ingredients, grown locally by Wendy Nairn, and this explains firstly why her food always has a vibrancy and freshness about it: it seems to reflect and express the sunshiney, youthful nature of the Wicklow hills.

To this, she brings a degree of invention and expressiveness — and an intuitive feeling for the architecture of taste — which few other country house cooks can match. Indeed, this sense of complex but compatible flavouring in her food is reminiscent of the structure of a perfume, with alluring scents and mellifluous taste structures to be enjoyed both in main dishes and in their compatriot sauces, a full vegetarian menu might include: spicy leek, parsnip and apple soup; egg purses with fresh herbs and tomatoes on a piquant beansprout salad; an Andalucian pancake — a wholemeal pancake stuffed with sweet red peppers, garlic and cucumber in a tomato and fresh basil sauce; finishing with elderflower bouquet — a confection of fresh elderflower fritters, elderflower sorbet with rich vanilla ice cream and Langues de Chat tuiles.

The extension of the dining room has gifted the Old Rectory with greater light, perfect for a cuisine of such delicacy.

Open 8pm Sun–Thurs, 7.30pm–9pm Fri–Sat. Closed Nov–Mar. Average Price: dinner under £30, B&B over £30. Visa, Access/Master, Amex. On the left hand side of the road as you drive into Wicklow town heading south.

# County Clare

## BALLYVAUGHAN

Café
### AN FEAR GORTA
*Pier Road Tel: (065) 77023 Fax: 77127 Catherine O'Donoghue*

An Fear Gorta is a splendid and beautiful tea rooms-cum-restaurant with a gorgeous conservatory at the back which is one of the nicest dining places you will find.

Sitting here at lunchtime in the summertime, surrounded by members of the judiciary, assorted Cosmo bike-girls with their Amy Tan novels, earth mothers and others of the odds and sods found in Ballyvaughan during the season, all munching on their pristine salads, scoffing their all-too-super cakes and bakes, is a total joy.

Catherine O'Donoghue's food is full of taste, full of fun, and the staff are great, especially the elderly Miss Tiggywinkle who waits on table with such beatific kindness that you want to insist she sits down while you get her a cup of tea.

Open 11am–5.30pm Mon–Sun. Closed Sept–May. Average Price: lunch under £5. On the quayside at Ballyvaughan.

Snack Bar/Shop
### AILWEE CAVE COMPANY
*Ballyvaughan Tel: (065) 77036 The Johnson family*

A tour of the Ailwee cave complex is thrilling, maybe even slightly chilling as you delve deeper and deeper into this extraordinary series of excavated caves. After you emerge into daylight, the visitors' centre offers not just splendid crafts and books but also an excellent tearooms/café, with hunger-slaughtering food that is carefully made and enjoyable and, a few hundred yards down the hill, Ben Johnson makes Burren Gold, a tender, buttery, Gouda-style cheese, which is for sale alongside other desirable comestibles.

Open 10am–5.30pm Mon–Sun. Average Price: meals and snacks under £5. Access/ Master, Visa, Amex. Very well signposted in the area.

Hotel
### HYLAND'S HOTEL
*Ballyvaughan Tel: (065) 77037/77051 Fax: (065) 77131 Marie Greene*

This is a cosy little hotel, just the right place to find yourself in when in Ballyvaughan. Although much of their cooking centres around fish and shellfish — the bowls of chowder are legendary — they do a fine gâteau au crepes — layers of crepes alternated with creamed spinach, lentil purée and garlic mushrooms, the sublime concoction topped with Parmesan cheese then oven baked and, finally, served with a crispy orange and sunflower salad.

Open Feb–Xmas. Average Price: lunch under £10, dinner under £20, B&B under £30. Visa, Access/Master, Amex. In the centre of Ballyvaughan

Restaurant and Craft Shop
## WHITETHORN RESTAURANT AND CRAFTS
*Ballyvaughan Tel: (065) 77044 Fax (065) 77155 John O'Donoghue*
Eating dinner in The Whitethorn as the sun sets over the bay is impossibly romantic, and they take great care with the cooking, take care that their vegetarian choices — strawberries and cucumbers in a mint vinaigrette; tagliatelle with tangy stir-fried vegetables; vegetable and mixed nut stroganoff with herbed rice — should be as enjoyable and satisfying as everything else. Excellent crafts are also for sale in the shop.

Open 7 days high season. Just outside the village of Ballyvaughan.

# BRIDGETOWN

Food Producer
## THE POT-POURRI
*Bridgetown Tel: (061) 377443*
County Clare's own herb grower, with a splendid list that encompasses regular kitchen herbs such as chives, fennel, parsley and marjoram and extends and extends to such luxuries as French tarragon, camomile, bergamot and Corsican mint.

Sold locally as well as in the Galway Saturday Market.

# COROFIN

B&B with Restaurant
## CAHERBOLANE FARMHOUSE
*Corofin Tel: (065) 37638 Brid Cahill*
By itself, Caherbolane is a modest farmhouse, just a quartet of unadorned rooms upstairs for guests and a dining room below. But the energy and good cheer of the Cahills is addictive and the cooking by Patricia Cahill in the front room they convert to a restaurant is excellent: spinach casserole — a creamy confection of spinach and noodles in a cheese sauce baked under a topping of breadcrumbs and pecans and walnuts; cheese raviolis with coriander pesto; or vegetable samosas with a saffron and lemon beurre blanc; a perfect chocolate and Grand Marnier mousse. The welcome and the quality of the cooking makes for a priceless base from which to scoot around the county.

Open 7.30pm–9.30pm Mon–Sun. Closed Nov–Easter. Average Price: dinner under £15, B&B under £15. No Credit Cards. Look for the signpost three miles outside Corofin on the road to Gort.

# DOOLIN

Café
## THE DOOLIN CAFÉ,
*Doolin Tel: (065) 74429 John & Josephine Clinton*
For a cup of tea and a relaxing browse through assorted papers and
books, the Doolin Café is hip and friendly, with good breads and good
coffee flowing freely.
Open 9.30am–2pm, 6pm–9pm May–Sept.

# KILNABOY

Farmhouse Cheese
## BARTELINK
*Poulcoin, Kilnaboy Annaliese Bartelink*
Annaliese Bartelink has been making cheese in Ireland for about
fourteen years, and her cheese has a depth and complexity of flavour that
comes from deep experience as a cheesemaker.

These gouda-style cheeses can be richly, vibrantly fulsome and loaded
with fine, mineral notes. One look at the rocky surroundings all about
her Hansel-and-Gretel farmhouse and you can see how the rich flora of
the Burren gifts the milk with these floral, erudite tastes, but the surprise
is just how creamy the cheese can be, for this is rocky land, and you
assume pastures are scarce and poor.

Like all the creamy, buttery Irish gouda-style cheeses, Annaliese's
cheeses are at their very best with a good deal of ageing: when over
twelve months old — admittedly and unfortunately it is difficult to find it
this old — it is truly memorable. But, even if bought young in the locality,
it's a cheese that reflects the smells and scents of the Burren, and this is
its singularity. Try both the cow's and goat's cheeses with different
flavourings, but the expertise of the Bartelinks often leads you back to the
original, unflavoured, cheese where the good Burren flavours come
through unchallenged.

# ENNIS

Delicatessen & Cooked Food Shop
## ABBEY MEATS — THE FOOD EMPORIUM
*Abbey Street Tel: (065) 20554 T.J. McGuinness and Brenda Dearing*
Don't be put off by the name, there is much more than meat on the menu
at Abbey Meats. It is, as the second part of its moniker suggests, an
emporium, a truly surprising place, a shop that fuses the elements of a

trâiteur and a patisserie: excellent baking and a fine display of deli foods and good vegetables. Very useful for making up a picnic lunch.

Open 9am–6pm Mon–Sat. Ennis town centre.

Restaurant and Pub Food
## THE CLOISTER
*Abbey Street Tel: (065) 29521 Jim Brindley*
Go any time in the afternoon for the bar menu, served around the bar itself as well as in the patio with its surround of a high walled garden, servicing locals as much as it does blow-ins, plane hoppers, travelling salesmen, those who are simply hungry.

Open noon–9.45pm (pub food), 7pm–10pm (restaurant) Mon–Sun. Closed Xmas. Average Price: restaurant under £20, bar under £10. Visa, Access/Master. At the first roundabout coming into Ennis from the Galway direction, turn left at the bridge.

Wholefood Shop
## OPEN SESAME
*29 Parnell Street Tel: (091) 31315(home) Sally Smyth*
Sally Smyth sells the organic vegetables of local grower Helga Friedmacher and the local Kilshanny cheeses in her cute little shop.

Open 10am–1.30pm, 2.30pm–6pm Mon–Fri, 10am–6pm Sat. Ennis town centre.

# ENNISTYMON

Bakery
## UNGLERT'S BAKERY
*Tel: (065) 71217 Mr Unglert*
Continental breads, such as those flavoured with rye flour are the speciality of this German bakery in the pub-filled town of Ennistymon. You can also eat in here, in a little café which is attached to the bakery and have coffee to go with your cake.

Open 9am–7pm Tue–Sun. Ennistymon town centre.

# INAGH

Farmhouse Cheese
## INAGH FARMHOUSE CHEESES
*Inagh Tel: (065) 26633 Meg and Derrick Gordon*
If Meg and Derrick Gordon moved to Kowloon, or maybe Madagascar, and brought their herd of beautiful goats with them, the cheese they would make in their new location, be it Des Moines or Dubai, would be just like the cheese they make in Inagh. Other cheesemakers utilise the strengths of the environment in which they work, and to this add a

soupçon of personality. With The Gordons, their goat's milk cheese seems to be the product more of themselves than of their environment, though that must, of course, play a role.

But, for the most part, this is a cheese which you feel you could almost have a conversation with, if you have met the cheesemakers and can hear their chirpy voices ringing in your head as you take a bite. The Inagh cheeses are alive with a wiry, sparky zestfulness, a sharp and laconic attitude, an ironic and well-versed fluency.

All the cheeses, whether the Lough Caum semi-hard cheese with its marbled paleness, or the St. Tola log, white like the sun behind the clouds, or the little crottins of soft cheese pressed in paprika or crushed peppercorns or fresh herbs, offer a concentrated and evocative lushness, a tingling satisfaction that becomes a tremor. You can use the St. Tola for cooking, and it is fresh and rich with pasta, superb grilled on a barbecue or with some dressed salad leaves as a starter, even a raspberry vinaigrette. The Lough Caum suits a wintry evening and a good cheese knife with which to peel off slices as you demolish a bottle of claret. And all the time you hear the voices of its makers in your head, that babble of life right through the ballet of tastes.

Inagh cheeses are available throughout the country, and are sold from the farm. Ask directions in the village of Inagh. You can also have the cheese sent through the post, which is surprisingly efficient. Telephone for details.

# KILSHANNY

Farmhouse Cheese
## KILSHANNY FARMHOUSE CHEESE
*Derry House, Lahinch Tel: (065) 71228 Peter and Aaron Nibbering*
There are a quintet of different flavours used by father-and-son Peter and Aaron to make the much-respected Kilshanny. The plain cheese has a lush and up-front milkiness, especially when young. The pepper version gives a spicy, but not too spicy, kick to the milkiness, whilst it is the cheese flavoured with garden herbs which is perhaps the most appealing, for the greenness of the flavouring seems very suitable for such a pasture-rich cheese. The cumin cheese has a pronounced savoury note which suits red wine, and the garlic cheese is pungent but still controlled. You will find the Kilshanny cheeses much in evidence in County Clare, where they are well supported, and they are for sale on Saturday mornings at a small stall in the Limerick market. If you are on the hunt for cheeses which are more mature, then it is perhaps best to follow the signs for the farm and to buy them there.

The Nibberings are delighted to sell from the house, which is well signposted ('Derry House') from Kilshanny village. Coming from Lahinch, go north. Cross over the bridge and take a right turn before you come to Liscannor. Otherwise the cheese is available from most of the surrounding supermarkets and many restaurants in the area.

# KILRUSH

Farmhouse cheese
## ST MARTIN CHEESE
*Carnanes, Kilrush Tel: (065) 51320 Eileen O'Brien*
Eileen's cheese is a simple and soulful product, not much seen except in the locality — look out for it in the Supervalu in Kilrush — and maybe as far away as Ennis in Knox's, but it is rich and buttery in flavour, great for picnics.

Cheese can be bought from the farm which is just outside Kilrush. Telephone for details and directions.

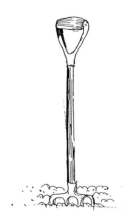

# LAHINCH

Restaurant
## BARRTRA SEAFOOD RESTAURANT
*Lahinch Tel: (065) 81280 Paul & Theresa O'Brien*
They are clever restaurateurs, Paul and Theresa O'Brien. In the offshoot of their house which is the little collection of tables known as the Barrtrá Seafood Restaurant, overlooking the peaceful and endearing calm of Liscannor Bay, the menu is a clever reflection of both their culinary strengths and their culinary experiments.

Their strengths lie with the eternal verities — good breads; good soups — and, especially, the fact that they offer a full vegetarian menu: beetroot soup; courgette and spinach soup; avocado salad; tomato and brazil nut pancake; steamed cabbage parcels with red pepper sauce; baked stuffed courgette with fresh tomato sauce; aubergine fritters with peanut sauce on a bed of spinach. Clever cooking, as you would expect, and terrifically generous and thoughtful.

Open 12.30pm–2.30pm Mon–Sun, 6pm–10pm Mon–Sat. Closed weekdays off season & Jan–17 Mar. Average Price: lunch under £5–under £10, dinner under £20. Signposted from the Lahinch-Milltown Malbay Road.

# County Cork

## NORTH CORK

## BALLINGEARY

Farmhouse Cheese
### CARRAIG GOAT'S CHEESE
*Ballingeary Tel: (026) 47126 Aart and Lieke Versloot*
Come rain or come shine you will find Mr Versloot with his little stall of goat's milk cheeses at the Bantry Friday market. A mountainy man, his clothes and beard perfumed with turf, he makes an instinctive, expert cheese that is fresh with the goodness of the Ballingeary hills, the after-taste furnishing a mellow cleanness. Carraig cheese is sold when it has aged a matter of weeks, usually somewhere around about seven weeks, but it will happily last much much longer, developing smoothly and richly into something special.

## BALLINEEN AND ENNISKEANE

Organic Eggs, Cheese and Vegetables
### MANCH ESTATE ★
*Manch, Ballineen, Tel: (023) 47507 Fax: 47276 Iris, Janet & Oliver*
The waxy organic Desiree potatoes that you can buy on the farm in Manch are each and every one immaculate. Seamus O'Connell in The Ivory Tower Restaurant in Cork uses them to make a crispy, ruby-tinged potato cake, and they're made for both mashing into a smooth, milky purée and for baking into a slumberously dry mouthful.

But it's not only the potatoes that are expertly produced. The cheese, made from sheep's milk is creamy white, clean tasting and can sink perfectly into an olive oil, garlic and herb coating and the Sunflowers burst with joyful colour and, even on dull days, remind you that it is summer.

Manch is a few miles east of Dunmanway, with a sign at the entrance to the farm saying Free Range Eggs (due to be changed sometime this year to give details of Manch Farm). Janet and Iris also sell their produce at the Tuesday market in Macroom and in the Cork Covered Market

Farmhouse Cheese
### ROUND TOWER CHEESE
*Bride View House Enniskeane Tel: (023) 47105 Nan O'Donovan*
Thanks to Nan O'Donovan's unceasing energy, wedges of Round Tower Cheese can be found for sale all over the county. Round Tower could be described as a classic Irish Gouda, the taste always gentle and milky, a

bundle of sweet and communing tastes which remain very fresh. If you can ever get the chance to try it, do look out for, or do inquire about, the small cheeses which Nan matures for up to nine months, for one then sees an entirely different Round Tower: forceful where the young cheese is mild, concentrated where the milkiness of the young cheese is diffuse, altogether something special and marvellous.

# COOLEA

Farmhouse Cheese
## COOLEA CHEESE
*Coolea Tel: (026) 45204 Dick and Helene Willems*
Such an extraordinary concatenation of tastes are contained within a properly kept, happily aged Coolea that it can seem almost impossible to enumerate them.

One finds the smell of sweetly old Parmesan, the buttery redoubt of Cheddar, the wise satisfaction of an Appenzeller, the cleanness and perfect construction of a good Gouda, the intensity of flavour of a Tomme or a Reblochon. But these names, and the styles of cheesemaking they signify, are no more than allusive signposts to the specific and special nature of Dick and Helene Willems' cheese, its essential uniqueness

Sometimes you think it is like a concentration of toffee — this perhaps if you buy one that is eighteen months old — other times the cheese will be cake-sweet, a sugary confection of milk, a baby-pleasing piece of utter delight, kaleidoscoping with lush, sexy flavours. More than perhaps any other Irish farmhouse cheese — though Coolea's near-neighbour Ardrahan does manage to achieve something similar — Coolea is a deep, deep concentration of tastes and flavours, so tongue-ready and upfront that they may leave you tongue-tied.

# KANTURK

Farmhouse Cheese
## ARDRAHAN CHEESE ➡
*Ardrahan House Tel: (029) 78099 Mary & Eugene Burns*
"I never met anyone in the cheese business who wasn't nice", says Eugene Burns. This comes as no surprise, for when you meet Mr Burns you can't be anything other than nice, for so charming and hospitable are both he and Mary that the devil himself would have to respond warmly to them.

Like all of the farmhouse cheesemakers, the cheese they make is constructed from their personalities as much as their skills, and Ardrahan is a mirror to Eugene and Mary and the essence of the country: intense, splendid, something instinctive and organic and devoid of artifice. The milk from this part of North Cork has long been celebrated for its richness and its complex flavours, and these powerful tastes make their way into Ardrahan, allying with Mary's skill as a cheesemaker to create a semi-soft cheese that can exhaust the senses with delight.

Country House & Restaurant
## ASSOLAS COUNTRY HOUSE
*Kanturk Tel: (029) 50015 Fax: (029) 50795 Joe and Hazel Bourke*
Assolas is gifted with being one of those houses that makes you feel very glad you are there. It is dashingly romantic, whether at night when the house is dappled with lights and you wander alongside the river, or on a warm morning amidst the sprucely manicured hedges and shrubs as you maybe swing on the tree swing and think of your salad days.

It is welcoming, thanks to Joe and Hazel Bourke and their assiduous and assured youthful energy, their easy wit and style. Mrs Bourke cooks, and she does so with a great feeling for both acuity of flavour and texture in a dish. With a twice-baked soufflé made with Mary Burns' Ardrahan cheese, the effulgent, energetic flavours will be tempered with a subtle cream sauce ringed around the soufflé. But where Hazel Bourke's cooking demonstrates her confidence best of all is with her use of the fresh herbs, many of them grown out back in Assolas' vegetable garden.

Such wonderful food, enjoyed in the quiet comfort of the red-walled dining room, makes you doubly glad to be at Assolas and, days after, images from the visit come back into the mind: the whites-clad cook walking back across the lawn after collecting herbs; the sea-green colour of a bowl of asparagus soup; the bursting orange and red colours of a breakfast compote; the lush comfort of the rooms. Precious memories.

Open 7pm–8.30pm (non-residents booking essential). Closed Nov–mid Mar. Average Price: dinner under £30 B&B over £30. Visa, Access/Master, Amex. Assolas is signposted from the N72, as you approach Kanturk, coming both from Mallow and Killarney. The house is a few miles outside town.


## NORTH CORK CO-OP SOCIETY LTD
*Kanturk Tel: (029) 50003 Sean McAulis.*
The milk collected from farmers within a ten mile radius of Kanturk is pasteurised by the Kanturk Dairy in exactly the same way as any other milk in any other dairy. So, how then is one to explain why the Kanturk Dairy milk is richer, creamier, more satisfying than other commercial milks? Heaven only knows, but better it is, with a fulsomeness and sweetness beside which other milks seem positively emaciated. The milk and cream — sold as North Cork Co-Op Society — can be found in Millstreet, Macroom, Kanturk and the small villages creeping into west County Limerick.

Millstreet, Macroom, Kanturk and the small villages creeping into west County Limerick.

# MACROOM

Oatmeal
## MACROOM OATMEAL

*Walton's Mills, Manor Villa Tel: (026) 41800 Donal Creedon*

You just can't hurry Donal Creedon's delicious oatmeal. Like many of the best breakfast foods — still-warm soda bread, slowly coagulated scrambled eggs — it needs the indulgence of time. So be wise, then, and indulge it, take the time to prepare this artful, artisan food, for nothing else in Ireland so repays the expenditure of effort, so rewards the indulgence in minutes.

To get it at its best, soak a few spoonfuls in water overnight. In the morning, pour off any excess water, then mix the appropriate quantity of fresh water — you can use a portion of milk to make it creamy — and add some salt. Slowly, slowly bring it to the boil, then slowly, slowly simmer it, with the little puckering popfuls of hot air breaking the surface. Stir every so often. Wait for it to achieve a creamy, gentle emulsion, which may take fifteen, maybe twenty minutes.

Then spoon it into a bowl, and scatter rich brown sugar on top. Pour on sinfully thick cream, and do not spare it, for this is no penitential Calvinistic food, but a serene, indulgent, sweet thing of joy. Eat it slowly, and savour the sustenance of deep flavour, with the fresh warmth of oats to warm every part of the soul. There is nothing else like it.

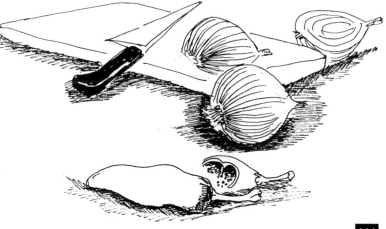

Market
## MACROOM TUESDAY MARKET
*Macroom Town Centre*
Each and every Tuesday there is an all-day street market in Macroom town. On one side of the street you find the conventional growers, selling brilliant orange carrots and snowy white parsnips gathered together by their feathery green leaves, sacks of potatoes and whatever else might be in season. On the other side of the street you find the artisans led by the marvellous Manch Estate growers.

# MALLOW

Restaurant & Country House
## LONGUEVILLE HOUSE AND PRESIDENT'S RESTAURANT
*Mallow Tel: (022) 47156 Fax: 47459 William and Aisling O'Callaghan*
William O'Callaghan is an outrageously talented cook, and his culinary fluencies seem to know no boundary. He manages with each dish to use his technique to evoke the inherent flavours and strengths of the food, and in the case of Longueville this has particular resonance, for the house is almost self-sufficient and in eating here one eats the food of the area in the area.

This unity — the son of the house cooking where his father taught him and exploiting the produce of the farm — is of great importance to William O'Callaghan, for he is obsessive about ingredients. "The cucumbers coming in now, the taste of those is just incredible", he says. "You can't compare the spinach we have here and the stuff that comes in plastic bags". And there are the trips a little further south to gather chanterelles and perhaps one day he will even find truffles "We have a lot of beech and oak around the property, no reason why they shouldn't be there".

One hopes so, for whilst most chefs dream of working with truffles, most of them in reality wouldn't be able to exploit the elusive and haunting flavour to the full. William O'Callaghan has such ability that you hope he can get his hands on the finest things, and you will happily abnegate any responsibility in his presence: if he wants to cook it, then you want to eat it.

Here are some of his vegetarian dishes: tartlette of tomato with star anise and basil sauce; terrine of garden vegetables set in a tomato concasse with a herb vinaigrette; vegetable broth; garden leek quiche with salad; tartlet of wild chanterelles with wild mushroom sauce; mousse of Ardrahan Farmhouse Cheese.

Open to non residents for dinner, if pre-booked. Closed mid Dec–mid Mar. Average Price: dinner under £30, B&B over £30. Visa, Access/Master, Amex, Diners. 3 miles west of Mallow on the N72 to Killarney.

Asparagus Grower
## JUNE WILLIAMS
*Doneraile Tel: (022) 24316*

Perhaps it is the painfully short season which makes the pert shoots of asparagus seem so precious when they do duck out from under the soil late in April and early in May.

Maybe it's their not-too-sweet cleanness of taste, or the promise of dishes to come as you bring them home: steamed then served with scrambled eggs; in a sharp green soup; with just a hollandaise sauce; maybe nothing more than a knob of butter on top oozing over the stalks and the dark tips.

Like corn, they are best eaten as soon out of the ground as possible, so heading to North Cork to buy some stalks freshly cut by the Williamses is great fun.

Telephone to inquire about availability and to get directions.

# EAST CORK

# FERMOY

Restaurant
## LA BIGOUDENNE
*28 McCurtain Street Tel: (025) 32832 Rodolphe & Noelle Semeria*

La Bigoudenne restaurant is as prototypically French as the queer-shaped pointed hat which gives the restaurant its name.

During the day it is a simple cafe, serving filled baguettes and home-made soups, while at night the menu becomes rather more formal. The speciality of the restaurant, however, and one that makes it worthy of a vegetarian's attention, are the northern French crêpes, sweet ones — filled with stewed apple, chocolate, pear and ice cream and savoury ones — egg and cheese, salad and blue cheese. They are splendid on-the-road food, giving the energy a lift, brightening the soul.

Open 12.30pm–5.30pm, 7pm–10pm Tue–Sat. Open for Xmas, closed 2 weeks end Sept. Average Price: lunch under £5–under £10, dinner under £15. Visa, Access/Master. On the main street in Fermoy.

# MIDLETON

Shop & Restaurant
## THE FARM GATE
*Coolbawn Tel: (021) 632771 Kay Harte & Morag O'Brien*

Flowers everywhere, food books and magazines scattered around and about, some unknown string quartet sawing away happily on the stereo, a great big table of desserts laid out to make you salivate the second you walk in, a giddy assortment of sculptures and paintings for decoration.

It is a happy space, the Farm Gate, very feminine, very understated, and how very nice it is to be here. They do nice things to simple food, they know how to make a proper sandwich and their pancakes and pastas are flavoursome, friendly, food to spend time over.

Out front, meanwhile, the Farm Gate shop is packed with choice cheeses, cakes, bakes and bread, good vegetables and comestibles. Do note that the girls have now opened a second restaurant in the Cork Covered Market.

Open 9.30am–6pm Mon–Wed, 9.30am–5pm, 7.30pm–9.30pm Thurs–Sat. Closed Xmas. Average Price: lunch under £10, dinner under £20. Visa, Access/Master.

Distillery
## JAMESON HERITAGE CENTRE
*Midleton Tel: (021) 613594*
The home of the tortuously expensive Midleton Single Malt, and nowadays the site of conducted tours which explain the magical process of distilling.

Open 10am–4pm Mon–Sun. Closed Nov–Mar except for bookings.

# SHANAGARRY

Country House & Restaurant
## BALLYMALOE HOUSE ➡
*Shanagarry Tel: (021) 652531 Fax: 652021 Ivan and Myrtle Allen*
Pythagoras was amongst the earliest vegetarians, refusing to eat meat due to his philosophical belief in the transmigration of souls.

Myrtle Allen has a philosophy of food which, though not exclusively vegetarian, evokes many of their environmental and social concerns.

Firstly, encourage a circle of producers around and about you to produce the very best foods they can manage and, vitally, support them as best you can. In addition to this, you should attempt to be as self-sufficient as you can: grow your own spuds, make your own chutneys, produce as much of the food you need through your own endeavours as is possible.

Then, when it comes to the cooking of this food, do it from scratch and do it with ingredients which are as pristinely fresh as possible, allow the food to speak of itself. Then, when it comes to serving the food, do it simply, but courteously and as graciously as you can, with the maximum dialogue between customer and cook, a culinary conversation.

This is a simple modus, and Myrtle Allen has never lost sight of this creed of simplicity, in more than twenty five years. During that time, the philosophy of Ballymaloe has remained consistent: respect for the fruits of the land, air and sea. Respect for the long-held culinary codes which best transform these fruits. Respect for the person who will enjoy the fruits of the cook's labours and, just as important, respect demanded for the efforts of the cook and respect for the culinary arts.

The Ballymaloe philosophy is a logical, conscientious, concerned and kind way of working with the world and it is this deep thread, just as much as the delicious presentations on a plate or the baleful comfort of the house, which makes Ballymaloe special.

Pythagoras, it must be noted, would have been well pleased, for Ballymaloe is one of the few restaurants to offer a complete vegetarian menu every evening.

Open buffet lunch 1pm, dinner 7pm–9pm Mon–Sun (buffet dinner Sun). Closed Xmas. Average Price: lunch under £20, dinner under £30. Visa, Access/Master, Amex, Diners. Ballymaloe House is signposted from the N25.

Cookery School
## THE BALLYMALOE COOKERY SCHOOL
*Kinoith House, Shanagarry Tel: (021) 646785 Darina & Tim Allen*
"Real food with true flavours" is the simple ethos of the Ballymaloe School an ethos reflected in the annual vegetarian cookery courses they run as part of their programme each year.
Telephone or write for their annual brochure.

Kitchenshop
## BALLYMALOE KITCHEN SHOP
*Ballymaloe House, Shanagarry Tel: (021) 652032 Wendy Whelan*
Behind the excellent craftshop at Ballymaloe there is an excellent kitchen shop. It's one of those places that, no matter how many times you return, you always find some new discovery, some exciting new implement.

But nothing is chosen for its gimmick value, from a simple nutmeg grater, to a pizza stone, to the complete range of le pentole saucepans, everything here will work when you take it back to your own kitchen, everything is bought because it's built to last. The shop echoes the philosophy of Ballymaloe itself, simplicity, excellence, and great fun.
Open 9am–6.30pm Mon–Sun

Preserves
## BALLYMALOE RELISH
*Caherlog, Glanmire Tel: (021) 353358 Yasmin Hyde*
The principal ingredient of Ballymaloe relish is tomato, red-ripe tomato. The texture is of soft chutney punctuated by the odd well-cooked sultana and the occasional spice seed. The recipe for the chutney was an original Myrtle Allen concoction, and, says her daughter Yasmin "It was always an essential part of the table, even before the restaurant opened".

Recently, Wendy has developed a new pickle — spicy green cucumber relish, a crunchy amalgamation of vegetable and spices that can be turned into a green salad, served in a sandwich, or used to brighten up a plate of, well, anything, in fact.

Ballymaloe Relishes are sold in shops and supermarkets throughout the country.

Pottery
## STEPHEN PEARCE POTTERY
*Shanagarry Tel: (021) 646807*
Stephen Pearce's traditional design of pottery has been much imitated, but never improved on. The calming russet-tinged colour of the local clay, dug near the river Blackwater, needs nothing other than the occasional swirl of pale white to bring it to life. Best of all, just as the clay colour evokes the essential earthiness and ruddiness of the potter's art, Mr Pearce's work also has a deeply pleasing grainy tactility and weight in the feel of the plates and jugs and cups, an honest feeling.

Open 8am–5pm Mon–Fri, 10am–5pm Sat, 2pm–5pm Sun.

Mustards & Preserves
## BRECON LODGE PRESERVES
*East Ferry, Midleton Tel: (021) 652352 Robert Nunn*
A broad and popular range of mustards — they actually grow the seeds for the mustards themselves — chutneys and savoury jellies, widely available in supermarkets and choice delis.

# YOUGHAL

Restaurant/Pub Food/Accommodation
## AHERNE'S SEAFOOD BAR
*163 North Main Street Tel: (024) 92424 Fax: 93633 The Fitzgibbon family*
Each and every year new followers are added to the fold of those for whom Aherne's personifies bliss itself. Charmed by the intimacy of the dining room, succoured by the comfort of the food, lulled by the promise of the wine list, they speak afterwards in enraptured tones. No-one, it seems, is immune to the charms of the pinky art-decked dining room, or the cosy bar where you are left alone to drink in the atmosphere.

Aherne's specialises in fish, but give notice of your vegetarian prefer-ences and no doubt you will join the legion of fans of Aherne's who come to give homage and enjoy themselves.

Open 12.30pm–2pm, 6.30pm–9.30pm Mon–Sat, 6.30pm–9.30pm Sun (pub food available 10.30am-closing time). Closed Xmas. Average Price: lunch under £10, dinner under £20. Visa, Access/Master, Amex, Diners. On the Main Street in Youghal at the Waterford end of town.

Goat's Milk and Cheese
### ARDSALLAGH
*Kornelius Korner Ardsallagh House, Youghal Tel: (021) 92545*
Farmhouse goat's milk cheeses, some soft, some hard and also goat's feta. Some of them flavoured, some spiced in oil, goat's yogurt, and goat's milk and goat's butter. Found in the locality, and occasionally in Cork city.

# CORK CITY

# RESTAURANTS

## ARBUTUS LODGE
*Montenotte Tel: (021) 501237 Fax: 502893 Michael & Declan Ryan*
Recent years have seen a greater informality make its way into the serving of food in Arbutus and, nowadays, one of the biggest attractions of the hotel is the very modern and delicious dishes served in the bar at lunchtime.

Whilst relatively simple food there is always a vegetarian option and it is always executed with professionalism and is just as suitable as the more formal cooking of the dining room when it comes to matching a good bottle of wine from the extraordinary wine list to accompany it.

Open restaurant: 1pm–2pm, 7pm–9.30pm Mon–Sat, bar lunch 12.15pm–2.30pm Mon–Sat. Closed Xmas. Average Price: bar lunch under £10, restaurant lunch under £20, dinner under £30, B&B over £30. Visa, Access/Master, Amex, Diners. Cork city centre, signposted from the Cork-Dublin road.

## CLIFFORD'S
*18 Dyke Parade Tel: (021) 275333 Michael and Deirdre Clifford*
Michael Clifford's cooking strikes a perfect balance between competing disciplines.

Whilst it is sumptuous and comforting, it is based on relatively simple ingredients. His work is cosmopolitan, yet never happiest than when working with something grown and produced as close to the restaurant as possible. His food is modern in style and technique, but he can manage to evoke a taste that seems age-old and yet — and this is vital — he avoids any sense of that dread nostalgia which so restricts Irish cuisine.

All of this skill is met by typical Clifford thoughtfulness when it comes to cooking for vegetarians: ring up in advance and they will discuss details with you for a complete dinner, and you can see the free-flow of ideas in Mr Clifford's work in all their splendour.

Open 12.30pm–2.30pm, 7pm–10.30pm Tue–Sat. Closed Xmas Day and bank holidays. Average Price: lunch under £15, vegetarian dinner under £20. Visa, Access/Master, Amex, Diners. Clifford's is a minute's walk from Jury's Hotel: turn left, then right and at the first set of traffic lights you will see the restaurant on the corner.

## ISAAC'S BRASSERIE AND HOSTEL
*MacCurtain Street Tel: (021) 503805 Canice Sharkey*

It's an awkward thing, deciding just what time of day it is that you most prefer to go to Isaac's.

This big tall room is a splendid place and the food — even though the vegetarian choices are limited — is full of suggestions which inspire the appetite: some colourful fresh pasta ribboned on the plate, swathed with fresh asparagus and parmesan or freshly festooned with pesto sauce, green beans and potato.

If you wish to make the most of the atmosphere, then the rooms in the Isaac's hostel are simple, spotless, reminiscent of a European pensione, and a valuable remembered taste of your salad days. It's the kind of place where the sound of some trumpeter playing some cool jazz may come quietly drifting across the quad as you lie on your bed on a warm afternoon and you ask yourself, just who was he?, that young man that you once were.

Open 10am for coffee, 12.30pm–2.30pm, afternoon tea, 6.30pm–10.30pm Mon–Sat, 6.30pm–9.30pm Sun. Closed Xmas. Average Price: lunch under £10, dinner under £15 B&B under £20. Visa, Access/Master. Cork city centre, north of the river.

## THE IVORY TOWER RESTAURANT ★
*Exchange Buildings, 35 Princes Street Tel: (021) 274665 Seamus O'Connell*

"I would like to open people's minds about food. I find there is no one who is really surprising people with cooking, challenging people with new ideas".

Other chefs say similar things to this all the time, but there is a difference when someone like Seamus O'Connell says it, for he is an almost preternaturally gifted cook. In the, simple, almost minimalist room that is The Ivory Tower, Mr O'Connell strives for a restaurant where "the diners would have such confidence in that they would come regardless of what is on the menu.

"I could say, 'Look, I'm just doing one menu a night with maybe three choices at a set price'. Then I would have free rein to follow the seasons, and to organise what I want to".

This is a good stratagem to follow with Mr O'Connell, for his food is devilishly exciting, right from the thrill when you first see a menu he has prepared: sun-dried tomato hummus and crudities; pumpkin squash and pesto soup; felaffel, tajine and cous cous tzatsikas; aubergine burrito, Salsa and sour cream; split pea and rice burger and mushroom stroganoff.

But not only can he write them, he can cook them and Mr O'Connell is as individual and as exciting a cook as you will find anywhere in Ireland.

Open noon–4pm Mon–Sat, 6.30pm–11pm Wed–Sun. Closed Xmas and 2 weeks Jan. Average Price: lunch under £10, dinner under £20. Visa, Access/Master. Princes Street leads off St Patrick's Street.

## JACQUE'S

*9 Phoenix St Tel: (021) 277387 Jacqueline and Eithne Barry*

In Cork, restaurateurs are not allowed the luxury of fence-sitting or laurel-resting and thus, after more than a decade in business, Jacque's has been newly refurbished by Jacqueline and Eithne into a lean, modern, minimalist space with cool lighting and the right sort of stylish, unadorned decor that suits the keenly motivated ambience of the restaurant.

The menu is quietly flamboyant in the modern international style, with thoughtful and creative vegetarian dishes like an aubergine sandwich with a spicy tomato tagliatelle, or grilled polenta with parsley pesto and a green salad, or hot vegetarian hors d'oeuvres. The staff are grace itself, and the charm of the dining room makes for a fine evening out.

Open 12.30pm–2.30pm Mon–Sat, 6pm–10.30pm Tues–Sat, lunch under £10, dinner under £20. Visa, Access/Master.

## CAFÉ PARADISO ★

*16 Lancaster Quay, Western Road Tel: (021) 277939 Denis Cotter*

Denis Cotter's Café is a simply decorated big room, facing immediately onto the street, filled with tables and chairs, with a simple counter at the end from which waitresses fetch food, and a cooking area into which you can expectantly peer to see the cook at work.

For what Mr Cotter does and for the way Mr Cotter cooks, this space proves apposite and appropriate. His cooking is quiet and effective, with little in the way of frills and needless gestures, but it is annotated by a broad vision and underpinned by a serious devotion to good flavours. He is also a harbinger of what is to come, for Café Paradiso is a vegetarian restaurant, but even the carnivore who eats here will not find that there is anything missing from the food. This cuisine is complete of and unto itself, and Café Paradiso is an exemplar of the genuine creativity within vegetarian cookery in Ireland.

Mr Cotter has opened his style up to the influences of the New World: a house soup elsewhere would be stodgy carrot, but here it has the svelteness of coriander to lift its profile and, with a baked croissant sandwich with brie, fresh and sun-dried tomatoes and salad sidled into it, it makes for a superb lunch.

There may be a salad of wild and basmati rices or a lovely peppery leek and peppercorn tart. In the evening the menu opens out: vegetable stir-fry in a hot and sour black bean sauce with roasted cashews and fragrant rice; a gougère pastry ring filled with Gabriel cheese, Thai cashew and tofu sandwich fritters; fresh spinach tagliatelle with mushrooms in a red wine sauce; broccoli and blue cheese filo pastry pie with a potato, aubergine and coriander stew. The desserts are jaw-droppingly fine: Tia Maria iced cream bombettes; butterscotch and walnut cheesecake; ginger sautéed pears with iced mascarpone. Incidentally, it can appear in here, at times, that smoking is compulsory: don't worry, it's not.

Open 10.30am–10.30pm (lunch 12.30pm–3.30pm, dinner 6.30pm–10.30pm) Tue–Sat. Closed Xmas week. Average Price: lunch under £5 dinner under £15. Visa, Access/Master. Opposite Jury's hotel.

---

### Denis Cotter's Aubergine, Lentil and Goat's Cheese Charlotte in Coriander Custard

**7oz (200g) brown lentils**
**6 Sun-dried tomatoes**, chopped
**2 medium aubergines**, sliced into quarter
inch thick rounds
olive oil

**The Custard Ingredients:**
**1 egg**
**2 cloves garlic**
**Scant three-quarters pint(400mls) yoghurt**
**3 and-a-half oz (100g) cream cheese**
**salt and cayenne pepper**
**small handful fresh coriander**

Cook the lentils and stir in the sun-dried tomatoes. Combine the Custard ingredients in a blender. Grill or roast aubergine slices, brushed with olive oil until browned.

In six individual deep soup bowls or large ramekins layer the aubergines, lentils, custard, cheese. Repeat. Add one more layer of aubergine and bake in a bain marie for 30–40 minutes. Invert onto a serving plate and serve with a lightly spiced tomato sauce.

---

Vegetarian Restaurant and Wholefood Shop

## QUAY CO-OP ➡

*24 Sullivan's Quay Tel: (021) 317660 Arthur Leahy, Maura O'Keefe*
The Co-Op has for many years been a reliable destination for wholesome wholefood, always managing to furnish its punters with good food even through a series of changes in direction and orientation.

During the day it operates as a self-service restaurant, offering tried and tested vegetarian staples cooked by Ann-Marie Friend: sweet and sour tofu with vegetables and rice; chickpea burgers; vegetable lasagne. At night the menu explores some of the newer ideas to influence vegetarian cuisine, offering table service and a moody, dusky ambience that invites you to open up a bottle or two. The shop downstairs is an excellent source of good foods, organic vegetables and occasional exotica.

Open shop 9.30am–6.30pm, restaurant 9.30am–6.30pm self-service, 6.30pm–10.30pm table service Mon–Sun. Closed Xmas. Average Price: lunch under £5, dinner under £10–under £15. Visa, Access/Master. Just south of the river in the city centre.

Café
## THE CRAWFORD GALLERY CAFÉ
*Emmet Place Tel: (021) 274415 Rory O'Connell*
The Gallery is a lovely space, femininely alert and appealing, with food to match. The café is a scion of the great Ballymaloe clan and much of the food in here comes from there, not just physically, but temperamentally and creatively as well. This is comfort cooking: crumbly brown breads and cakes to accompany coffee, soulful pancakes, zappy sandwiches with cheese and Ballymaloe Relish. At lunchtime it is a delightful place in which to consider and recharge.

Open 10.30am–5pm (lunch served 12.30pm–2.30pm) Mon–Sat. Closed Xmas and bank hols. Average Price: lunch under £10. Visa, Access/Master. The restaurant is on the ground floor of the gallery, near the Opera House.

Bakery and Café
## THE GINGERBREAD HOUSE
*Paul Street Tel: (021) 276411 Barnaby Blacker*
Now housed in new premises, Barnaby Blacker's Gingerbread House is still a slightly excitable space, full of good baking, good preserves and excellent filled sandwiches. Croissants and pain au chocolat can all be taken away or eaten in.

Open 9am–6.30pm Mon–Sat

Pub
## THE LONG VALLEY
*Winthrop Street Tel: (021) 272144*
Weirdly wonderful pub with terrific sandwiches, terrific pints.

Pub food served all day.

Wine Shop/Off Licence
## GALVIN'S OFF LICENCES
*37 Bandon Road Tel: (021) 275598; Watercourse Road Tel: (021) 500818; 22 Washington Street Tel: (021) 276314 Barry Galvin*
The range of both wines and spirits in Barry Galvin's shops is splendid, a keen balance struck between easy-going quaffers at decent prices and the

more serious wines which need age and a more profound financial supplement on the part of the customer.

Open 10.30am–11pm Mon–Sat, noon–2pm, 4pm–10pm Sun

Wholefood Shop
## NATURAL FOODS
*26 Paul Street Tel: (021) 277244 Wendy O'Byrne*
Wendy O'Byrne's little nook and cranny of a shop may well be the best wholefood bakery in the country. If this summons images of well intentioned but crushingly dull baking, think again. The breads and cakes here — sourdoughs, wholemeals, pittas, famous cherry buns, sweet slices of apricot bake — are executed with an alert and well-tempered hand, and at lunchtime they are formed into truly fine sandwiches. The shop is a busy warren of good things, with organic vegetables for sale, bags of Macroom Oatmeal, many of the good foods of the county.

Open 9.30am–5.30pm Mon–Sat.

Market
## CORK COVERED MARKET
The Cork Market, confusingly known also in local parlance as the Old English Market, can seem at first glance like little more than a cross between abattoir and emporium. Meat dominates most counters, and much of it is grimly unappetising, but a little patience unearths the jewels in this crown: the cheeses, the buttered eggs, the stall of Asian foods. It is an eternally lively place, reverberant with noise and activity, the don't-touch! looks of some stallholders, the pell-mell come-and-go of lively shopping and gossiping.

### Mr Bell's
Spices and all the sorts of stuff you need for cooking and eating Eastern: couscous, Shaosing wine, pulses, the lot.

### The Farm Gate Restaurant
Kay Harte & Morag O'Brien have brought their Farm Gate restaurant from Midleton (where the original still flourishes) to the gallery overlooking the fountain in the Cork Market. An excellent location, there are always lengthy queues for the creative yet understated lunches that they serve to an eager and appreciative public.

### Maucnaclea Farm Cheeses Tel: (021) 270232 Martin Guillemot & Anne-Marie Jamand.
Within the world of Irish farmhouse cheesemakers, the work of Martin and Anne-Marie is unique. Rather than concentrating obsessively on a single style of cheese and concentrating then on replicating it each and every day, they experiment according to the amount of milk they have, strolling effortlessly between creations

that use cow's milk and those that use goat's milk, ageing some cheeses while others are sold with the bloom of freshness.

Is there anything that unifies their work? The answer is that the Maucnaclea cheeses are unified by Martin and Anne-Marie's staggering skilfulness, their ability to create and mature cheeses to immaculate fullness of taste, precise exposition of flavour and break-heart beauty. One day you buy a piece of goat's milk camembert and also a slice of camembert made with cow's milk: the former is flinty and oozing, the taste balanced between careful acidity and a fresh completeness, the latter will be rich and evocative, the saltiness summoning the concentrated flavours of the milk out of the cheese.

But then, you also buy some cottage cheese, and a tub of cream and butter and what-have-you, for these cheeses, perhaps more than any others in Ireland, can genuinely be classified as irresistible, sublime, plangent. The stall is open 10am–5.30pm Wed–Sat.

*Iago, Tel: (021) 277047 Fax: 277750 Sean Calder-Potts.*
Imagine being able to fax in your orders to the Old English Market. Sean Calder-Potts allows you to do this. On sale are pasta and ice cream from Isaacs, unusual breads and an expanding selection of Irish farmhouse cheeses, including rarities like raw milk Cashel Blue and Silke Cropp's Corleggy cheese from Cavan. Lavazza coffee is perfectly served with the right cups, the right saucers, the right little doiley, and even the right tiny bite-sized macaroon. In fact, everything they do, they do The Right Way. It may seem obvious, but it's something that in fact takes years of travel, years of reading and plenty of care to achieve.

*Moynihan's Buttered Eggs Tel: (021) 272614 Mr Moynihan*
Buttering the eggs helps to keep them fresher for longer, but it also seems to impart a buttery character to the eggs. Open Mon–Sat.

# CASTLEWHITE

Farmhouse Cheese
## CHETWYND IRISH BLUE
*Castlewhite, Waterfall Tel: (021) 53502 Jerry Beechinor*
Jerry Beechinor's mild blue cheese is made with pasteurised milk and has a quiet, tongue-teasing contrast between the spicy saltiness of the roquefort blueness and the alloyed canvas of the milk on which the blue rests. Widely available, it is vastly superior to any imported blue cheese, swapping the blandness of the foreign cheeses for a considerate and gentle texture and taste.

# SOUTH & WEST CORK

# BANDON

Pottery
## THE BANDON POTTERY
*82–83 North Main Street Tel: (023) 41360 Robin & Jane Forrester*
The intense blueness of Jane Forrester's work is as much of a signature as the unmistakable cuspy orange hued apples which are found on all the Bandon Pottery products.

The many pieces made by the Forresters are pleasing and tactile, but should not be regarded purely as ornaments: these are plates and dishes intended to be used. You can deliberate decisively about what to snap up in the shop whilst you enjoy their coffees and home baking and peruse the other crafts, Jerpoint glass, Con Doyle Woodcraft, handwoven scarves, silk, wool, leather and candles which they sell.

Open 9am–6pm Mon–Sat. The shop is just on the way out of Bandon, heading west after the traffic lights.

Country Market
## THE BANDON FRIDAY MARKET
The Ladies in the print dresses and the sensible cardies run the Bandon market with a firm hand, the array of cakes and sweet things, the table of fresh eggs, the fine organic vegetables and the lovely Jersey butter — this and many of the vegetables produced by Kim Lois and Ian Paul in Ballineen — are all lined up lovely and inviting, on best behaviour.

Friday 2pm–4pm The Hall has a sign at the top end of the main street, just around the corner.

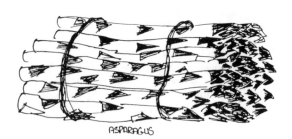
ASPARAGUS

Restaurant
## DUNWORLEY COTTAGE RESTAURANT
*Dunworley, Butlerstown, Co Cork Tel: (023) 40314 Katherine Noren*
The disciples of Dunworley point eagerly and hungrily to its protean perfection and they go quiet with awe at the purity of taste which every morsel of the food Asa Helmerson cooks exhibits so perfectly. They go wide-eyed in explanation at the elemental wildness in which the restaurant is located, and how this is so decisive and important an influence on the foods which Mrs Noren collects and cooks. If there should, ideally, be a dialogue between every restaurant and the environment from which it sources and secures its foodstuffs, then Dunworley expresses that dialogue with the finesse of a Shakespearian ode.

Whilst vegetarian choices are somewhat limited — salad plates; stir-fries; vegetable fritters — they are delicious, and as unimpeachably sourced as everything else. The famous Dunworley nettle soup, of course, is not to be missed.

Open summer lunch 1pm–3pm, dinner from 6.30pm Wed–Sun. Closed Nov and Jan–early Mar. Average Price: lunch under £10, dinner under £20. Visa, Access/Master, Amex, Diners. Signposted from just outside Clonakilty.

# CARRIGALINE

Country Market
## CARRIGALINE COUNTRY MARKET
*The GAA Hall, Crosshaven Road Tel: (021) 831340*
"Please no shopping until 9.30, except for flowers", pleads the felt-tip sign on the table as you walk into the Carrigaline community hall and wait for the Friday morning market to kick off.

It's a necessary commandment, for retaining self-control when faced by the disarming riches of the biggest and best Country Market in the country presents enormous difficulties. You want to hoover up yardarms of lolloping flowers, grab reams of vegetables all spruce and happy in their fresh glory. Caution, and calorie counting, can go hang whilst you deliberate over whether to get one chocolate topped sponge or two, or just one and a battenburg, or a battenburg with a gooey Swiss roll.

And then there are the obligatory additions: some of Pat O'Farrell's Carrigaline cheeses, made just up the road outside the town. Some candle-white beeswax. A jar or two of orchard-brown apple chutney.

The market is a riot of good food, food which is not just good to taste but is good in every sense. Local food, made by local folk, sold at its best in the locality from which it has drawn its character.

Like the other markets scattered throughout the country, Carrigaline is a splendidly pleasurable place in which to shop. The atmosphere is punctuated with kind advice and the comfort of close friends, fresh gossip, the goings and comings of the community, the expectation of fresh new foods as they come into season. Whether or not you actually buy anything, a stroll around the Carrigaline Community Hall on a Friday morning is delightful.

Friday mornings 9.30am–10.30am For details Tel Catherine Desmond: (021) 831340

Farmhouse Cheese
## CARRIGALINE FARMHOUSE CHEESE
*Marello, Leacht Cross Tel: (021) 372856 Pat O'Farrell*

This cheese represents the epitome of a farmhouse operation. Pat O'Farrell milks the cows, makes the cheese with his wife, and then can be relied upon to promote the cheese at great lengths at food fairs around the country. One wonders when anyone gets a chance to sleep in this household. The cheese itself is mild in taste, as gently flavoured as Pat's accent is whisper-soft, and comes under an enveloping wax coating. Some of the cheeses are flavoured with garlic and herbs.

Preserves
## OWNABWEE PRESERVES
*Ballynametagh House Tel: (021) 372323 Phil Thompson*

Phil Thompson's Ownabwee Preserves can be relied on to give the professionalism of a cottage industry allied to the taste of jams and jellies that could have been made on the kitchen stove.

# CLONAKILTY

Restaurant
## FIONNUALA'S
*30 Ashe Street Tel: (023) 34355 Fionnuala*

Fionnuala cleverly describes her raggle-taggle collection of tables, chairs, and candle-wax encrusted Chianti and Amarone bottles as a "Little Italian Restaurant", clever because this spells her culinary strengths. Pizzas and pastas are generous with spicy flavours, food that is comforting at lunchtime, and fun for the evening. The dining room, with its appropriately well-worn feel, looks like the stage set of some amateur dramatic production, but there is nothing stagy about the friendliness and the good heart of the cooking.

Open 12.30pm–2.15pm, 6pm–9.30pm Tue–Sun. Limited hours in winter. Average Price: lunch under £10, dinner under £20. Visa, Access/Master. On the main street.

# COURTMACSHERRY

B&B with Restaurant
## TRAVARA LODGE
*Courtmacsherry Tel: (023) 46493 Mandy Guy*
"With advance notice we do our best to accommodate any requests, i.e. ground floor room, cots, baby sitters, sea view, dogs, vegetarian meals, packed lunch, early breakfast etc", says Mandy Guy in this manifesto-like statement, and she means it.

Travara Lodge sits looking out onto the sea in the beautiful, pastel-painted village of Courtmacsherry, and Ms Guy works hard, extra hard, to make a success of both the little restaurant downstairs and the rooms upstairs. Monday night in the restaurant is dedicated to vegetarian cooking and, like all other times, is a fun time.

Open Mar–Oct. Average Price: dinner under £20, B&B under £20. Visa, Access/Master. Overlooking the waterfront in Courtmacsherry.

# OYSTERHAVEN

Restaurant
## THE OYSTERCATCHER RESTAURANT
*Oysterhaven Tel: (021) 770822 Sylvia & Bill Patterson*
You could be forgiven for feeling a pang of trepidation when you first see the Oystercatcher Restaurant.

Its complete and utter cuteness — a necklace of spangly coloured lights hanging just under the lip of the roof, the gently arcing white-faced cottage lamp-lit at the windows, its ideal location at the crown of the road in this serene fold of the Cork countryside — promises something altogether too perfect, and you fear the reality cannot possibly live up to the first impression.

But, walk inside and the simplicity of the design, the lack of anything contrived or unnecessary in the layout of the single room, and one is reassured. On the tables, tall gobletty glasses spell out their seriousness of purpose, and the happy sound of whisking and whirring that falls out from the swing doors which hide the kitchen banishes any fears, any trepidation. Bill and Sylvia Patterson's Oystercatcher is a well-considered, considerate place, a quiet culinary adventure.

Bill Patterson enjoys any sort of culinary challenge and cooking a perfect vegetarian dinner is a task he approaches with humour and verve. He understands that vegetarians get a poor deal in many a restaurant and does his best to redress using all the tricks — soufflés, sauces, patisserie, confectionery — at his disposal to give you a memorable meal. Just do make sure to give him plenty of notice of your needs and desires.

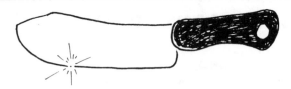

The service is perfect, never intruding on the intimately romantic ambience of the restaurant, and the whole experience is blissful, balmy.

Open 7pm–9.15pm Mon–Sun, May–Sept. Open for lunch high season. Closed Nov–Apr (but will open for private bookings). Closed Xmas, also Tue & Thur in Winter, and the month of Jan. Average Price: dinner: under £30. Visa, Access/Master. Follow signs for Oysterhaven, and the restaurant is just on your left before you go over the bridge into the village.

# TIMOLEAGUE

Restaurant & Hostel

## LETTERCOLLUM HOUSE ★

*Timoleague, Co Cork Tel: (023) 46251 Con McLoughlin & Karin Austin*

"God, it's gorgeous!"

When your lunch companion utters something as effusive as this, having gone no further into lunch than to break off and bite into a single piece of bread, then it is time to pay serious attention.

So, you break off and bite into a piece of bread and, as the rush of yeasty liveliness assails your taste buds and the great span of flavour just goes on and on, try to see if you can resist such exclamations of delight. You won't get very far, believe us.

Total deliciousness is the template and tenor of Con McLoughlin's cooking: a perfect salad composée; smooth courgette soup; gorgeously creamy spanokopitta; the amazement of a plate of vegetables which have dawdled in from the walled garden and been transformed into a festival of fresh tastes; buckwheat crêpes with spinach and wild mushrooms; cannelloni of goat's brie and spinach with a tomato coulis.

Food this simple and pure is always a treat, no matter how often you eat it, and perfect desserts like lemon tart or floating islands with home-made vanilla ice-cream merely cap the innocent joy of eating at this funky, splendid place.

If you are five or fifty, rich or poor, frail or sound in limb and wind, Lettercollum promises delight for all. It is, probably, the most demo-cratic dining room in the country, with all ages, creeds and complexions wrapped up by the carefree nature of the House and the "God, it's gorgeous!" food. The rooms upstairs are simple, priced just right, perfect for families.

Open 7.30pm–9.30pm Tue–Sun, 1.30pm–3.30pm Sun (check times out of season). Closed Xmas day. Average Price: lunch £10, dinner under £20. Visa, Access/Master, Diners. Just outside Timoleague, driving west, and clearly signposted.

*Karin Austin's Hazelnut and Mushroom Roast*

**The Loaf:**

8oz (225g) brown rice, cooked
1 large onion, finely chopped
6oz (170g) mushrooms, finely chopped
2 medium carrots, grated
2 sticks celery, diced
4oz (110g) wholemeal breadcrumbs
4oz (110g) hazelnuts, ground
1 dessertspoon fresh thyme or
1 teaspoon dried thyme
1 tablespoon soya sauce
1 teaspoon yeast extract
3 fl oz (85ml) hot water
salt and pepper
sunflower oil to sauté

**The Sauce:**

1oz (30g) butter
4 oz (110g) mushrooms, sliced
1 tablespoon sherry
half-an oz flour
half-a pint (290ml) vegetable stock, hot
3 spring onions, chopped
salt and pepper
handful fresh parsley

Use a food processor to grate the carrots, grind the nuts and — using the pulse so that you don't annihilate them — chop the mushrooms. Sauté the onion and the celery in the sunflower oil for a few minutes, then add the grated carrot and cook until the carrots are just soft. Add the mushrooms and soya sauce and cook for a couple of minutes longer. In a large mixing bowl mix the rice, breadcrumbs, nuts and thyme with all the vegetables. Dissolve the yeast extract in the hot water and mix thoroughly with the rice mix. Oil a 2lb loaf tin and press the mixture firmly in. Bake at 180C, 350F, Gas 4 for about 1 hour.

To make the sauce: Sauté the mushrooms and spring onions in butter for a few minutes, then add the sherry and cook a further few minutes before adding the flour. Cook for 1 minute then whisk in the vegetable stock. Cook for a further few minutes to cook the flour then whizz the whole lot in a liquidiser or food processor. Stir in chopped parsley and serve.

# THE FAR WEST PENINSULAS

## Bantry And The Sheep's Head Peninsula

# AHAKISTA

Japanese Eating House

### SHIRO JAPANESE DINNER HOUSE ★

*Ahakista Tel: (027) 67030 Kei and Werner Pilz*

There are only two tables in The Shiro Japanese Dinner House, each in separate rooms and each available only to a single party each evening, there is only Kei and her husband Werner, and their food is quite extra-ordinary, something that demands the realm of the sexual vocabulary to express adequately the pleasure it gives.

Here, an ideal of heightened, almost narcotic delight is orchestrated by Kei Pilz by means of a sinuous procession of dishes, each of them separate but, ultimately, sympathetic. Culinary alchemy in The Shiro is conceived as a broad canvas, with a final sense of satisfaction arising only at the conclusion of a meal.

With every delicious morsel parcelled exquisitely, the procession parades food that is a delight to the eye — the filigree fans of vegetable tempura served on a wooden board, tenderly carved vegetables, a soup with tofu and cabbage greens — a delight to the palate. Through the course of the evening, it seems to motivate and arouse, and ultimately exhaust, every sense in the body.

Open 7pm–9pm Tue–Sat. Closed Xmas and Jan. Average Price: dinner over £30. Visa, Access/Master, Amex, Diners (payment by credit card incurs an additional charge of 5%). Signposted from the Cork-Bantry road and from the village of Durrus.

# BALLYLICKEY

Handmade Knives

### HAND CRAFTED KNIVES

*Ballylickey Tel: (027) 50032 Rory Conner*

"I read an article about knifemaking and took a fancy to it", says Rory Conner of his introduction to the world of hand-crafted knives. "My first attempts were terrible, disastrous! But I read everything, anything I could get my hands on and bombarded American knife makers with letters, got a few more scars and improved".

Today, Mr Conner's craft is as far removed from the familiar mass production of cooking and eating implements as one could imagine. This is knife-making as art.

Everything he makes is done to order — there is a minimum three month waiting list — and the process is uniquely personal. The process of ordering a knife from Rory is quite painstaking, with drawings and silhouettes swapped back and forward until the customer is happy with the shape, the length, the type of wood, the weight. "Then we start grinding, hours and hours of grinding".

The knives are made from a stainless steel that is specially manufactured for knife making. For the handles he uses a range of different materials and decorates the knife with a hand-carved illustration.

For the kitchen he makes a cook's knife, a cheese knife, a paring knife, as well as knives made to order. Such work is not cheap, of course, but given the sheer amount of labour involved, and the beautiful results, prices are reasonable.

Rory's workshop is at the entrance to Sea View Hotel: take the right fork.

Food Emporium
# MANNING'S EMPORIUM
*Ballylickey Tel: (027) 50456 Val Manning*
Val Manning's famous Emporium hibernates during the winter. After his second Food Fair in December — a quiet day of good crack and polite wine swigging — the slow days of wintertime see the shop batten down for the duration.

Then, come Easter, and the arrival of the Goat's milk cheeses and the beginning of the herbs and the Irish vegetables, and Val and his staff set about the spring cleaning with a vengeance: rub-a-dub, scrub-a-dub into the wee small hours, and out of its quiet cocoon this brilliant butterfly of enthusiasm, fine food and boundless hospitality comes into its own.

The best way to get the measure of Manning's is simply to loiter around it for as long as you can, looking at this, deciding to buy that, having a taste of this cheese or that cheese or whatever. That way, listening to the greetings and the gossip, you realise that Manning's is less like a conventional shop and more like an unconventional drinks party: everyone in here is a friend and at any minute you are likely to be introduced to someone new, someone nice.

Someone wrote to us once and, in the course of a eulogy about West Cork, praised Val Manning for being "an excellent host". For this is what Mr Manning is. Host to his customers. Host to the carefully chosen, carefully nurtured foods he sells. Host to a vision of the shopkeeper as a focus for a community in which he plays a vital part. Host, above all, to enthusiasm for, and devotion to, good food.

Open 9am–9pm Mon–Sun (longer hours in the summer, shorter hours in the winter, but like all good country shops everything is a bit flexible).

Herbs and Herb Pates

## MEADOWSWEET HERBS

*Ballylickey Tel: (027) 66024*

Jeff and Jenny Startup are not just fine herb growers — you will find their excellent herbs and herb mixtures in neat little plastic bags in a variety of shops in the area — but they also make unusual and unusually good vegetarian pâtés, found in shops in little tubs with a Meadowsweet label stuck on the top. Hazel nut and sage, peanut and parsley, mushroom and mixed herb are just some of the ingenious concoctions Jeff works on devotedly, but each time you meet him there is some new experiment, some new confection of herbs and pulses from which to fashion a perfect picnic, a fail-safe starter.

B&B

## RIVER LODGE

*Pearson's Bridge Tel: (027) 66148 Gudrun Bernard*

This handsome stone house, a few miles off the road from Ballylickey bridge, is principally a bed and breakfast for vegetarians, with produce for meals coming from their own organic garden. Gudrun specialises in breakfasts — strawberries from the garden; muesli; fresh grapefruit — but they do their best at all times to make everyone welcome. This is a fine base for exploring the mellifluous delights of the area.

Turn right at the Ballylickey bridge, and look for the sign.

# BANTRY

Organic Grower
## PAUL SCHULTZ
*Ardnageehy Beg, Bantry Tel: (027) 51158*
Paul Schultz's work is a brilliant example of the diversity which organic methods of agriculture promote, and a testament to his own devilishly hard work. He grows anything, everything, all of it on a mere few acres just outside Bantry and it is inevitably perfectly delicious: swollen courgette flowers, bright sweet peas, tender little courgettes, floury potatoes. His vegetables, found for the most part in Manning's Emporium and the Supervalu in Bantry, can also be bought from the farm and visitors are most welcome.
Telephone for directions. The farm is a few miles west of Bantry.

Café
## 5A CAFÉ
*5a Barrack Street Cookie Susukie*
A laid-back, inexpensive little vegetarian café, where Cookie dreams up contenting soups, good breads (which can be bought to take away) and good salads. The buzz, from the assortment of intriguing odds and sods who hang out here, is always good.
Open 9am–5.30pm Mon–Sat.

Wholefood Shop
## ESSENTIAL FOODS
*Main Street Tel: (027) 61171 (home) Alan Dare*
You need to get here early in the morning on the days when the organic vegetables arrive, for the early risers of Bantry make determined efforts to snap up the pick of the vegetables in Alan Dare's shop.

It's a good practice, therefore, to introduce yourself to the proprietor and his cohorts and to find out what is expected, and when. That way, they may be persuaded to hold back some bright tubs of purslane for you, some crisp-as-altarcloth leeks and lettuces, some muddied Cara or Scarlet Pimpernel spuds. Mr Dare has been slowly improving the shop, ever since he opened, so there is usually some nice surprise in store in the store.

Open 10.30am–5pm (closed lunch 1pm–2pm and half day Wed) Mon–Sat.

# DURRUS

Farmhouse Cheese
## DURRUS FARMHOUSE CHEESE
*Coomkeen Tel: (027) 61100 Jeffa Gill*

The secret strength of Jeffa Gill's cheese lies with its subtlety and its confident but gradual exposition of flavours. Find one of the rounds in peak condition — the outside dusty white like a Bakewell tart, the top mottled like a cooling fruit gratin, the cheese moderately tall and with enough surface to allow the tastes inside to conjoin — and the traces of clean mustard and field mushroom, followed then by apples and pears come creeping into the taste buds as the cheese is eaten.

The backdrop for this splash of flavours is a subtle creaminess on which everything rests, but the wizardry of Durrus lies in keeping this lactic energy contained, using it as a carrier for the fruit and savoury notes which a good cheese delivers.

Perhaps it is the fact that she only ever uses morning milk that allows Jeffa Gill to achieve this subtlety, but it is very pleasing, as pleasing as the fact that Durrus has been perhaps the most steadily improving of the Irish farmhouse cheeses over the last few years.

The farm is two and a half miles up Coomkeen hill: take the right fork in Durrus village, turn right at the Church of Ireland, drive straight until you see the sign, then look for the marked entrance.

## Glengarriff and The Beara Peninsula

# ALLIHIES

Artichokes
### ALLIHIES GLOBE ARTICHOKE CO-OPERATIVE
*Reentrisk Tel: (027) 73025 Tony Lowes*
This is the perfect Co-Op, for it is run by one man, Tony Lowes, and thus concord and harmony reign. All you need in order to get the best out of Allihies — modestly described by Mr Lowes as "the globe artichoke capital of Ireland" — is to climb out of the car, grab a knife and start cutting some artichokes. Tony also sells the crown sections of the plants through the post.
Follow the signs on the right hand side of the road as you drive from Allihies to Eyeries.

SPRING ONIONS

# EYERIES

Farmhouse Cheese
### MILLEENS
*Eyeries Tel: (027) 74079 Veronica and Norman Steele*
Veronica Steele's Milleens was the first of the Irish farmhouse cheeses, and it will forever hold a special place in the hearts of many for originating what has turned out to be one of the most wonderful parts of Ireland's food renaissance over the last fifteen years.

The cheese itself has come a long way in that time, changing from something with run-away softness and a charged lactic ooziness into a more conventional, rather more sober cheese. On occasion, one can find a Milleens with the old characteristics and the true nature of the Vacherin style to which it is often compared — apparently these can often be found in the Neal's Yard cheese shop in Covent Garden in London — and when you come across one of these the cheese is simply unforgettable.
Telephone first if you want to buy cheese from the farm, and to get directions as finding it is tricky: you turn left at the graveyard then take the second on the right.

# The Schull Peninsula

# BALLYDEHOB

Restaurant
## ANNIE'S

*Main Street Tel: (028) 37292 Annie Barry*

Annie Barry has the best, the nicest, manner of any restaurant owner in the country. Her pacific nature with kids is legendary — though Mrs Barry herself is too modest to agree with this — but she works the spell on adult kids with the same surreptitious ease, and quickly has you goo-goo with anticipation for the treat that is dinner in Annie's.

The restaurant is just a single room with tables in multiples of pairs, nice and bright in summertime if you choose an early evening dinner. Mr Barry doesn't try to do too much — and doesn't need to do too much — to coax the very best from his good ingredients and vegetarian requests are treated with the same care and hospitality as everything else. There is a brand new coffee shop next door to the restaurant, with books and whatnot to peruse.

Open 6.30pm–10pm Tue–Sat. Closed Oct and limited hours off-season. Average Price: dinner under £20. Visa, Access/Master. In the centre of Ballydehob.

Pub
## LEVIS'S

*Main Street. Julia Levis*

This timeless, quiet pub might remind you of an Irish dancehall from the 1960s. On the right side, lined along the wall, is the bar, with its masculine bottles arraigned on shelves, the whole lot facing across to the left wall, where a spread of feminine groceries sit contentedly staring across the dancehall flatness of the floor at the boozy male counter.

It's a delightfully innocent yin and yang arrangement that may have you wondering whether the pint of Murphy's will ever get up and ask the packet of Rich Tea to dance, and the Ms Levis's themselves delightfully complement the elemental simplicity. "Been here long?" a visitor asks. "All my life" replies Julia with the assurance of experience. "And my mother before me" she adds, for good measure. Evenings in Annie's restaurant usually begin here, but Levis's lovely pub has its own, intuitive, menu.

Wholefood Shop
## HUDSON'S WHOLEFOODS

*Main Street Tel: (028) 37211 Gillian Hudson*

Gillian Hudson's shop combines the local with the international: dried herbs from all parts of the globe, and fresh herbs grown by west Cork organic growers. Sea weeds from Japan, and some which is locally collected: West Cork wakame and kombu as well as dilisk and carrageen. Cheeses come from the next door villages of Schull, from where Bill Hogan brings country butter along with his Gabriel, Desmond, Raclette and the rare Mizen, in effect a vegetarian parmesan, and there is some of Jeffa Gill's cheese from Durrus. There is real ice-cream, Cork-made tofu — both fresh and fermented — local juices, and flour from the south east and from further fields. The noticeboard outside the shop is always a fascinating bricolage of the wild and the weird.

Open 10am–6pm Mon–Sat (closed lunch 1.30pm–2.30pm).

# DUNBEACON

Goat's Cheese
## DUNBEACON GOAT'S CHEESE
*Dunbeacon, Tel: (027) 61025 Francie Bainbridge*
The cheese produced on this happy farm is a soft, lightly pressed goat's cheese that teams superbly with the white sourdough rolls from Adele's in nearby Schull.

Cheese can be bought from the farm at all times, as long as there is somebody there.

# SCHULL

Home Bakery, Restaurant & Coffee Shop
## ADELE'S
*Main Street Tel: (028) 28459 Adele Conner*

Just as Adele's is someplace that is ever youthful, so you will be stolen back to your short-trousered days the instant you bite into something creamy and over-the-top in this cosy café, and exhale then with adolescent delight at the indulgent sweetness of this fine baking. A bite of a chunky vegetable pastie can seem an evocation of simpler days, when your Mammy was there to save you from your own stupidity, some tea and a jammy scone a comfort you might have enjoyed when school was over and you were at the kitchen table.

This is the secret of Adele's: the baking is utterly expert — that crumbly, rich carrot cake, that testy and tingling lemon cake, those soft sourdough rolls — but it is also very maternal, very involving, very pleasureful.

As if this was not enough, Simon Conner, Adèle's son has opened up Adèles during the evenings. A simple menu revels in clean, vibrant tasting starters, taste-suffused pasta dishes, syrupy desserts, and the whole thing has added a splendid new dimension to this splendid place. Mr Conner will roast red and yellow peppers and pair them with some feta cheese and a light dressing for a famishsome starter. His pasta dishes can include a truly fine spaghetti with parsley pesto. The teaming of everything, from pasta to sauce, from dressing to dish, right down to the crockery and the wines on offer, is splendidly appropriate.

Open shop and café open 9.30am–7pm, restaurant open 7pm–10.30pm Tue–Sat, 11am–7pm Sun. Closed Dec–Easter. Average Price: café under £5 restaurant under £10 to under £20 B&B under £20. No Credit Cards. On the main street in Schull, at the top of the hill.

Delicatessen & Bakery
## THE COURTYARD
*Main Street Tel: (028) 28390 Dennis & Finola Quinlan*

Here is a Courtyard story.

Bill Hogan, local cheesemaker, tells Dennis Quinlan that he is making enormous new cheeses called Mizen. They weigh forty five kilos, they take two years to mature, and in circumference they are simply huge. "I'm afraid they won't fit into your cheese cooler", says Bill. "No bother", says Dennis. "We'll get a bigger cooler", Later, Bill Hogan mentions to Finola that Dennis has said that they will get a bigger cooler just to accommodate the new Mizens. "Oh, we will", says Finola.

This sense of encouragement, this sense of excitement, lies behind everything the Quinlans do in The Courtyard. The shop reveals a simple truth about them: they love good things, and they want to sell them. This makes The Courtyard a true cornucopia, for it is packed to the rafters with the finest Irish foods, many of which have to do little more than travel a few miles from up or down the road, for this area is rich in fine things, some of which have to do no more than be carried in from the back, for Jackie Bennett bakes stoic, sweet loaves, kneaded by hand, out in the bakery.

As if this wasn't enough, the food served in the bar and in the café is terrific: beautiful and bounteous ploughman's lunches with a posse of farmhouse cheeses and soft bread to soak up some Murphy's, crisp salad leaves with melting mushroom vol-au-vents, buttery doorstops of sandwiches. All these good things, all this good work, all under one roof.

Shop open 9.30am–6pm, bar food available 10am–7pm Mon–Sat (food available until 4.45pm off season).

Farmhouse Cheese
## GUBBEEN ★

*Gubbeen House Tel: (028) 28231 Giana and Tom Ferguson*

The progress of Tom and Giana Ferguson's Gubbeen cheese is a parallel of the development of Ireland's food culture during the last decade.

Gubbeen was central amongst the farmhouse cheeses in marking a break from the uniformity of mass produced food which so seduced the country during the 1960s and '70s, and in stating that here was a food which could stand comparison with the most celebrated foods made anywhere in the world. Not only that, but the cheese made a positive feature of the characteristics of the local climate, the local grass, the local milk, and stated that these were an integral element of good food. Local, pure, hand-made. It may seem strange now, but those notions were considered passé only a decade ago, when the bright future beckoned us on into a bland and monotonous diet.

The Fergusons drew on their own resources when making the cheese, for it reflects their own determination and intelligence, their discrimination and affection for natural things. You might compare it to a pont l'eveque, except that such comparisons are by now largely redundant when one discusses Irish cheeses, for they are their own thing, they speak of their own place. The skills in curing which bring out the bloom of a Gubbeen, the skills of the cheese-smoker which Chris Jepson contributes to the smoked Gubbeen, exploit the benefits of dairy science, yet at bottom they remain instinctive, natural.

Gubbeen and Smoked Gubbeen are available throughout the country.

Farmhouse Cheese

# WEST CORK NATURAL CHEESE ★

*Ardmanagh Tel: (028) 28593 Bill Hogan & Sean Ferry*

On a cheesemaking day, Bill Hogan's blue-painted cheesemaking room seems to contain all the excitement and promise of a railway station in the early morning. There is the hiss of steam from the ancient and beautiful boiler, the gurgle of pipes as water heats up, the sense of a beginning, a journey beginning.

And this is no idle emotion, for each of the cheeses made by Bill and Sean have a lengthy road to travel: some of the Desmond cheeses will be ready in six months, some of the Gabriel cheeses will take nine months, but the newest cheeses which they have been making here —Mizen cheeses weighing no less than 45 kilograms — will start out on a long journey, for they will not be mature for at least two years.

"They are promises at the horizon of what could happen in Ireland", says Mr Hogan, who learnt his skills in both Switzerland and Costa Rica, way up in the mountains, making thermophilic cheeses that age slowly, patiently. "We are dedicated to our own obsessions", he adds, and one would need to be, for making super-hard cheeses of this nature is terrifyingly hard work. The heat as the milk is warmed, the grain-like elusiveness of the curd as it is stirred, the sheer physical strength required to lift such a volume of curd and then to set it inside a wheel as it is shaped is enormous, exhausting.

But every bit as enormous is the reward. Take a slice of aged Gabriel and the mouth is assailed by scents and tastes as sweet as pineapple, a sort of volatile super-sugar, and as fine-edged as walnut. A small Mizen is buttery, lush, calling out for a glass of champagne, a Desmond more subtle, a perfect match for a floral wine from Alsace. It is in their synthesis of maturity and freshness that the West Cork Natural Cheeses leave most others standing, for they don't become mere blunderbusses as they age, but instead acquire a subtlety, a persistence that puts one in mind of fine Burgundy: power with finesse.

"My teacher Joseph Durbach described these cheeses as 'stored-up sunshine'", says Bill Hogan, and their encapsulation of summer meadows, rich milk, sun-filled days warms the soul when you eat them.

# SKIBBEREEN

Hotel and Restaurant
## LISS ARD LAKE LODGE

*Skibbereen, Co Cork Tel: (028) 22365 Claudia Meister*

In the glorious Liss Ard Lodge, you will find some of the most singular, singularly impressive cooking in Ireland.

Claudia Meister's recipes do not use animal fats in their preparation, a bold move which forces both the chef and her assistant, Fred, into a free-fall of creativity with every single dish. What is most impressive, aside from the solid seizure of flavour which the food exhibits so boldly, is the fact that the cooking is not an abstract exercise. It is powerful, absorbing food, beautifully orchestrated and achieved.

Ms Meister achieves her ambition of cooking in a style which allows one to contemplate the beauty of the preparation — that startling sea-vegetable sculpting which is the leek and pine kernel cannelloni; an amazing pavé of chocolate which might have been designed by the extraordinary Japanese costume designer Eiko Ishioka — but which never masks the beauty of the flavours which the food contains. This cooking is intricate and feminine.

Creativity and originality runs rampant through the six courses of dinner: a pithivier of vegetables in a pin-cushion pastry; little tortellinis like bishops' hats atop a chessboard of pulses and tapenade; a hot calvados soufflé shaped like a cossack hat.

And you do not, at the end of dinner, feel that you have missed anything, or that something has been lacking. The tastes are so direct, the preparations so exquisite, the choreography of dinner so expertly conceived and executed, that you are lost in admiration. Ms Meister's food points a way forward for Irish cooking, away from the dead-hand of emulsions, the shout of butter, the cloud of cream. Anyone who wants a taste of the future — a gorgeous taste of the future — will get to Liss Ard as soon as possible.

Open 7pm–10.30pm Mon–Sun (booking essential). Closed Xmas day. Average Price: dinner under £30. Visa, Access/Master, Amex, Diners. Leave Skibbereen on the Tragumna road, the house is signposted, and their tower gates — a folly — are very distinctive.

Shop
## THE KITCHEN GARDEN

*North Street Tel: (028) 22342 Jenny Mass*

Jenny Mass's shop is one of the most pristine and polished you will find anywhere. The window is dressed with a cornucopia of fresh vegetables, while inside every requisite and necessity proffers itself to you with wanton energy. Packets of pulses are arranged standing to attention. Fruits and veg are as much of a decoration as a do-consider. Herbs and spices are parade ground perfect, and the wheels and truckles of cheese, the fresh golden butter are anticipatory and salivatory.

Open 9am–8pm Mon–Sat.

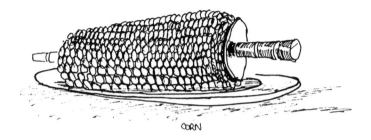

CORN

Shop
# FIELD'S

*26 Main Street Tel: (028) 21400 J.J. Field*

Though one could call J.J. Field's shop a supermarket — it has trolleys and miles of aisles and folk in white coats to point you in the direction of whatsoever you might want — it is still nothing so much as a great big local store.

The chatter of the locals as they line up, the unflustered queues at the checkouts as the girls speed the goods through with a word of gossip; the feeling that everyone knows everyone else, or at least will come to know them sometime soon, none of this spells out the modern, anonymous supermarket. And Field's also shows its sense of locality in its support for locally produced foods: there are always locally grown organic vegetables and herbs. It's a happy shop, a happy place, a happy space, a market that is undoubtedly super.

Open 9am–6.30pm Mon–Sat ('till 7pm Fri).

Off Licence
# O'BRIEN'S OFF LICENCE

*29 Main Street, Skibbereen Tel: (028) 21772*

Generously and rather broad-mindedly, O'Brien's nice little shop sells not only a decent selection of decent bottles of wine and crates of cans of beer, it also sells home brew kits for folk who want to make their own concoctions, a curious case of a shop drinking the hand that feeds it. They also have lots of pipe smoking paraphernalia, cute Swiss army knives, sherries and ginger wine for maiden aunts and bottles of De Kuyper gin with its life-enhancing message engraved on the side of the handsome green bottle: "He who De Kuyper nightly takes, soundly sleeps and fit awakes".

Open 9am–8pm Mon–Sat, limited hours on Sun.

Accommodation

## GABRIEL COTTAGE

*Smorane Tel: (028) 22521 Suzanne Dark & Dominic Lee*

Somewhat better known as Irish Peddlers, Dominic and Suzanne organise the dream of the gleam of the open road seen from the saddle of a bike. If you wish to escape from it all and slow down to a human pace, head here for a cycling holiday.

You stay in either the restored stone barn or in the house itself, in rooms that are sugar-sweet nice. Suzanne and Dominic describe their rooms as reflecting "our love of simple country style", but this undersings the dreamy, cosy, out-of-it-all nature of the rooms, and the dapper perfection of the farmhouse.

You will get to know the house because super meals — always vegetarian meals — are served around the big old table at the end of a hard day hacking the roads of West Cork, and staunch breakfasts will set you off at a fast pedal in the morning.

Open for dinner for guests. Closed Oct–Apr (other times by arrangement). Average Price: dinner under £10–under £20, B&B under £20. Visa, Access/Master. Cycling holidays include 3 evening meals, cycle hire, loan of waterproofs and route planning. On the Clonakilty/Skibbereen road, a mile or so east of Skibb.

Herb Farm

## WEST CORK HERB FARM

*Church Cross, Skibbereen Tel: (028) 22299 Rosarie O'Byrne*

A sign on the main road from Skibbereen to Ballydehob points you to the West Cork Herb Farm, and when you turn off the road you drive into an enclave of good things. The O'Byrnes mastermind this essential organisation with the dynamism and determination, and quiet achievement, that has always signalled their work, painstakingly restoring this collection of houses, organising a shop, laying out the grounds, and selling vibrant and lovable herbs of every hue and colour.

There's a race to buy their honey, their bees are feasting on borage and thyme when other hives have to content themselves with ivy, and their daughter's special recipe for Clara's cooked pesto sauce is something they are all rightfully proud of.

Open 10am–6.30pm Mon–Sat, 12.30pm–6.30pm Sun. (Winter hours noon–5.30pm Mon–Sun).

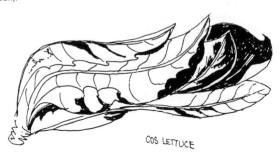

COS LETTUCE

# County Kerry

## DINGLE

Restaurant
### BEGINISH RESTAURANT

*Green Street Tel: (066) 51588 John & Pat Moore*

Pat Moore's food is hungrily inquisitive, full of those little gestures which announce, quietly, the improvisations and experimentations of a cook who wants to learn more and more.

Where this comes most actively to play is in her appreciation for flavour, and the need to maintain the integral flavour of an ingredient whilst contrasting or comforting it with an apposite sauce. Her vegetarian pot-pourri, served with two sauces, is a perfect indicator of her strengths as a cook and desserts are another ace card of the Beginish: a rhubarb soufflé tart so shockingly light as to beggar belief, and home made ice-creams that are childishly scoffable.

Recently the Beginish have opened modern self-catering apartments. Suitable especially for couples, they are the perfect base for exploring this wondrously beautiful peninsula.

Open lunch and dinner Tue–Sun. Closed Dec–mid Mar. Average Price: lunch under £10, dinner under £20. Visa, Access/Master, Amex, Diners. Almost opposite the Catholic church in Dingle town.

Café & Bookshop
### AN CAFE LITEARTHA

*Dykegate Street Tel: (066) 51388 Seoirse O Luasa*
One of Dingle's two splendid bookshops-cum-cafés.
Open 9am–5.30pm Mon–Sat. Dingle town centre.

Wholefood Shop
### AN GRIANAN

*Dykegate Street Tel: (066) 51910 Elaine Avery*

Elaine's shop houses a vast array of wholefoods and some speciality items, but is especially valuable for fine yeasted and sourdough breads, baked locally and delivered warm each morning. There is also carrot cake, vegan samosas and slices of pizza topped with masses of vegetables. Rocky Avery, meanwhile, completes this happy picture of local industry by providing the organic vegetables for the shop.

Incidentally, Kerry is famous for the fact that many seasonal restaurants open up each year, and the fact that many of them are vegetarian. But, they are often places which open for only a single year and then close. If you wish to know who or what is new and where, then Elaine should be able to inform you.

Open 10am–6pm Mon–Sat. Dingle town centre.

Restaurant, Bar, Bookshop & Café
## THE ISLANDMAN
*Main Street Tel: (066) 51803 Karl Frolich*

The Islandman is a supersmart quartet of temptations. The bar is continental in character and perfect for a glass of wine first thing, an aperitif before dinner or a digestif last thing at night. The café is ideal for good apple pie and coffee at eleven, maybe a chocolat just before bed, or a sandwich at lunchtime.

The restaurant produces contenting, simple food at most times of the day, and the book shop diverts your gaze with neatly arranged titles that summon your attention. It is a brilliant combination of functions, all of them carried out in an atmospheric series of rooms whose considered design is accented by fastidious housekeeping.

Open 9am–11pm Mon–Sun during the season (more limited hours in winter). Average Price: meals under £5–under £10. Visa, Access/Master. Dingle town centre.

B&B
## THE OLD STONE HOUSE
*Cliddaun Tel: (066) 59882 Michael and Becky O'Connor*

Michael and Becky O'Connor's cosy little cottage is a good base, and their extraordinary fund of knowledge about the peninsula is a boon to travellers. Please note this is a No Smoking B&B.

Open all year, including Xmas. Average Price: B&B under £20. Visa, Access/Master. 2.5 miles from Dingle town, on the main road west to Ventry, the house is on the right and signposted.

# THE RING OF KERRY

# BLACKWATER

Farmhouse Cheese
## CAPPAROE GOAT'S CHEESE
*Greenane, Blackwater The Hensel Family*

The Hensel family make a deliciously rich and unctuous soft goat's cheese, which they pack into jars and cover with a darkly yellow organic olive oil. If you find it, don't miss it, for the richness and purity of the flavour is totally distinctive, as is the neat hand-script which they use on the label to describe the cheese.

You can often buy the cheese in The Pantry in Kenmare, otherwise ask locally for "The Bicycling Germans".

# CAHIRCIVEEN

Restaurant
## THE OLD SCHOOLHOUSE
*Knockeens, Cahirciveen Tel: (0667) 2426 Ann O'Kane*
There is much thoughtfulness about the Old Schoolhouse, and they do
work hard to please as much as they can in this easy-going, good time
place.

Open 11am–9pm Mon–Sun. Closed Nov–Mar. Average Price: lunch under £10, dinner
under £20. Visa, Access/Master, Diners.

# CAHERDANIEL

Restaurant
## LOAVES AND FISHES
*Caherdaniel Tel: (0667) 5273 Helen Mullane & Armel White*
They are a good twosome, Helen Mullane and her man Armel White.
Armel White's food is deeply flavoured and prices are splendidly modest.
Vegetarians are advised to mix and match from the first courses, whilst
everything dances to life from the use of fresh herbs: "We here have
always kept a corner of the garden to grow herbs. The air is permanently
scented by a dozen or so herbs which we use in our cooking to add a
note of sweetness, delicacy, bitterness or pungency to achieve the desired
effect". Helen Mullane, meantime, orchestrates everything with perfect
sweetness.

Open 6pm–9.30pm Tue–Sun, Closed end Sept–Easter. Average Price: dinner under £20.
Visa, Access/Master. Caherdaniel is on the Ring of Kerry about 45 mins from Kenmare.

# KENMARE

Restaurant
## THE LIME TREE
*Shelbourne Street, Tel: (064) 41225 Fax: (064) 41402 Tony Daly*
The Lime Tree has recently re-opened under the ownership of Tony and
Alex Daly — Tony is also the General Manager of the Park Hotel just
behind the restaurant. Their Head Chef is Michael Casey, who has
worked in country houses and hotels all over the country, and the menu is
a homely selection of classics, from which vegetarians can choose dishes
like ragout of wild mushrooms with puff pastry and fresh herb cream, or
vegetable stir fry with wild and steamed rice, in a soybutter sauce.

Open 6pm–10pm Mon–Sun during the high season. Closed Nov–Feb. Average Price:
dinner under £25. Visa, Access/Master, Amex, Diners. At the top end of town, just
beside the Park Hotel.

Restaurant
## AN LEITH PHIGIN
*Main Street Tel: (064) 41559 Con Guerin*

Con Guerin's restaurant may be one of the best kept secrets in Kenmare, even though it has been operating now for almost ten years. They specialise in a style of northern Italian cooking, and produce rare delights such as ravioli with a filling of aubergine and courgette in a creamy white wine sauce scented with thyme; tortelloni filled with ricotta and spinach with a sage butter; tagliatelle with a basil and pinenut pesto; a quattro formaggio pizza. To suit this individual, creative cooking, the wine list is rich in choice Italian wines, some of them quite rare.

Open lunch and dinner during the high season (dinner only in winter). Average Price: meals under £15. Visa, Access/Master. Kenmare town centre.

Restaurant
## D'ARCY'S
*Main Street Tel & Fax: (064) 41589 Matthew d'Arcy*

Matt d'Arcy has been best known over the last years as the head chef in the illustrious Park Hotel. The attraction of this happy town must be strong, for Mr d'Arcy has moved no further than just up the street to open The Old Bank House.

His new premises may be simpler than the grandeur of The Park, but the strengths of d'Arcy's cooking, strong flavours, impressive technical command of his craft and a flair for complicating and combining, are every bit as evident here as before. Vegetarian food is always available, but for special requests and strict diets, it helps to give notice.

Open 6pm–11pm Mon–Sun (closed Sun off season). Closed Xmas. Average Price: dinner under £20. Visa, Access/Master. At the top end of Main Street.

Wholefood Shop
## THE PANTRY
*30 Henry Street Tel: (064) 41320*

A useful shop for hunting down local foods and splendidly vibrant organic vegetables.

Restaurant
## PACKIE'S
*Henry Street Tel: (064) 41508 Maura Foley*

The trip to Kenmare to eat Maura Foley's food is one of the most worthwhile, pleasure-promising and well-rewarded trips you can make.

This a happy, up-for-it place to eat, with great staff, great prices and a wonderful bistro buzz. Simple foods cooked in here seem almost a revelation, their taste is so real, so true. Pasta. Omelettes. Salad. Vanilla ice-cream. You name it, and you will scarcely be able to remember when you last ate it so good. It was a desire to simplify her food and to cut prices which led Maura Foley to begin this smashing venture, and this foresight reveals the same stroke of simple genius that you find in her cooking.

Open 5.30pm–10pm Mon–Sat. Closed end Dec–end Feb. Average Price: dinner under £15. Visa, Access/Master. Kenmare town centre.

Bistro
## THE PURPLE HEATHER BISTRO
*Henry St Tel: (064) 41016 The Foley family*
A few doors down from the Foley family's Packie's restaurant, and motivated by the same concern for thoughtful, good food.

Open noon–6.30pm Mon–Sat. Closed Xmas. Average Price: lunch under £5. Visa, Access/Master.

# THE REST OF KERRY

# KILLARNEY

Restaurant and Hostel
## THE SUGAN
*Lewis Rd Tel: (064) 33104*
The Súgán has transmuted over the years from a vegetarian restaurant and shop into a vegetarian restaurant and independent hostel. Very much a fixture of Killarney life, with plenty of crack and music to be expected.

Open May–Oct, 6pm–10pm Tue–Sun, dinner under £10, B&B under £10.

Restaurant
## SWISS BARN SPECIALITY RESTAURANT
*17 High Street Tel: (064) 36044 The Veillard family*
Daniel Veillard used to run the Swiss Barn way up north in the wind-blown wastes of County Mayo, so his move from there to the bustle of Killarney could hardly represent a greater climactic and social change. In fact, it represents something of a homecoming, for Killarney was the first place he worked in when he came to Ireland in 1968.

His cooking has not changed however, and is still as individual and distinctive as ever. Vegetarian choices are limited — king-sized salad; vegetable platter; vegetarian curry — but in a town where conventional restaurants often pay scant attention to vegetarians, they are valuable.

Open 12.30pm–3pm, 6pm–10pm. Average Price: lunch under £10, dinner under £20. Visa, Access/Master. In the town centre.

# KILLORGLIN

Farmhouse Cheese
## WILMA'S KILLORGLIN FARMHOUSE CHEESE
*Ardmoniel, Killorglin Tel: (066) 61402 Wilma Silvius*
Found in local shops and beginning to make its way further afield, Wilma's is a rich and buttery gouda-style cheese, with nice traces of peppery sharpness. Do look out in particular for the cheese sold marked as "mature", for then the meld and blend of flavours are at their best.

# TRALEE

Farmhouse Cheese
## KERRY FARMHOUSE CHEESE
*Coolnaleen Tel: (068) 40245 Sheila Broderick*
Sheila Broderick's cheddar-style cheeses are earthy and agrestic, whether the plain Kerry cheese or those flavoured with a variety of ingredients. The plain cheese suits a fair bit of age to get the very best out of it, so it can be a good idea to buy from the farm in order to get the level of maturity you want.

Thirteen miles along the Tralee-Listowel Road you will see a sign for Lixnaw. Take the road on the right, go up the hill, past two houses opposite one another. The Brodericks' is the next painted entrance on the right.

Wholefood Restaurant
## ROOTS RESTAURANT
*76 Boherbue Tel: (066) 22665 Ruth O'Quigley*
A few little tables in a little room, with nicely satisfying wholefoods cooked by Ruth — courgette and cauliflower lasagne; cracked wheat; shredded carrot salad; celery and apple bake; mushroom and tomato quiche; vegetable and pasta soup. The locals sit around and talk about Vishnu, whilst this little place runs along at its own tender speed. Age does not wither Roots, and fashion is something they pay no heed to.
Open 10.30am–5.30pm Mon–Sat.

Restaurant
## BRATS
*The Square, Tralee*
Wholefood and vegetarian lunchtime restaurant, upstairs at the end of a small shopping mall.
Open 11am–5pm Mon–Sat.

Shop
# THE WHOLEFOOD BAKERY
*24 Upr Castle St Tel: (066) 27430*
Kieran O'Callaghan's baking, the slabs of soda made with wholemeal
flour, white flour and yellowmeal (maize flour), his French sticks, the rye
bread and the cakes, flavoured with ginger, porter and carrot and
coconut, have all been bought and enjoyed around Tralee for some years.
In 1991, however, he brought together the whole works under one roof,
in his new premises, the Wholefood Bakery. The bread is still baked in
Castlegregory, and distributed throughout the town, but for a complete
range of his produce, including pizzas, apple squares, tarts and
turnovers, you will find everything here.

# TUOSIST

Farmhouse Cheese and Home-Prepared Takeaway Food
## LISETTE & PETER KAL
*The White House, Tuosist Tel: (064) 84500 Lisette & Peter Kal*
Lisette Kal discovered the recipe for their Old Ardagh cheese in a Dutch
cheese cookery book, but this is not, in fact, a Dutch recipe. Rather, the
recipe was that for a cheese made by Irish monks in Ardagh, who would
no doubt be glad that the tradition still survives. It's a semi-hard goat's
cheese that matures to perfection.

Lisette and Peter also make wondrous sweets and desserts, including
Speculaas, the rich Christmas sweetmeat which must be eaten all year, a
concoction of spices and handmade marzipan, and you can find hand-
made chocolates, jams, cheesecake and birthday cakes made to order.
The Kals' cheese is on the cheeseboard at both the Park and Sheen Falls. In Kenmare the
Pantry sells their cheese, O'Sheas sell the chocolates. Otherwise you can order direct from
the house. Everything is very reasonably priced.

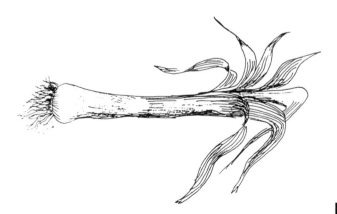

# County Limerick

## ADARE

Restaurant
### THE MUSTARD SEED
*Adare Tel: (061) 396451 Dan Mullane*

There is a simple answer to the public relations and culinary difficulties which bedevil County Limerick.

Celebrated as somewhere which is unlikely to detain the traveller and the travelling eater overlong, Limerick should — tomorrow — appoint Mr Daniel Mullane as President and Main Man of the county. His seal of office will allow him carte blanche to improve the quality of life in this strange, strangely bourgeois county.

Mr Mullane's qualification for ascending to the job is, simply, that he runs a restaurant — The Mustard Seed — which is not just one of the best in the country, but which, in its thoughtful, considered, creative way of working, shows every other place in Limerick up for the hole-in-the-wall joints they are.

He will solve the matter of crime by using the same charm with which he suffuses his restaurant: no one could cause trouble under the gaze of Mr Mullane's ministrations. He will attend to the matter of the county's less than picturesque towns and villages by designing them to look as much like Adare as possible, for Adare is heartbreakingly lovely. Any difficulty with bureaucrats, roads, water and so on will be solved by the efficiency which Mr Mullane and his chef, Michael Weir, attend to every business.

Mr Weir cooks impressively for vegetarians — a mélange of roasted vegetables on a base of tomato tagliatelle with a roast pimento sauce; twice baked spinach and Gruyère soufflé with lasagne of garden vegetables on a tomato purée, are just some of his inspired creations — inventive, individual cooking, but food that never looses off its notes of comfort and homeliness. Mr Weir strives to make his dishes "full of flavour, colourful and interesting, as I feel too often that vegetarian dishes are dull and thrown together in the kitchen at the last minute and this should not be so".

Which is just how the restaurant itself functions: comforting, homely, welcoming.

Could there possibly be a greater electoral platform?

We would have to insist, of course, that Mr Mullane's duties did not take him away from the Mustard Seed. Saving Limerick may be important. But it's not that important.

Open 7pm–10pm Tue–Sat. Closed Xmas. Average Price: dinner under £30. Visa, Access/ Master, Amex, Diners. In the centre of Adare village opposite the Dunraven Arms pub.

# CRATLOE

Sheep's Cheese
## CRATLOE HILLS

*Cratloe Tel: (061) 87185 Sean & Deirdre Fitzgerald*
The best known Cratloe is a pale-white sheep's milk cheese which, unusually perhaps, is made in a shape reminiscent of a blancmange dessert. Whilst it is subtle and light in flavour, do try to seek out that cheese, in the shape of a small curling iron or a small gouda, which the Fitzgeralds age for a longer period of time. With a caramel brown coat and a harder, leaner consistency, this Cratloe develops a much greater spread of flavour and shows sheep's milk at its best.

# KILMALLOCK

B&B
## CUSSONS COTTAGE

*Ballygrennan, Bulgaden, Kilmallock, Co Limerick. Tel: (063) 98926*
*Ita*
A peaceful B&B run by vegetarians, the cooking is provisioned by the produce of their organic garden — cucumber soup with coriander leaves and wholemeal bread, leek and garlic pie in a wine sauce with spring greens, lemon glazed carrots and roast potatoes. In the morning you can "combine your own muesli", mixing together a choice of grains, seeds and fresh fruits. Then at the end of a day's walking in the Ballyhoura and Galtee mountains, take comfort that you are just a few minute's walk from the local pub.

There are family rooms, a sun lounge and, as the rooms have their own separate entrance you can come and go as you please.

Open all year, including Xmas. Average Price: dinner under £10, B&B under £15. No credit cards. Just outside the village of Kilmallock, ask for detailed directions when booking.

Farmhouse Cheese
## GLEN-O-SHEEN

*Ballinacourty, Kilmallock Tel: (063) 86140 Matthew & Margaret O'Brien*
Glen-o-Sheen must be one of the last unpasteurised cheddars to be made and sold in these islands, impressively handsome and tall in big truckles of up to 30lbs in weight.

Do be patient with it: the buttery, buttercup yellow cheese is at its best after many months of ageing, when the milkiness first of all subsides a little, but then reappears as a rich, buttery melt.

Take the road to Kilfinnan from Kilmallock, and when you come to the townland of Glenroe, Glen-o-Sheen is signposted both on the road and at the farm.

# LIMERICK

Producer's Market
## LIMERICK SATURDAY MARKET

The Limerick market is an ambling sprawl of cars and carts, stalls and set-ups which snakes around the city first thing on Saturday morning. Best things to look out for are bakes and preserves, and maybe some good tufty carrots or other root vegetables. Kilshanny farmhouse cheese makes its way down from Lahinch and mingles with the other artisan products. Do be warned that the Market, which is near the town centre, is amazingly difficult to find, even if you have been there before, and it is usually necessary to ask directions, possibly — indeed probably — three or four times.

NASTURTIUM

Wholefood Shop
## EATS OF EDEN

*Spaight's Centre Tel: (061) 419400 Nancy Flexman & Rita O'Mahony*
Not just the familiar paraphernalia of a wholefood shop, but good also for organic vegetables, breads and other local foods.
Open 9am–6pm Mon–Fri, 9am–6.30pm Sat

Cooked food and Delicatessen
## IVAN'S

*Caherdavin, Limerick Tel: (061) 455766 Ivan Cremins*
"This is a shop that does everything", says Ivan Cremins, and he is just about right. The shop has an instore bakery, a deli counter and a sand-wich bar. The breads are conventional soda plus breads flavoured with walnuts and oatmeal. The deli counter sells the Abbey Burren jams made from apricot and almond, apple and cinnamon, some farmhouse cheeses, particularly Cooleeney from Mrs Cremins home-county of Tipp, plus hand-made cooked foods and salads. It's a good, buzzy sort of place.
Open 7am–11.30pm Mon–Sun

# County Tipperary

## BORRISOKANE

Country House
### BALLYCORMAC HOUSE
*Aglish, Borrisokane Tel: (067) 21129 Herb & Christine Quigley*
Herb and Christine are excellent, enervating cooks, and their skill and enthusiasm extends to creative vegetarian dishes.

"We tend to cook both Indian and Italian cuisine", Christine says, "as both lend themselves to full meals without meat, and you don't feel you're skimping. We cook pizzas and pastas — last year I made a cannelloni stuffed with chard in a walnut sauce which I was particularly pleased with. And we make risotto. Then we cook a lot of Indian food and Herb makes home made naan bread to go with it". Enthusiasts for Herb's bread should note that they run classes on breadmaking in the early part of the year.

Open all year except Xmas. Average Price: dinner under £30, B&B under £30. Visa, Access/ Master. Take the Portumna Road out of Borrisokane, for half a mile then take the first turn right. Keep going to the end of this road (about three miles) and then follow the signs for the house.

---

*Herb Quigley's Apricot and Chocolate Soda Bread*

**3 and a half cups strong white flour**
**1 heaped teaspoon baking soda**
**1 teaspoon salt**
**4 tablespoons caster sugar**
**2 tablespoons butter**
**half a cup of dried apricots**
**quarter of a cup of chopped bittersweet chocolate or tiny chocolate chips**
**1 and a half cups buttermilk**

Sift together the flour, soda, salt and sugar. Cut in the butter until the mixture looks like fine crumbs. Stir in the fruit and chocolate and make a well in the centre. Pour in the buttermilk and mix until a light dough forms. It should look like thick porridge. Grease a seven-inch cake pan and pour in the dough; sprinkle with a little flour. Bake at 425F for 10 minutes. Reduce the heat to 400F and bake for 40–45 minutes. The bread is done when brown and sounds hollow when tapped on the bottom. Remove bread from the pan and wrap lightly in a tea towel to cool.

# CAHIR

Organic Farmer
## BALLYBRADO HOUSE
*Cahir Tel: (052) 66206 Joseph Finke*
Joseph Finke grows and gathers wheat, oats and rye from his own fields and the fields of other organic farmers, and distributes the flour and the oatmeal throughout the country under the Ballybrado label.

The Ballybrado operation is a visionary adventure, for it is organic farming practiced on a fairly large scale, rather than the conventional man-wife-dog-and-three-acres set up which is so commonplace. Mr Finke's work offers a vision where organic farming is the norm, and not something left-field or alternative. Indeed, the efficiency and independence of the Ballybrado operation demonstrates that we should regard so-called "conventional" farming as something illogical and, these days, effectively nonsensical.

Ballybrado flour is widely available throughout the country.

# CASHEL

Restaurant
## THE SPEARMAN
*Main Street Tel: (062) 61143 The Spearman family*
As an on-the-road stop between Dublin and Cork, The Spearman is a godsend, for service is speedy and the restaurant is a calm space in which to loosen up and stretch the legs. The food is zappy with flavour.

There is always at least one vegetarian choice at lunch and dinner: courgettes parmiggiana with tomato sauce; baked aubergine; fettucini al fredo for dinner; mushroom and leek tart, omelettes and salads at lunchtime. Do note that they use chicken stock in the soups, so if you wish to avail of the full menu, advance notice solves any such problems.

Open 12.30pm–3pm, 6.30pm–9.30pm. Closed Xmas. Average Price: lunch under £10, dinner under £20. Visa, Access/Master. Just off the main street running through Cashel.

# CLOGHEEN

Farmhouse Cheese
## BAYLOUGH CHEESE
*Mount Anglesby, Clogheen Tel: (052) 65275 Dick & Anne Keating*
The Keatings' territorial-type cheeses are buttery and gentle in flavour, blessed with the aromatic scents of flora which their good pastures gift to their milk. They have often been compared to a good Cheshire cheese,

and whilst the consistency of the cheeses is vaguely Cheshireish, the tastes are stronger and more lactic than you will find in an English cheese.

Baylough is usually sold when still very young but, as they are wrapped in black and yellow plastic coats, they are easy to age, and then the flavours mellow and intensify, and call out for a good glass of red wine. Much of the cheese is sold in Peter Ward's shop, Country Choice, in Nenagh.

# CLONMEL

Market, Shop and Restaurant

## CLONMEL ORGANIC MARKET, THE HONEY POT AND THE BEE'S KNEES RESTAURANT

*14 Abbey Street Tel: (052) 21457 Jill Sandvoss*

On Thursdays and Fridays the lucky citizens of Clonmel are treated to the joyous sights and zestful smells of an organic market, replete with all manner of vegetables, each in numerous varieties.

One Friday in September there were no less than four types of potato, four types of apples, two types of beans, as well as onions, shallots, garlic, tomatoes and cherry tomatoes, Swiss chard, cabbages and cheese. Everything is symbol standard organic or, indeed, of bio-dynamic standard.

The Honey Pot operates as a wholefood shop and the Bee's Knees restaurant is open throughout the week. So go for their lovely potato nests, where hats of mashed potato are stuffed with carrot, marrow, celery and broccoli, in a tomato sauce, served with an excellent potato salad and a crisp tomato and onion salad.

Market 10am to 6pm on Thurs and Fri. Restaurant open 1pm–3pm, 7pm–midnight. Average Price: meals under £5–under £10. No credit cards.

# FETHARD

Farmhouse Cheese

## CASHEL BLUE

*Beechmount, Fethard Tel: (052) 31151 Jane & Louis Grubb*

Jane and Louis Grubb's Cashel Blue is now so famous that, along with Veronica Steele's Milleens, it is effectively synonymous with the Irish farmhouse cheese movement. Like Milleens, it has a mighty reputation abroad, and at home it is the second-biggest selling farmhouse cheese.

Like any good cheese, it is temperamental, and needs careful handling to allow the blue veining to seep through the curd and saturate every inch of the cheese with salty, potent tastes.

You find it reaches this ideal state at about three and a half months old, and if you can arrange to get a cheese at this age it should promise flavours and satisfactions that are almost addictive. At Christmastime, of course, a Cashel Blue is almost de rigueur, so to get the best try to order a cheese from the farm, or from Peter ward in Country Choice in Nenagh, and arrange for it to hit its peak on the happy day.

# NENAGH

Delicatessen and Coffee Bar
## COUNTRY CHOICE
*25 Kenyon Street Tel: (067) 32596 Peter Ward*
If you went into Peter Ward's shop looking to buy a particular farmhouse cheese and the man himself said something like "Well, I'm not sure that that one is quite ready yet, but there is a lovely cheese here that is just right, do you think you might like to try that?", you will think: If Peter Ward says it is not ready, it is not ready, and if Peter Ward says this one is ready, is at its best, then that is the one to buy.

Mr Ward, though he would be too modest to admit it, is an Irish affineur, a cheese expert, a man who can tell just by feeling and smelling a cheese whether it is ready to be cut and served and sold. His feeling is quite instinctual, but deadly accurate, and his instinct for good food, for things served at their best, is the animus of this wonderful shop.

The goods on the shelves are splendid, the coffee shop in the back is great for a snack, great for lunch, and invaluable if you are travelling anywhere near to Nenagh and need a break from driving. And his professionalism and dedication give Country Choice a marvellously motivated atmosphere: it is fun to shop here, fun to allow yourself to be persuaded that the cheese you wanted is not ready and to enjoy the delight of trying something unexpected. The shop, by the way, is particularly excellent for sourcing high quality foods for Christmas baking.
Open 9.30am–6.30pm Mon–Sat. Nenagh town centre.

Mustards & Salad Dressings
## LAKESHORE FOODS
*Coolbawn Tel: (067) 22094 Hilary Henry*
Hilary Henry is a determined woman. Meet her and you will be in no doubt that if Mrs Henry has a plan, some new venture, some new mustard or condiment or dressing which she wants to create, then that mustard or whatever will be created, will be invented, and will then be sold tirelessly and professionally at food fairs throughout the country. The Lakeshore foods are splendid things: faultlessly made, very alluring and pleasing, and very individual and artisan.
Lakeshore mustards and dressings are available throughout the country.

# ROSCREA

Flour
## ABBEY STONEGROUND WHOLEMEAL FLOUR
*Mount Saint Joseph Abbey Tel: (0505) 21711*
"Milled for the Cistercian Monks of Mount St Joseph Abbey, Roscrea" announces the bright blue and white two kilo bags in which Abbey Stoneground is sold and, as if this monastic seal of approval wasn't enough, the label, reassuringly, also states; "Ingredients: Wheat". The brothers themselves use the flour to bake splendidly sensual bread, which you can buy from the Abbey and the guesthouse.
The flour is available in shops throughout the country.

# THURLES

Farmhouse Cheese
## COOLEENEY CHEESE
*Cooleeney House, Moyne, Thurles Tel: (0504) 45112 Breda Maher*
Get one of Breda Maher's camemberts when it is at its creamy, oozy best and you get one of the finest foods you can buy in Ireland. The rich pastures and boggy depth of the land in this part of Tipperary allow Mrs Maher to make one of the most effulgent, lurid, and insolently powerful cheeses in Ireland, something so good you would walk a country mile in the rain to eat it again.

How do you get a Cooleeney in this state? If you don't have the good fortune to know a good shopkeeper, then buy the small Cooleeneys, the ones in the ash boxes, when they are right at their sell-by date, and then hold on to them for a few days. Otherwise, travel to the farm and pick up one yourself — this, of course, is the awkward but ideal thing to do. Get it once when it is perfect, and you will chase that perfection for the rest of your days.
Cooleeney House is about three miles off the main N7 Dublin-Cork road. Take the turning opposite Mary Willie's Roadhouse, go straight for three miles, and you will see Cooleeney House right in front.

# County Waterford
# CAPPOQUIN

Apple Juice
## CRINNAGHTAUN JUICE CO LTD
*Cappoquin Tel: (058) 54258/54962 Julia Keane*
Julia Keane's apple juice is especially good, thanks to the fact that it is made from 100% pure apple juice, and not from reconstituted

concentrate. As she uses natural juice as it flows from the press, the juice is, therefore, naturally cloudy and golden, and it is not refined. Ms Keane uses Bramleys and Cox's Orange Pippins from her own orchards and they are pressed traditionally, and pasteurised in the bottle.

Sheep's Cheese
### KNOCKALARA IRISH SHEEP'S CHEESE
*Cappoquin Tel: (024) 96326 Wolfgang & Agnes Schliebitz*
If it is the handsome label drawn by Agnes Schliebitz which first draws your eye towards Knockalara — a beautiful pencil drawing of mummy sheep, daddy sheep and baby sheep — it will be the clean, refreshing, almost lemony taste of this sheep's milk cheese which will draw you back.

Fresh, limber, and filled with bright flavours, with a little ageing the curdiness of the cheese begins to bind together, knitting together the sharp, cool tastes. When young, it works beautifully in a summer green salad, much better than any imported feta cheese, and marrying perfectly with olive oil dressings. Wolfgang also imports some German wines, including some interesting red wines which are rarely seen.

The cheese is available in good delicatessens. As the farm is difficult to find, if you wish to visit it is necessary to telephone first for directions.

# DUNGARVAN

Farmhouse Cheese
### RING FARMHOUSE CHEESE
*Gortnadiha House, Ring Tel: (058) 46142 Eileen and Tom Harty*
Tom and Eileen Harty's cheese is as up-front and no-nonsense as the couple themselves. A spicy, tongue-coating brew that fills the mouth with clean mineral tastes that reside along with the sharp, lactic tension of the cheese, you will find that you will need something tough and tannic to drink with this handsome effort, easily recognisable in its great big orange-coated truckles.

Something from the Rhone Valley or a New World Shiraz is probably called for, something that has a length of taste that lasts as long as the cheese itself, for Ring has a concentration of flavour that persists and persists.

Gortnadiha House is just off the N25, a couple of miles west of Dungarvan, and the cheese can be bought from the farm. Telephone to arrange an appointment and to get precise instructions on how to find the farm.

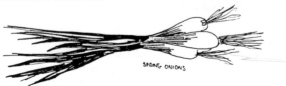

SPRING ONIONS

# KNOCKANORE

Farmhouse Cheese
## KNOCKANORE CHEESE
*Ballyneety, Knockanore Tel: (024) 97275 Eamonn Lonergan*
Eamonn makes plain, herbed and smoked cheeses from cow's milk, in
a Port-Salut style. Knockanore is the younger version, Ballyneety the
more aged, and perhaps more interesting, version.
The cheeses are widely available.

# WATERFORD

Restaurant
## OPUS 1
*18 High Street, Waterford, Co Waterford Tel: (051) 57766 Michael Quinn*
Michael Quinn has a restless, hungry culinary character. His background
in food is rock solid — he rattled the pots and pans on the stoves in
Ballymaloe House, in County Cork, in recent times — but even there he
took time out to see the goings on of fine chefs such as Simon Hopkinson
in London and Shaun Hill in Devon, and to pick up the tricks of a smart
food operator such as Anthony Worrall-Thompson.

His cooking in his brand-new restaurant in High Street, which cheekily
adapts the name of the famous wine made collaboratively by Robert
Mondavi and Baron Philippe de Rothschild, shows a cook eager to
extend his education in Ballymaloe. "I cook the stuff I like cooking — it's
sort of salady, tasty food that won't break the bank. It's healthy", he says.
It's also fun: fine bruschetta with herbed mushrooms, olives, sun-dried
tomatoes and Parmesan cheese; a soulful leek and potato pie served with
salads; a great lunchtime dish of mixed bean stew with buffalo chips.

This is zappy, up-front cooking, and main courses maintain this devotion to flavour: roast red pepper, lentil and goat's cheese salad; home-
made fettucine with a red pepper sauce, or tagliatelle with tomatoes and
basil. Not just good food, but accessible, satisfying, welcoming food, food
that you find you want to eat morning, noon and night.

And does the wine list include Opus One? Well, go to Opus 1 and you
will see . . .

Open noon–2.30pm, 6.30pm–10pm Mon–Sat. Closed Xmas and bank holidays. Average Price:
lunch under £5, dinner under £20. Visa, Access/Master. High Street runs parallel to the Quay
in Waterford town centre. Take the turn off heading towards the new city square car park.

Delicatessen
## CHAPMAN'S DELICATESSEN
*61 The Quay Tel: (051) 74938/76200 Mr Prendergast*
Home-made fudge and mascarpone, soured cream and liquid glucose,
country butter, farmhouse cheeses and wholefoods, crystallised fruit and

fresh-ground coffee, preserves and breads. Chapman's is a super shop, full of foods for cooks and bakers, full of the foods of the area as well as select stuff from the rest of the globe.

At the back of the shop there is a café, Chapman's Pantry, which sells soups, good sarnies, pies and quiches, with teas and coffees.

Open 9am–6pm Mon–Thur, 9am–9pm Fri, 9am–6pm Sat. Pantry open from 8am–6pm Mon–Sat.

Wholefood Shop
## FULL OF BEANS
*9 George's Court Ian & Sonia McLellan*
Look out for the local Dunmore East Yogurt if shopping in Ian and Sonia's nifty little wholefood shop, where you can also find organic vegetables — grown by themselves — good oils and pulses, breads and whatnots.

Wholefood Shop
## NATURE'S REMEDIES
*Michael Street Tel: (051) 78350 Teresa Murphy*
Good local wholefood store which is a member of the Irish Association of Wholefood Stores.

Restaurant, Hotel and Country Club
## WATERFORD CASTLE
*The Island, Ballinakill Tel: (051) 78203 Paul McCluskey*
Though Waterford Castle looks like to be somewhere that demands a Rolex, a Roller and a roll of folding stuff before you make your way on the ferry over to the island, this bourgeois paradise should not blind the inquisitive to the fact that the food and the wines here are worthy of anyone's attention and, if you choose carefully, you can enjoy superb food and brilliant wines without having to mortgage the house.

Paul McCluskey's cooking is innovative but thoughtful: he prepares excellent vegetarian pastas. This is intelligent cooking that benefits greatly from impeccable ingredients, and the short ferry journey across, and the panelled dining room, add to the sense of fun and romance.

Open 12.30pm–2pm, 7pm–10pm Mon–Sun (Sun 'till 9pm). Open for Xmas. Average Price: lunch under £20 dinner over £30. Visa, Access/Master, Amex. Some three miles outside the town, and well signposted on the Dunmore East road. The little ferry will come and collect you when it sees your car arrive at the pier.

Bistro
## THE WINE VAULT
*High Street Tel: (051) 53444 David Dennison*
There isn't a great deal of choice amongst the vegetarian dishes in David Dennison's bistro — stir-fried vegetables; Mediterranean salad; spring roll with a dressed salad — but it is a fun, happening place, with great wines and good crack.

Open 10.30am–midnight, Mon–Sat.

# County Cavan

## BALLINAGH

B&B
### BAVARIA HOUSE
*Garrymore Tel: 049) 37452 Rolf and Ilse Kleiber*
Rolf and Ilse's home is a 19th century Georgian house, and the grounds supply the organically-grown vegetables, fruits and herbs which they use in their vegetarian cooking. Both of them are vegetarian, "and we love cooking", says Ilse, so there are homemade breads, jams and wine also. They are happy also to cater for macrobiotic tastes, indeed, to do their very best to make sure you have the best time.

Open Apr–Oct (winter months by appointment). Average Price: dinner under £15, B&B under £15.

## BELTURBET

Farmhouse Cheese
### CORLEGGY FARMHOUSE GOAT'S CHEESE ➡
*Corleggy, Belturbet Tel: (049) 22219 Silke Cropp*
It is impossible to divorce the happy and instinctive tastes of Silke Cropp's Corleggy goat's milk cheeses from the environment where they are made. On a small farm just outside Belturbet, with the River Erne speeding lazily past down at the bottom of the pastures.

Corleggy is made with a vegetarian rennet and sea salt, and the taste is fresh and unalloyed, very precise and clean, perfect with a glass of claret after dinner but also surprisingly good to cook with.

Silke also makes a cow's cheese in the winter season, and there are soft goat's cheeses preserved in oil, these often decorated with borage and other flowers, for Mrs Cropp has an artist's spontaneous grasp of colour and appearance, and other soft goat's cheeses sold in little crottins. All of them are subtle but very pure in flavour, allowing tastes to emerge and unfold cautiously as you eat them, but it is the pillars of Corleggy which are the perfect product of this perfect farm. Dubliners can buy the cheeses at the fortnightly Dublin Food Co-Op, but the farm is distinctly worth a visit, just to see a protean vision of an organic farm, and to take away with you a memory that will taste good for years.

In Belturbet take the road beside the cinema — it is the road on the right as you come into town by the N3 from Cavan — which runs down to the River Erne, then at the bridge turn left and continue for about one-and-a-half miles until you see the sign saying "Corleggy Cheese". Visitors are welcome to the farm to buy cheese and vegetables and to see the farm itself — groups should ring beforehand to arrange a visit.

" WHAT LOVELY THINGS
THY HAND HATH MADE: .... "

W. de la M.

# BLACKLION

## MACNEAN BISTRO

*Blacklion Tel: (072) 53022 Vera and Neven Maguire*

Neven Maguire's culinary star is in the ascendent. This demure, boyish young man has been knocking the socks off the locals of Blacklion for some time now. But, with his success in the Young Chef of the Year competition in 1994, the word about this stellar young talent is moving abroad.

The restaurant is little more than a small front room on the main street in Blacklion. The cooking is shared by Vera and Neven, mother and son. There are two menus, an à la carte and the "chef's special", and it is to the latter that you are urgently directed. The "chef's special" is the responsibility of Maguire Jnr., a cook who, according to Mr Maguire Snr. "goes to bed with cookery books".

The vegetarian choices are limited, but expert: avocado stuffed with ratatouille in filo pastry on a tomato coulis; broccili and cashew nut bake; a fine vegetable curry; sweet and sour vegetables with rice; or garlic potatoes or potato puree. But it is in the desserts that Mr Maguire's skills are best exemplified. A chocolate plate collection of white, milk and dark chocolate confections is exquisitely beautiful, whilst nougat ice cream wears a Philip Tracey hat of spun sugar. You leave the restaurant on a veritable high, the narcotic delirium of these desserts coursing through your veins.

Open 5.30pm–9pm Tue–Sat, 12.30pm–9pm Sun. Closed Xmas. Average Price: dinner under £20, Sun lunch from £10. Visa, Access/Master. On the main street in Blacklion.

# CAVAN

Wholefood shop
## BACK TO NATURE
*Main Street tel: 049) 61019 Christine McGuinness*
The complete range of wholefoods and whatnots can be found in Christine's shop.

Restaurant
## THE OLDE PRIORY RESTAURANT
*Main Street Tel: (049) 61898 Samuel and Marie Schwab*
Perhaps the best choices in Samuel Schwab's restaurant, aside from the big puff pastry filled with asparagus or mushrooms on a white wine and cream sauce — lies with some of his pizzas: the vegetarian, which has mozzarella, tomato, mushrooms, sweetcorn, onion and peppers; the Margherita; or the special, which allows you to compose your own favourite. The wine list actually contains some wines from Switzerland which they import themselves: Dôle Du Valais Les Raccards — Dôle is a blend of the Pinot Noir and Gamay grapes — and Johannisberg Du Valais, Vent D'Est — the Johannisberg better known perhaps as the Sylvaner grape.

Open 12.30pm–10pm Tue–Sat, 6pm–10pm Sun. Closed Xmas. Average Price: lunch under £5 dinner under £10–under £20. Visa, Access/Master. At the Cathedral end of Main Street in Cavan town.

# CROSSDONEY

B&B
## LISNAMANDRA HOUSE
*Crossdoney Tel: (049) 37196 Bert & Iris Neill*
Bert and Iris Neill's house, just south of the complex of lakes, is famed principally for the gargantuan breakfasts they offer to the sodden fishermen, healthy walkers and holiday-makers who make their way here — the list of options is as long as a telephone directory but a lot

more interesting — but they deserve their fame every bit as much for the spontaneous charm which they gift to the house.

Open May–Oct. No evening meals (suppers and flask-filling offered). Average Price: B&B under £20. No Credit Cards. Lisnamandra House is clearly signposted on the Crossdoney Road leading from Cavan town.

# VIRGINIA

Farmhouse Cheese
## RYEFIELD FOODS

*Ryefield House Tel: (049) 47416 Anne & John Brodie*

The energy of the Brodies is only miraculous. At home all week long working the farm, milking the cows to make the orange-coloured and black plastic-clad Ryefield, a sweet and understated territorial cheese which can be compared to a good cheddar, they scoot up the N2 and down to Dublin at the weekends to run splendid stalls at the Mother Redcap market.

Here, alongside their own cheeses in both the matured and fresh styles and the Boilie cheese, soft little balls of cheese preserved in oil which is their latest addition, they sell many of the other farmhouse cheeses and a host of other foods which Anne organises and collects and coaxes out of her neighbours.

At Christmas time a visit to the Ryefield stalls reveals the magnificent panoply of Cavan farmhouse foods: plum puds laced with liquor, fruit-packed Christmas cakes, newly baked biscuits and breads and cakes, hand-made fudge and other sweets, jars of carefully prepared preserves, the whole lot of it exploding out of Anne's stall and brimful of good cheer, just like Anne and John themselves.

See entry for Ryefield Foods in the Dublin chapter.

# County Donegal

## BRUCKLESS

Restaurant With Rooms
### CASTLEMURRAY HOUSE

*Dunkineely Tel: (073) 37022 Thierry Delcros*

Thierry Delcros is a superb cook, and a Frenchman who cooks as if he was still back in his native land. His ability to conjure French tastes out of Irish ingredients is nothing short of spectacular, and the lovely dining room in Castlemurray, with its staggering views across the bay, is the best place in which to enjoy his creations.

Typical of a French orientation, the menu concentrates on fish and meat, but M Delcros' skill can produce delightful vegetarian dishes, such as a vegetarian gateau, and the eggs and coffee at breakfast-time are already legendary.

There are splendid, simple, affordable rooms to stay in, which are a perfect base for exploring the county and a perfect balm for the conscience to know that they are upstairs at the end of a boozy dinner.

Open 7pm–9.30pm ('till 10pm Sat and Sun) Mon–Sun. Closed Xmas and Mon–Wed off season. Average Price: dinner under £20, B&B under £20. Visa, Access/Master. Signposted just after the village of Dunkineely, heading west out of Donegal town.

## DONEGAL

Wholefood Shop
### SIMPLE SIMON

*Anderson's Yard, The Diamond Tel: (073) 22687 Andrew Cape*

Andrew Cape's shop continues to expand like hard wood: slowly, painstakingly, but solidly. There is now a regular supply of organic vegetables which are exported northwards from County Leitrim, there are farmhouse cheeses, good natural yogurt and a well made carrot cake. In the front of the shop there is an area selling Traidcraft goods, and the air of quiet co-operation which the shop enjoys is always delightful.

Open 9.30am–6pm Mon–Sat. Signposted in The Diamond.

Pub Food
### STELLA'S SALAD BAR, MCGROARTY'S PUB

*The Diamond Tel: (073) 21049*

This is one of few pubs which makes a conscious effort to cook something original and creative. Stella is in charge of the food in this friendly boozer and her stir-fried vegetables, wrapped up in a pouch of pitta bread, are a delight, the soups are warming against the chill of a Donegal morning, her main dishes simple and trustworthy.

Open for lunch Mon–Fri.

# FAHAN

Restaurant
## RESTAURANT ST JOHN'S

*Fahan Tel: (077) 60289 Reggie Ryan*

Reggie Ryan and his chef Phil McAfee have been in control since Restaurant St. John opened in 1980, and whilst their joint operation is as seamless as any you will find, it has never become soulless. St. John still has a sharp, buzzy feel to it, and there is considerable motivation evident, a considerable desire that the customer should have a good time and leave the restaurant happy.

The food has evolved slowly over the years — it could be described as old-fashioned, if it had any truck with fashion in the first place — and the vegetarian choices — stir-fried vegetables with rice; vegetables in a puff pastry parcel — are as ageless as everything else. The devoted clientele enjoy a splendid, very keenly priced wine list, and the suburban styling of the dining rooms and the bar area completes the agelessly conservative attraction of St. John.

Open 6pm–10pm Tue–Sun. Closed Xmas. Average Price: dinner under £20. Visa, Access/Master, Amex, Diners. Clearly signposted in Fahan village.

# GLENCOLUMBKILLE

Tea Rooms and Food Shop
## GLENCOLUMBKILLE FOLK VILLAGE

*Glencolumbkille Tel: (073) 30017 Christina Daly*

The tea rooms in the Glencolumbkille folk village are a welcome haven for decent tea and Guinness loaf or home-made soup and sandwiches. In the shebeen behind the tea rooms you can buy wine made from seaweed and other unlikely ingredients, and dilisk is also available in its raw form. Jars of butterscotch and a mouth-tingling fudge should have the children bawling happily in half an hour's time.

Open from 10am–6pm, Mon–Sat, noon–6pm Sun. Closed end Sept–Easter. Average Price: meals under £5. Visa, Access/Master.

# GLENTIES

Bio-dynamic farmer
## THOMAS BECHT

*Dorrian, Glenties Tel: (075) 51286*

It is rare to hear farmers praised by their peers, but we've heard much praise from other farmers, as well as customers, of Thomas Becht's careful work on his mixed farm in Glenties. For his labours he has earned both the Organic Trust symbol, and the hard-fought Demeter symbol of Bio-Dynamic farming.

For sale at the farm are vegetables in their season, and some dairy produce: farm country butter, milk and cheese. Cow's milk is made into a semi-hard cheese, and the milk from the goats is sold as a fresh cheese. You can buy Mr Becht's butter in Simple Simon in Donegal town, and wizard chef Thierry Delcros uses much of the Becht produce in his restaurant, Castlemurray House.

There are no official opening times to buy produce, and there's usually someone there to help you. But it's always a good idea to telephone first.

# KERRYKEEL

B&B
## KNOCKALLA FARM
*Ballynashannagh Tel: (074) 59105 Tim Spalding & Norah Newell*
Way, way up the gorgeous Fanad peninsula, but adroitly adjacent to the road as it courses through this chauvinistically beautiful countryside, is Knockalla, a handsome farmhouse announced by the happy field of organically grown vegetables which stretches enticingly out in front of it.

Tim and Norah offer Bed and Breakfast — there are four rooms in the main house and a further three in a converted wing — and also evening meals, specialising in wholefoods and using their own organic produce — the owners themselves are vegetarian.

So, begin the day with a vegetarian fry-up of potato cakes with fresh herbs, scrambled eggs, mushrooms and tomatoes.

What counts in Knockalla, however, aside from the wit of the owners (their little card, with a drawing of the house on standard grey paper, announces at the bottom: "100 per cent recycled, naturally") is the quality of the ingredients used: eggs from their own flock of chickens, fresh herbs plucked from the garden, their own organically grown produce and fresh bread made with yeast and soda.

In the evening, at dinnertime, this happy transport of tastes is in full play: chilled cucumber soup, or a summer tomato soup; leek stuffed pancakes in a cheese sauce; baked stuffed marrow with potatoes, beetroot and runner beans; lemon soaked sponge; chocolate mousse. "In general", they write, "our meals are made using whole ingredients which have not been processed and which contain no artificial ingredients. We are proud to be able to use only fresh herbs in our cooking".

Fanad is one of the most alluringly seductive of the Donegal peninsulas, and touring it offers endless delights and diversions and also, in late autumn and throughout winter, a wind so lazy that rather than wafting around you as you walk on the beaches, it just piles straight through into your bones.

Open Mar–Nov. Average Price: dinner & B&B under £14. No Credit Cards. Signposted at the crossroads three miles from Kerrykeel, on the Ramelton/Portsalon road.

# LETTERKENNY

Restaurant
## CAROLINA HOUSE
*Loughnagin Tel: (074) 22480 Mary and Charles Prendergast*
Though Carolina House is sveltly modern, Mary Prendergast's orientation is towards the verities of Irish cooking, a direction abetted by her Bally-maloe Cookery School background, and supplemented by her devotion to fine ingredients. Vegetarian dishes are only cooked on request, but they enjoy the same enthusiastic preparation visited on everything else.

Open 7.30pm–9.30pm Tues–Sat. Closed Xmas. Average Price: dinner under £20. Visa, Access/Master, Diners. Carolina House is just off the Derry to Ramelton road, near the golf course.

Shop
## THE NATURAL WAY
*Lower Main Street Tel: (074) 25738 David Foley*
Wholefood Shop which is a member of the Irish Association of Healthfood Stores.

# Northern Ireland

## BELFAST RESTAURANTS

### ANTICA ROMA

*67/69 Botanic Avenue, BT7 Tel: (0232) 311121 Tony Mura*

Antica Roma is where Italy meets Hollywood. You could come here just for the surreal indulgence of the décor and the ecstatic energy of the diners, but the food, happily, is not just hype or spectacle. Specialist Italian restaurants have been signalling the death of trattoria food for some years now, and Antica Roma shows that even in these great big Italian joints, tratt grub is passé.

Vegetarians are catered for mainly by the pasta dishes — the restaurant otherwise shows a strong leaning towards the meat and fish dishes beloved of its customers — but there are plenty of options and the staff are helpful. The wine list has some dry, cussedly fruity Sicilian wines which are rarely seen, the service is splendid, prices are keen and the atmosphere, particularly at the weekend, is a subdued riot.

Open 6pm–10.45pm Mon–Sat. Closed Xmas week, 12 Jul. Average Price: dinner under £20. Visa, Access/Master, Amex. Half way up Botanic Avenue, just up from Shaftesbury Square.

### MANOR HOUSE

*47 Donegal Pass, BT7 Tel: (0232) 238755 Tony Wong*

The Manor House may have the most God-awful location of any restaurant in the country — smack opposite an intensely fortified police station on a road replete with speed barriers — but the zingy, flavour-filled Cantonese food you can enjoy in here makes it worthwhile to stroll down this godforsaken pass.

The restaurant is a standard laminate-and-lacquer array of rooms, and whilst you can of course opt for familiar Chinese food, the real fun happens when you to put them to their mark and put yourself on the culinary edge.

Order the unusual dishes, ask for them to be done in the real style with lots of chillies, and then enjoy the energy and excitement of this confident Chinese cooking. This sort of adventure allows you to get the best from the Manor House, and to find some of the best Chinese food in the North. Vegetarians should try to give them a little notice, as this means they can offer a full range of choices from their vegetarian menu.

Open noon–midnight. Closed Xmas week. Average Price: lunch under £10, dinner under £15. Visa, Access/Master. Donegal Pass runs off Shaftesbury Square.

## NICK'S WAREHOUSE

*35/39 Hill Street, BT1 Tel: (0232) 439690 Nick & Cathy Price*

Years ago, Nick Price used to cook in a restaurant and pub called Daft Eddie's on Sketrick Island, on Strangford Lough. Simple stuff, really, but the food was as effective and happy an assault on the taste buds as you could imagine. In little or no time, Price had gifted to Daft Eddie's an almost mythic status: back in the bad old days of Ulster food, his was cooking that kept a close and fastidious eye on matters as obvious as freshness, motivation, concern.

Years later, and several moves on from Sketrick, Nick Price is still cooking, and cooking as well as ever. His food is always approachable and always correct, and in Nick's Warehouse he has a funky, lean, dining space which suits the spirited effectiveness of his work.

His vegetarian dishes have the same super-charged flavourfulness you find in everything else: courgette lasagne; cannelloni with ricotta and spinach; a lentil and mushroom loaf; a gulyas of mixed mushrooms with pasta; a bulgur wheat pilaf — spoon lickin' stuff.

Nothing much has changed with the way Nick Price cooks, and nothing needs to. He manages to offer a more intricate menu in the Warehouse, but no matter what you eat, the essential truths remain and the utter wit of his notes on the wine list is almost as much of a pleasure as the plonk you eventually choose. Anyone could try to do this sort of thing — providing super food in a super space — but no one else could do it with the grace, good sense and good humour that Nick and Cathy Price can.

Open noon–3.30pm Mon–Fri, 6pm–9pm Tue–Sat. Closed Xmas and 12&13 July. Average price: wine bar under £10, restaurant under £20. Visa, Access/Master (note: card purchases under £10 subject to 50p surcharge). Hill Street is off Waring Street, just behind St. Anne's Cathedral, just down from the offices of The Belfast Telegraph, near the ring road that connects with the M2.

## ROSCOFF

*7 Lesley House, Shaftesbury Square, BT2 Tel: (0232) 331532 Paul & Jeanne Rankin*

In Roscoff, the most influential restaurant to have opened in Ireland in the last decade, as stylish and cool an eating space as you will find anywhere in the country, Paul and Jeanne Rankin offer instinctual, artistic food, with a minimum of fuss and self-consciousness, with a maximum of concentration on achieving a hard-held vision of the pleasures which food should offer. That they are able to concoct a cuisine of such depth after such a relatively short period of time is little short of miraculous.

Paul Rankin's cooking strives towards presenting a series of delicately and precisely realised tastes, thereby creating a momentum and a rhythm to a meal which arouses and placates, stimulates and satisfies. Best of all, his food is disciplined and his considerable skills are never wasted on fashionable concoctions or experiments.

There are no formal vegetarian choices on the menu, but this is a kitchen which relishes cooking without meat: pappardelle with artichokes, mushrooms and pesto; sun-dried tomato and artichoke pastry turnovers; Oriental pasta with soya, ginger and stir fried vegetables.

Open 12.30pm–2pm Mon–Fri, 6.30pm–10.30pm Mon–Sat. Closed Xmas, Easter & 12 Jul. Average Price: lunch under £15, dinner under £20. Visa, Access/Master, Amex, Diners. Right in Shaftesbury Square, on Belfast's "Golden Mile" which leads from the city centre to the university.

# OTHER BELFAST RESTAURANTS

*The Ashoka, 363/365 Lisburn Road BT9 Tel: (0232) 660362*
Decently achieved Indian food in an enjoyably lively place.
Open noon–1.45pm Mon–Fri, 5.30pm–11.30pm Mon–Sat (10pm Sun).

*Bengal Brasserie, 339 Ormeau Road BT7 Tel: (0232) 640099*
Typically decent Indian vegetarian choices.
Open noon–2pm, 5.30pm–11.15pm (Sun 10.15pm).

*The Spice of Life 82 Donegal Street, BT1 Tel: (0232)332744*
One of the city's longest-established vegetarian restaurants.
Open 9am–5pm Mon–Fri, 'til 9pm Thurs.

*Villa Italia, 39 University Road, BT7 Tel: (0232) 328356*
Generates the longest queues of any eaterie in the city.
Open noon–2.30pm, 5pm–11.30pm Mon–Fri, 4pm–11.30pm Sat, 4pm–10.30pm Sun.

*Welcome Restaurant, 22 Stranmillis Road, BT9 Tel: (0232) 681359*
One of the better Chinese restaurants.
Open noon–2pm, 5pm–11.30pm Mon–Fri, 5pm–midnight Sat, 5pm–11.30pm Sun.

Pubs
## CROWN LIQUOR SALOON
*46 Great Victoria Street, BT2*
Not so much a pub as an institution, both for drinking and for the perusal of a grievously hallucinatory interior design. Having a drink in here on a Friday evening at five-thirty will explain the drive, energy and bonhomie of the people of Belfast quicker than any sociological treatise or front-line reportage by a visiting American writer.

## THE ROTTERDAM BAR
*Pilot Street*
Students of architecture may come here to marvel at how this building manages to stay erect — its weird location makes it seem as though it is being used as a prop in a Wim Wender's movie — students of design may

appreciate the ancient distillery mirrors, students of music may appreciate the nightly bands, but students of whisky will be most at home in The Rotterdam, for the range of malts and specialist hootches in Chris Roddy's bar is spectacular. At about five o'clock on a summer evening, sunlight distilling through the windows, and a glass of 36 year old Old Comber in your mitt, you may feel you have intruded upon the secret of existence.

Belfast Shops
## The Top of the Lisburn Road
It would be impossible to live in Belfast and to live without frequent trips to the wonderful collection of good food shops found near the top of the Lisburn Road.

Quite why and how these thoughtful, individual, characterful shops have gathered themselves together in such a small space is a mystery. But the mystery is of secondary importance to the thankful fact that they do exist and the fact that their proximity one to the other makes life so easy for the hungrily curious resident.

In Cargoes, a fine sense of discrimination abounds, from the careful selection of olive oils, to the handmade pasta, to the very tabletops in this café-delicatessen. The oils come mostly from Italy, imported to these isles by the Camisa family, as well as from Spain and Portugal. The tables are reminiscent of a Paris bistro with their aluminium tops on which to drink fine cups of strong coffee. A range of more than sixty cheeses mix good Parmesan with the best of the Irish farmhouse varieties, and everything underpins Rhada and her partners' desire to find food from "small family companies". Cargoes also offer outside catering and ready made freezer foods and desserts.

Arcadia, meanwhile — another deli with a treasure trove atmosphere — continues to thrive.

June's Cakeshop's cakes and breads — soft pancakes, triangles of soda, potato cake circles and wheaten wedges — are a good example of the North's particular baking culture. The breads and cakes up here are soft and welcoming. Mulholland's has the edge over other greengrocers by offering oyster mushrooms, local organic foods, seasonal berries and imported exotics. A little further down the road, Eatwell treads an expert line between the conventions of the standard wholefood shop and the imprimatur of the decent deli: good yogurts and creams, good sandwiches, good fruit and veg. Service everywhere is plain wonderful.

## CARGOES
*613 Lisburn Road BT9 Tel: (0232) 665451 Rhada Patterson*
Open 9.30am–6pm Mon–Sat
## ARCADIA
*378 Lisburn Road BT9 Tel: (0232) 666779 Willie Brown*
Open 7.30am–6pm Mon–Sat

## JUNE'S CAKE SHOP
*376 Lisburn Road BT9 Tel: (0232) 668886 June Henning*
Open 7.30am–5.30pm Mon–Sat

## MULHOLLAND'S
*382 Lisburn Road BT9 Tel: (0232) 381920 Jack Whiteman*
Open 9am–6pm Mon–Sat

## EATWELL
*413 Lisburn Road BT9 Tel: (0323) 664362*
Open 8.30am–6pm Mon–Sat

Chinese Supermarket

## ASIA SUPERMARKET
*189 Ormeau Road, Belfast BT1 Tel: (0232) 326396 Mrs Pau*
Krupuk udang from Indonesia. Long grain rice from Mississippi. Electric rice cookers from Japan. Under a single, capacious roof, the Asia Supermarket is a splendid bazaar of the bizarre and the commonplace. A place where agar agar sits beside salad cream in an ever-bustling warehouse of Asian essentials.

Hand-made dim sum await your steamers, fresh fruit and vegetables could be long long beans, watermelon, or perhaps four types of Chinese greens: choi sum, kai lau, bak choi or kai chi, each with its individual flower, mustardy taste and healthy green goodness even in the dragging chill of an Ulster spring. There are joss sticks and shoes, china bowls with gaudy plastic serving spoons, woks and bamboo steamers. The staff are giggly and friendly, making cracks as their customers dodge around the boxes being wheeled in and out as part of the wholesale business which runs side by side with the shop.
Open 10am–7pm Mon–Sun.

Kitchenware & Café

## EQUINOX
*32 Howard Street, BT1 Tel: (0232) 230089 Kay Gilbert*
Embarking on a caffeine crash course to find the finest cup of coffee in the country would throw up many delights, many disappointments, and few better cups of potently dark nectar than the coffee served in the café at the rear of Equinox.

Served in a thrillingly expensive Rosenthal little cup, the espresso here has the suppleness of deep roast and the energy of high altitude. Two sips, and the body is restored, the brain pulses clear, the blood rushes and rushes. It is a private, orgiastic excursion into the centre of one of life's great pleasures, a selfish culinary cocoon that lasts but a few seconds, and those few seconds are long enough.

In Equinox they annotate this joy with cool sounds, gorgeous croissants, splendid apple juices selected by variety, and other moderne dishes such as Tuscan bean soup. Even before this swish and inspired venture, Equinox kitchenware was an essential, albeit costly, necessity of life, but the café has turned it into a bedfellow.

Open Shop: 9.30am–5.30pm Mon–Sat ('till 9pm Thurs); Café: 9.30am–5pm Mon–Sat ('till 8pm Thurs).

Supermarket
## SUPERMAC
*Newtownbreda Shopping Centre, Saintfield Road, BT8 Tel: (0232) 491176*
Supermac scores over the droves of other Ulster supermarkets simply by virtue of the relaxed ambience, agreeable human scale and user-friendly staff who keep the oldest supermarket in Belfast ever youthful. In particular, the bread and cheese counters and the section devoted to specialist foods are invaluable, but it's always pleasurable to find yourself wheeling a wire trolley around this capacious space.

Open 8am–9pm Mon–Sat. At the top of the Saintfield Road, right on Belfast's A55 Outer Ring.

Vegetable shop
## SAWERS
*Unit 7, Fountain Centre BT1 Tel: (0232) 322021 Mr Graham*
A small shop which is stocked to the rafters with each and every manner of comestible: outside there is an array of fruit and vegetables, including organically grown vegetables, inside, at the back, there is a good cheese counter with a small but select brace of Irish farmhouse cheeses. In between there are certain surprises, and patient staff to assist you through the maze of makes and models.

Open 9am–5.30pm Mon–Sat

# BELFAST WINE MERCHANTS

There are many branches of the Winemark group dotted throughout Belfast, and they offer an increasingly fine range of wines.

## THE BELFAST WINE COMPANY
*130 Stranmillis Road, BT9 Tel: (0232) 381760*
Though the Belfast Wine Company has cashed in some of its singularity, and taken a turn down market in an attempt to broaden its cheaper and mid-priced range, it is still an attractive shop, with some classy clarets and the occasional offer worth being snapped up as you make your way home.

Open 11.30am–9pm Mon–Wed, 9.30am–9pm Thurs–Sat. Left hand side as you drive up the Stranmillis Road away from the city.

## DIRECT WINE SHIPMENTS
*5/7 Corporation Square, BT1 Tel: (0232) 238700 Kevin McAlindon*
Whilst brand new bridges dissect the air above and around it, Messrs McAlindon's shop stands still in its quiet, time-ignoring way. An echoey, arcane and splendid place to buy the fruit of the vine, they have everything from Tokaji Aszu to Tempranillo, and service is helpful and informed. Excellent wine classes and demonstrations are a constant theme of this energetic, absorbing organisation.
Open 9.15am–6.30pm Mon–Fri ('till 8pm Thurs), 10am–5pm Sat. Near to the car ferry port in Belfast's docks area.

## THE WINE GALLERY
*Boucher Road, BT12 Tel: (0232) 231231 Rory McNally*
This is a small, enthusiastic and friendly wine shop, set fast on the busy main strip of Boucher Road and featuring a small but attractive array of wines.
Open 9.30am–7pm Mon–Sat.

# BUSHMILLS

Distillery
## OLD BUSHMILLS DISTILLERY
*Bushmills Tel: (02657) 31521*
Highly organised and highly entertaining tours of the classic and handsome Bushmills Distillery — the oldest licensed distillery in the world — take place regularly during the day. At the end of a trudge around tuns and stills, there is the promise of a shot of the hard stuff to sip as you ponder the romantic concept of "The Angels' Share", that portion of spirit in the barrel which evaporates each year to succour the spirit world.
Open 10am–noon, 2pm–4pm Mon–Thur, 10am–noon Fri. No reservations necessary except for groups.

# LISBURN

Food Emporium
## GREEN'S FOOD FARE
*23 Bow Street Tel: (0846) 662124/662641*
This friendly rigmarole of a shop is little different from many standard supermarkets, but the fruit and vegetable section is always good and there is a small corner of speciality foods which may well contain some small, essential ingredient you desperately need.
Open 9am–5.30pm Mon–Wed, 9am–9pm Thurs, 8.30am–9pm Fri, 8.30am–5.30pm Sat.

# NEWTOWNABBEY

Japanese Restaurant

## THE GINGER TREE

*29 Ballyrobert Road Tel: (0232) 848176 Shotaro Obana*

Ulster's only Japanese restaurant plays a wonderful trick on the first time visitor, for inside this big house, from the road nothing more un-usual than a substantial farmer's dwelling, is an austerely minimalist dining room with Japanese prints, lean dark furnishings and a wooden floor.

Unusually, they puncture this contemplative and attractive space with inappropriate Western pop music, and this leavening of the atmosphere is echoed by Shotaro Obana's cooking, which despite its pure and traditional direction is rather more user-friendly than the food served in Japanese restaurants in the south of Ireland. Nevertheless, by choosing carefully, there are splendid tastes to be enjoyed. Prices are keen, both for lunch and dinner.

Open noon–2.30pm Mon–Fri, 7pm–10pm Mon–Sat. Closed Xmas and 12, 13 Jul. Average Price: lunch under £10, dinner under £20. Visa, Access/Master, Amex. Leave the M2 at the Glengormley junction, take the sign for Corr's Corner. At the next roundabout take the sign for Ballyclare, the restaurant is 2 miles further, on the right hand side.

Organic Farmer
## JOHN HOEY
*Shandon, Mallusk Tel: (0232) 832433 John Hoey*
With his bookish appearance and clubbable clothes, you could easily imagine John Hoey as a youthful don or someone who does something or other in the Jockey Club or a solicitor's firm.

Instead this quiet, thoughtful man is one of the major producers of organic food in the North, supplying his delicious herbs and vegetables direct to restaurants — the improvement in eating standards in Belfast owes a lot to Hoey and his close relationship with restaurateurs — and to certain shops. Like any good grower, his range is broad and diverse and dictated, happily, by the seasons.

# PORTGLENONE

Flour & Compost
## OUR LADY OF BETHLEHEM ABBEY
*Portglenone Tel: (0266) 821473 Father Jim Conlon*
Father Jim is something of a modest media star when he isn't out on the farm fiddling with the Bishop's Hat. If this sounds vaguely disrespectful, rest assured that the Hat is, in fact, an anaerobic digester, a splendid machine which not only heats the monastery — and thereby the shop and the tea rooms and the guesthouse which they also run — it also eventually produces the excellent Abbeygrow and Dungstead composts which the brothers sell. Their Abbeycorn wholewheat flour and porridge oats are resonant, reliable foods, blessing you with goodness.

Craft Shop (Tel: 0266 821754) Open 9.30am–5.30pm Mon–Sat, 1.30pm–5.30pm Sun (closed lunch hour 12.30pm–1.30pm) The monastery is just on the edge of the town and is clearly signposted from the road. The flour is also available in many supermarkets, the compost in many garden centres.

# PORTRUSH

Restaurant & Wine Bar
## RAMORE
*The Harbour Tel: (0265) 824313 (Wine Bar: 823444) George McAlpin*
The re-invention of the Ramore into a more informal dining space, with the kitchen fully open to view and a set of bar chairs at the counter, has lightened the atmosphere of this most swish of dining rooms, set high up in the harbour at Portrush.

Tumbling tresses of garlic, the bottles of oil, the dog-eared texts, are all on happy exhibition along with their white-clad employers who intersect with one another with the sure-footedness of dancers.

In parallel with the reinvented renovation, George McAlpin's cooking has shifted its concentration away from an obsessively detailed French style, bringing on board more of the vogueish influences of the pacific Rim: Japan, San Francisco, Thailand, Indonesia, with considered borrowings from the Mediterranean.

This lighter, light-hearted, style is delivered with confident aplomb, and whilst vegetarian choices are few, they are expertly and keenly achieved. Seasonal vegetables are summer-crisp, a garlicky purée of spuds babyful delicious, desserts of serene lemon tart and a cracking praline ice cream perfectly delivered. The staff are super, the wine list short and clever, breads are excellent, the whole organisation devoted to delivering a good time.

Open 6.30pm–10.30pm Tue–Sat. Closed Xmas. Average Price: dinner under £25. Visa, Access/Master. Right on the harbour in Portrush, as far down the one-way system as you can drive.

# County Down

## BANGOR

Off Licence
### THE AVA
*132 Main Street Tel: (0247) 465490 The Hillen Brothers*
"If there's anything you want us to get special, anything you find when you're away on holiday and you want it when you get back, then we will try to get it for you. Just give us a few days, and we'll try", said the kind lady behind the counter to the gentleman who confessed that he was making his first visit to The Ava.

Like the others of us who have maybe been in here dozens of times, he likely imagined he had stumbled upon an Aladdin's Cave of good drinks and hospitable service, for The Ava has that personality and personability which singles out certain shops and makes them worthwhile. The Hillen brothers try hard, and always try hard, and their sense of service and self-criticism means that the shop is steadily getting better, steadily adding more interesting spirits to an already enormous range, steadily adding new designer beers culled from all corners of the globe, working to expand their selection of wines and to line up and list Antipodean superstars, East European replicas of West European varietals, California classics, classy clarets.

Open 9.30am–9pm Mon–Sat. Bangor town centre, opposite the Post Office.

Restaurant
### SHANKS
*The Blackwood, Crawfordsburn Road Tel: (0247) 853313 Richard Gibson & Robbie Millar*
Shanks was always destined to success. Put together a smart team headed by Richard Gibson, a super-confident operator — and an excellent ship's cook on 'round the world races — and get Robbie Millar from Roscoff as your chief cook and an ex-Ballymaloe hand like Peter Barfoot also in on the act. Then get Terence Conran's interior design partnership, Benchmark, to design your interiors, and one might ask how you could fail?

Well, you could fail by not having sufficient ambition, despite the grandness of your surroundings, but the Shanks' team are as driven a bunch of blokes as you will find. Even in the basic business of serving a sandwich at the bar, they exhibit that meticulousness and invention which gladdens the heart. When the small things are so carefully attended to — they make the most glorious chips, for example, just brilliant — then you can relax, and tune in to enjoying the crescendo of excitement that is dinner.

Robbie Millar's food demonstrates that same drama between tension and release which has always been an integral part of Paul Rankin's cooking in Roscoff. Like Mr Rankin, Mr Millar does not offer vegetarian choices on the menu, so you need to tell them when you book, at which time they will discuss possibilities. This means, of course, that one gets extra special treatment, and extra special treatment from these guys is some sort of culinary carry-on.

This same unpredictability is found in the organic design by Conran, daringly minimal and dashingly romantic. Some don't like it, of course. Poor old them.

Open restaurant: 12.30pm–2pm Tue–Fri, 7.30pm–10.00pm Tue–Sat; Bar and Grill: 11am–11pm Mon–Sat. Closed Xmas. Average Price: Restaurant under £20, Bar and Grill under £10. Visa, Access/Master. On the main Belfast/Bangor dual carriageway, take the turning for Newtownards, a few miles before Bangor. Keep following the signs for Newtownards, and you will see the signs for Shanks.

Wine Warehouse
## STEWARTS' WORLD OF WINE
*116 Clandeboye Road Tel: (0247) 466909 Paul Abraham*
Although the range of wines and spirits on sale in the Stewarts' Warehouse is attractive, the capacious barn which encloses them has all the charm of an after-the-match football ground.

Airless, fluorescent-lit, with a jumble of cases piled on top of each other and a cold corner for beers, this is somewhere to go purely to see if there is anything at decent value and then to buy in bulk.

Open 9.30am–9pm Mon–Sat. At the top of the Clandeboye Road, past the football stadium, just off the Bangor ring road.

# COMBER

Herb Farm
## THE HERB FARM
*Cockle Point Cottage, 31 Ringneill Road Tel: (0238) 541992 Margaret McShane & Bill Franklin*
Margaret and Bill supply fresh herbs, some vegetables and flowers to restaurateurs, grown in their "high-rise" conservatory, known locally as Franklin's Folly.

Restaurant
## THE REFECTORY
*46 Mill Street Tel: (0247) 870870 Stephen Jeffers & Michael Thomas*
The principal space of The Refectory is a great big, ceiling-beamed, floor-planked room, bisected by the stairs. It looks and feels like the kind of room where you come to raise quiet havoc with your friends at the weekend, but a glance at the menu will reveal that Messrs Jeffers and Thomas are serious about their work, though not so serious that they don't want you to have a good time.

When the food arrives, one is struck, again, by the flair and competence of these Northern cooks. A fine dish of baked polenta and aubergine with a smart tomato vinaigrette is a good example of what they can achieve for vegetarians, and there can also be mushroom pasta in a parmesan cream sauce; bruschetta of mature goat's cheese dressed with sun dried tomato oil; a mille feuille of roasted vegetables in filo pastry, perhaps a vegetable stroganoff. Desserts, such as their special tiramisu, or a good, sharp lemon tart, are extra pleasing.

Open 6.30pm–10pm Tue–Sat, 12.30pm–3pm Sun. Closed Xmas. Average Price: Sun lunch under £15, dinner under £20. Visa, Access/Master. On the main road coming in from Belfast, look for the restaurant upstairs on the right, opposite the Burma Petrol Station.

# CROSSGAR

Wine Merchant
## JAMES NICHOLSON

*27A Killyleagh Street Tel: (0396) 830091 Fax: (0396) 830028 Jim & Elspeth Nicholson.*

Jim and Elspeth Nicholson's shop has a trade which increases at a rate of knots each year. They have managed not only to survive, but to veritably thrive in this apparently out-of-the-way environment. They have done this not only through the selection of wines sold, but also through careful thought of the design of the shop itself and through the excellent tastings and events which they organise. For, right down even to the quality of paper on which they print their list, Jim and Elspeth Nicholson do things right.

The distinctiveness which invades every part of the business, the sense of choice dictated by quality, tumbles resplendently over into the wines he sells and a list of the names of the great winemakers whose wine Nicholson sells reveals men with a headstrong, hands-on bent for both quality and personality: Aimé Guibert of Mas de Daumas Gassac, Henry Ryman of Chateau la Jaubertie, Gaston Huet from the Loire valley, Gerard Jaboulet and Etienne Guigal from the Rhône valley, Esme Johnston from Bordeaux, Paul Croser from Australia, Kevin Judd from New Zealand, Rainer Lingenfelder from Germany, the Bergqvist family from Portugal, Serge Hochar from the Lebanon. Who would not drive to Crossgar, to the Heart of Nowhere, to cull a case from this stellar line up?

Open 10am–7pm (shop), 9am–5pm (office). Killyleagh Street runs off the centre of Crossgar. Delivery free throughout the north for a minimum order of one case.

# DONAGHADEE

Ice-Cream Parlour
## THE CABIN

*32 New Street, Tel: (0247) 883598*

The Cabin is the original, and still the best, place to eat hand-made ice-cream. With its clean, unsophisticated shelves and old-fashioned counter, its jars of boiled sweets and a kindly lady to take your money, it is a slice of commerce that time forgot: frozen as perfectly as the crystals of milk in the ice-cream itself.

The gentle, white-coated old gentleman who makes it makes vanilla flavoured ice-cream, and that is that, though you can decide to stick a chocolate flake into it should you be less of a purist. Why is it so good? Because the innocence and mothers' milk goodness which ice-cream portends is made real here, reminding you of times when you were so much younger, and had cuts on your knees and ice-cream on your chin.

Open 11am–6.30pm Mon–Wed, 11am–9pm Fri–Sun. (Closed Thurs).

# DROMORE

Farmhouse Cheese
## CAORA & DRUMILLER CHEESE

*15 Leapoges Road Tel: (0846) 692211 John & Mary McBride*

Although John and Mary McBride pasteurise the sheep's milk they use to make both Caora and Drumiller cheeses, these pale, pale white log and feta cheeses still have the well tuned, slightly sharp and very cleansing pleasure which a sheep's milk cheese gifts to a salad — for which the Drumiller, particularly, is an invaluable asset. The Drumiller Greek-style yogurt is a deliciously real and satisfying transformation of the milk, splendid for cooking classic dishes such as Broad Beans and Yogurt, to garnish a moussaka, or to off-set a bowl of sweet summer berries.

# DUNDRUM

Pub & Restaurant
## THE BUCK'S HEAD INN

*Dundrum Village Tel: (039675) 868/859 Craig & Maureen Griffith*

Billowing lobelia interspersed with fuscia dangling from the window boxes, teams of white haired grannies with pleated checks and cardies arriving with their kids and grand-kids, give a clue to the fact that the Buck's Head is less a pub than a restaurant meets country tea rooms.

One of the three menus is vegetarian, so there is always plenty of choice, and it is fun to enjoy the food outside in the conservatory.

Open 12.30pm–2.30pm (lunch), 5.30pm–7pm (high tea), 7pm–9pm dinner Mon–Sat. 12.30pm–2.30pm (lunch), 5.30pm–8.30pm (high tea) Sun. Closed Xmas. Average Price: meals under £10. Visa, Access/Master. In the centre of Dundrum village.

# GROOMSPORT

Restaurant
## ADELBODEN LODGE

*Donaghadee Road Tel: (0247) 464288 Margaret & Dennis Waterworth*

The Adelboden is a wonderfully motivated restaurant. The Waterworths and their staff keep it bubbling along — enthusiastically! — for twelve hours a day offering first a lunch menu, then afternoon tea, then high tea and finally dinner. Vegetarians get their own full pasta, rice or crêpe menu and the verity of Margaret Waterworth's cooking is immensely pleasing to all tastes at all times of day.

Open noon–midnight Tue–Sat. Closed Xmas. Average Price: under £10–under £20. Visa, Access/Mastercard, Amex. Signposted on the coast road to Donaghadee, just outside Groomsport.

# HELEN'S BAY

Restaurant
## DEANE'S ON THE SQUARE
*Station Square Tel: (0247) 852841 Haydn & Michael Deane*
There are interesting and amusing influences visibly at work in Deane's On The Square. The semi-revealed kitchen harkens to a bistro ambience and the happy sounds of sizzle-sizzle that extrude from it serve to puncture the cloistered atmosphere of this manifest old station building, as do the picturesque but vaguely nervous waiters with their manes of ponytails.

Thoughtfully, Deane's offers a full vegetarian menu, with many choices: pasta with roasted vegetables; goat's cheese Niçoise; casserole of lentils and potatoes; a tian of roasted baby aubergines with sun dried tomatoes. This is creative, clever cooking, from a creative and clever team who relish their work, and it makes Deane's a fun place to eat.

Open 7pm–10pm Tues–Sat, 12.30pm–3pm Sun. Closed 2 weeks Jan. Average Price: under £20. Visa, Access/Master. The restaurant overlooks the station platform in Helen's Bay. Look for the newly-restored tower.

# HOLYWOOD

Café and Craft Shop
## THE BAY TREE
*Audley Court Tel: (0232) 426414 Rosalind MacNeice*
The cute little dining room in The Bay Tree nestles at the back of a cave of hand-thrown crockery and hand-threaded wicker baskets, a light, bright rinkydink of small tables that promises relaxation and fondly regarded food the second you walk in.

Sue Farmer's cinnamon scones and her sinfully rich carrot cake with its coxcomb of crushed nuts on top are vital staples for morning coffee or afternoon tea, and her lunch menus enjoy a quiet creativity, with vegetarian dishes like mushroom and broccoli croustade. "We don't serve any padding", says Ms Farmer, and nor do they: the bread is good, the salads crisp and fresh, and the affable feminine ambience makes The Bay Tree quite charming.

Open 10am–4.30pm, Mon–Sat. Set back from the street amidst a courtyard of shops.

Organic Grower
# HOLYWOOD ORGANIC FOODS
*23 Seaview Terrace Tel: (0232) 423063 John McCormick*
Saturday mornings find John McCormick in the big barn which doubles as an Organic Farm Shop on the Clandeboye estate, a couple of miles out of Holywood, a couple of miles out of Bangor, surrounded by a clatter of tables with his organic produce laid out on top.

There will be purply beets, soil-covered spuds, green broad beans, boxes of eggs, sharp red tomatoes, tightly-knotted heads of Little Gem and Sierra lettuces. The location seems an apposite and appropriate spot to buy his fine produce: the tactility of the wood and the logged trees outside adding to the earthiness of the experience.

Like the other principal organic growers in the North, John Hoey of Shandon and David Hawthorn of Derry, John McCormick's influence as a grower is much greater in impact than the modest size of his operation might suggest, simply because the produce of these growers is in such demand from smart restaurateurs and decent shops. It is thus easily accessible and not overpriced, for in a typical piece of Northern understatement they don't make a song and dance about it all. They just get on with the business of growing and distributing their glorious foods.

The Clandeboye shop is open on Saturday mornings and signposted from the road.

Bistro
# IONA BISTRO
*27 Church Road Tel: (0232) 425655 Bartjan Brave*
You bring along your own bottles of wine, sit on the steep stairs quaffing your plonk as you wait for a table, and then enjoy not only the rushy familiarity of a true bistro — gingham table cloths, candles stuffed into wine bottles, waiters who rush around the place, the hum of conversation, the steady backbeat of well-chosen music — but also food that is packed with true tastes. The blackboards offer a trio of starters and main dishes, with an unannounced vegetarian choice always available, and then probably a quartet of desserts, and no matter what you choose, the food in the Iona has always been distinguished by both simplicity and voluble, lively tastes.

Open 6.30pm–midnight Mon–Sat. Closed Xmas. Average Price: meals under £15. No Credit Cards. Holywood town centre, up the stairs over the Iona Wholefood Shop.

Specialist Shop
# THE IONA
*27 Church Road Tel: (0232) 428597 Heidi Brave*
The Iona shop combines food and crafts, and both sections display a selective and clear-visioned mind at work. The selection of organically-grown vegetables is small but always pristine — flootery rocket leaves, tiny courgettes, small bursts of seasonality in the shape of beans and

peas, fresh new spuds, crunchy apples — the breads are wholesomely efficacious, though perhaps a little worthy and old-fashioned, and all the essential ingredients to usher forth good cooking from soup to nuts are handsomely displayed and alluring. The crafts, likewise, are must-have, must-buy beautiful.

Open 9.15am–5.30pm Mon–Sat. Holywood town centre.

Delicatessen
## PANINI
*25 Church Road Tel: (0232) 427774 Tony McNeil*

Tony McNeil's shop combines a variety of Italianate leanings, with a tiny coffee bar with a scattering of seats at the far end, a healthy cold counter with good cheeses, prepared salads, a selection of Deli France and other part-baked breads, and staples such as oils, vinegars, teas and coffees

Open 7am–6pm Mon–Sat. Holywood town centre.

DANDELION

Restaurant
## SULLIVAN'S
*Sullivan Place Tel: (0232) 421000 Simon Shaw*

Sullivan's is Simon Shaw's first venture out on his own, after long tenures under Paul Rankin in Roscoff, just up the road in Belfast, as well as spells working in France and Switzerland. The restaurant's almost-instantaneous success has presented this amorphous village with a happy increase to its already considerable culinary riches.

Sullivan's works as a coffee shop by day and transmutes into a restaurant in the evening when the glasses and the napery come out. Mr Shaw's menus show the imprint of a solid, reassuring cook, though his trademark is a finesse with flavour which leaves ingredients to speak for themselves: a salad of roasted peppers and pinenuts, a wholemeal tartlet with crisp vegetables and parsley pesto or a spicy vegetable cous cous are some of his vegetarian dishes, and they will have the same goodness and instinctiveness he brings to everything he cooks.

Prices are very keen and the fact that you can bring your own wine allows for the cost of a cab fare to wherever you hail from.

Open 10am–4pm Mon–Sat, 6pm–10pm Tue–Sat. Closed Xmas and bank holidays. Average Price: lunch under £5, dinner under £15. Visa, Access/Master, Diners. Holywood town centre.

### Simon Shaw's Baked Tomato, Red Pepper and Garlic Soup

**2lb (900g) ripe tomatoes**
**2 red peppers**, roughly chopped
**half onion**, roughly chopped
**4 cloves garlic**, halved
**1 teaspoon olive oil**
**1 teaspoon tomato purée**

Sauté the onion and garlic in the olive oil until just softened. Add the whole tomatoes, the purée and the peppers and cook, uncovered for 5 minutes. Add 2 pints water and season with salt, pepper and sugar. Place in an earthenware dish, in a low oven for one-and-a-half hours. Liquidise to a smooth purée and serve.

# NEWRY

Bakery
## ARTHUR MCCANN LTD

*Victoria Bakery, Castle Street Tel: (0693) 2076 Christopher McCann*
McCann's brack is available in local shops, including the petrol station shops at the border. The portercake is widely distributed in tourist shops.

# NEWTOWNARDS

Shop
## HOMEGROWN

*66B East Street Tel: (0247) 818318 Trevor & Margaret White*
This busy, confident little shop is a treasure, simply because it is filled with foods that you both want and need. Lots of different types of onions, good garlic, in-season marrows, four or five varieties of potato, loads of good quality soft fruits and strangenesses such as mangoes, beans of all hue, salads which sit spanking fresh in their bowls, cooked meats that have a genuine, satisfying edge to their taste. Its location — right bang in the middle of a sullen housing estate — makes it a little awkward to find, but interestingly adds an ironic delight to the pleasure of being able to find here the foods you want, the foods you need.
Open 8am–5.30pm Mon–Sat. At the top end of the town, and hard to find.

# County Fermanagh

## BELLANALECK

Restaurant
### THE SHEELIN
*Bellanaleck Tel: (0365) 348232*

The Sheelin is probably as well known for the brown bread and the brown bread mixture sold in shops throughout Ulster as it is for the popular and familiar food it produces for its devotees.

Open Summer: 10am–6pm Mon–Tues, 10am–9.30pm Wed–Sat, 12.30pm–9.30pm Sun. Winter: 10am–6pm Mon–Thur, until 9.30pm Fri–Sat. Closed Xmas. Average Price: lunch under £10, dinner under £20. Visa, Access/Master, Amex. Just of the A509.

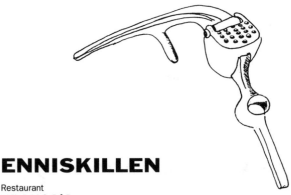

## ENNISKILLEN

Restaurant
### FRANCO'S
*Queen Elizabeth Road Tel: (0365) 324424 The Sweeney Family*

Bring a light-hearted mood to Franco's, maybe sometime late on a weekend night, and the jeans'n't-shirts of the staff and the customers, the waxy candles with their flickering light, the funky music and the fun ambience will seem just perfect.

They base their forays into Italian food firmly around pasta and pizza — although the restaurant is celebrated also for its fish cookery — and there are myriad manifestations of each métier on offer, and the occasional clever concoction intrudes from time to time amongst the daily specials.

Open midday–11.30pm Mon–Tues, 'till 1am Wed–Sat, 5pm–11pm Sun. Closed Xmas. Average Price: lunch under £10, dinner under £20. Amex. Walk down the hill behind the town hall and Franco's is on your left.

# IRVINESTOWN

Restaurant
## THE HOLLANDER
*5 Main Street Tel: (03656) 21231 Jim, Margaret & Stephen Holland*
"We try to cater for all" declare the trio of Hollands — Jim in the bar, Margaret and Stephen in the kitchen — and whilst their generous sized menu gushes with Saturday night certainties for the benefit of the locals, they cater for vegetarians thanks to the Hollander vegetable en croute — a selection of vegetables and seasonings topped with garlic mushrooms which is then encased in puff pastry.

You will need to order this in advance — preferably when ringing to make a reservation — but if you can't, they also make a dish of vegetables puffs, with pastry wrapped round a selection of thinly sliced vegetables.

Open 11.30am–2pm Mon–Sat, 5.30pm–11pm Mon–Sat, 6.30pm–10pm Sun. Closed Xmas and Mon & Tue Oct–Jun. Average Price: lunch under £10, dinner under £20, wine bar snacks under £5. Visa, Access/Master. On the main street in Irvinestown.

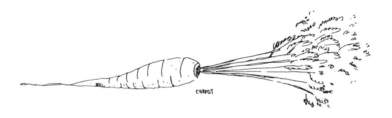

CARROT

# County Londonderry

# COLERAINE

Restaurant & Country House
## MACDUFF'S
*Blackheath House, 112 Killeague Road, Blackhill Tel: (0265) 868433*
*Joseph & Margaret Erwin*
Macduff's is the cellar restaurant of Blackheath House, a handsome, quietly unimposing Georgian rectory. Margaret Erwin's cooking is friendly and accessible, with the benefit of almost two decades of experience behind it. The house has six comfortably thoughtful rooms for those who are touring or who wish simply to make a proper night of it.

Open 7.30pm–9.30pm Tue–Sat (7 days Jul & Aug). Closed Xmas. Average Price: dinner under £20, B&B under £30. Visa, Access/Master. Just off the A29, seven miles south of Coleraine, four miles north of Garvagh.

# DERRY

Hotel/Restaurant
## BEECH HILL COUNTRY HOUSE HOTEL
*32 Ardmore Road, Derry Tel: (0504) 49279 Noel McMeel*

Quite how Noel McMeel manages to so confidently stride that danger zone, wherein a cook must satisfy the conservative demands of his customers and at the same time create food which inspires his own imagination, is one of the most intriguing questions in the world of Irish food.

But, however he manages it, his successful achievement of dishes which combine tried and trusted favourite tastes with forays into modern styling and technique is nothing but a joy, and it has been possible to see, on return visits to Beech Hill, that he has begun to transcend the lessons learnt at the hands of other fine chefs — a love of colourful complexity borrowed from Ian McAndrew, a love of earthy flavours brought from Paul Rankin — and has begun to sign dishes with his own signature.

His vegetarian dishes are as creative as everything else on the menu at Beech Hill: a warm salad of peppers and potatoes with a cumin dressing; a gratin of broccoli and cauliflower topped with smoked almonds; a tagliatelle of courgette mixed with carrot and a sundried tomato vinaigrette, are just some of his starter dishes.

Main courses continue these bold themes: a crispy potato nest with ratatouille on a bed of pommes purée surrounded by a herb jus; basil gnocchi served with a fresh tomato salsa; a filo of mushrooms served on a spaghetti of vegetables with a red pimento sauce.

Everything Mr McMeel cooks has all the elements which you associate with his work: gracefulness, strength of flavour and a dazzling capacity to invent. You don't expect food of this order in an hotel, and to find it in the romantic and innocent dining room in Beech Hill is a joy.

But can he bake a cherry pie? He can, and he can bake a rich, soft plum pudding with a thin brandy sauce or a lissom series of chocolate mousses that are ethereal confections. Derry just does not know how lucky it is to have this young man cooking such fine food a mile outside the city.

Open 7am–10am, 12.30pm–2.30pm, 6.30pm–10pm Mon–Sun. Closed Xmas. Average Price: lunch under £20, dinner under £20. Visa, Access/Master, Amex. Beech Hill is signposted from the A2, just past Drumahoe as you come into Derry on the main Belfast road.

# Index

# NOTES

NOTES